What's Wrong with Addiction?

What's Wrong with Addiction?

HELEN KEANE

NEW YORK UNIVERSITY PRESS
Washington Square, New York

First published in the U.S.A. in 2002 by
NEW YORK UNIVERSITY PRESS
Washington Square, NY 10003
www.nyupress.nyu.edu

Text © Helen Keane 2002
Design and typography © Melbourne University Press 2002

Typeset in 11/14 pt Sabon by Syarikat Seng Teik Sdn. Bhd., Malaysia
Printed in Malaysia by SRM Production Services

Library of Congress Cataloguing-in-Publication Data

Keane, Helen, 1964–
What's wrong with addiction? / Helen Keane
p. cm.
Includes bibliographical references.
ISBN 0-8147-4765-5 (pbk: alk. paper)—ISBN 0-8147-4764-7
(alk. paper)
1. Compulsive behavior-Moral and ethical aspects. 2. Compulsive
behavior-Social Aspects. 3. Compulsive behavior-diagnosis.
4. Addicts-Psychology. I. Title.
RC533.K425 2002   2001051424
616.86-dc21

Contents

Acknowledgements

THIS BOOK owes its existence to many people. It began as a doctoral thesis at the Centre for Women's Studies, Australian National University, where the generosity, enthusiasm and intelligence of my supervisors Jill Matthews and Barbara Sullivan were crucial to the development of my ideas. My thanks also to Jindy Pettman and Rosanne Kennedy for their support during my time as a student and staff member. The stimulating company of Christine Owen, Adele Stevens, Rebecca Cox, Berenice Carrington, Deb Clark and Michael Flood also made my time at the Centre memorable. At the National Centre in HIV Social Research I would especially like to acknowledge the friendship and encouragement of Catherine Waldby, Sue Kippax and Kane Race. I would also like to thank Valerie Walkerdine, Robyn Warhol and Robin Room for their support of my work. Robin in particular has been remarkably generous with his knowledge, time and expertise, and I have learnt a great deal from him. I am also grateful to Cindy Patton for her astute comments and help with Chapter 7.

There are many friends who have sustained and stimulated me during the production of this work. Elizabeth Wilson and Marsha Rosengarten have my enduring gratitude for their insights, intellectual generosity and friendship. I am also indebted to Nicole Vitellone, Lisa Adkins, Rosalyn Diprose, Anni Dugdale, Penelope Sinclair, Hilary Ericksen, Heidi Mellish and Jenny Chalmers for enhancing my life and work in different ways. Simon Philpott deserves special thanks. His love and encouragement kept me going during my often precarious progress and his contribution to this work is incalculable.

Di Piper of the Alcohol and other Drugs Council of Australia Resource Centre provided excellent research assistance and Christy Newman provided crucial help with preparation of the manuscript.

I would also like to thank John Meckan, Caroline Williamson and Gabby Lhuede of Melbourne University Press and Jennifer Hammer of New York University Press.

Finally, my deepest gratitude to Daniel Stoljar, for opening previously closed doors.

A different version of Chapter 6 has been published as 'Taxonomies of desire: sex addiction and the ethics of intimacy', *International Journal of Critical Psychology*, 1:3 (2001), and a different version of Chapter 7 as 'Setting yourself free: techniques of recovery', *Health: An Interdisciplinary Journal for the Social Study of Health, Illness and Medicine*, 4:3 (2000). Sections of Chapter 1 are drawn from 'Adventures of the addicted brain', *Australian Feminist Studies*, 14:29 (1999).

Introduction:
What's Wrong with
Addiction?

For there is no health as such, and all attempts to define a thing that way have been wretched failures. Even the determination of what is healthy for your body depends on your goal, your horizon, your energies, your impulses, your errors, and above all on the ideals and phantasms of your soul. Thus there are innumerable healths of the body; and the more we allow the unique and incomparable to raise its head again, and the more we abjure the dogma of the 'equality of men', the more must the concept of a normal health, along with a normal diet, and the normal course of an illness, be abandoned by medical men.

—Friedrich Nietzsche, *The Gay Science*

The question 'What's wrong with addiction?' seems almost too obvious to bother asking. There is certainly no shortage of answers already in circulation. In politicians' speeches, newspaper columns, medical journals, television documentaries, talk shows and self-help guides we are repeatedly told of the terrible consequences of drug and alcohol addiction. Introducing a special series of articles in the *Lancet*, psychopharmacologist David Nutt lists 'massive costs' in crime, loss of earnings and productivity, and social damage, as well as 'huge direct health costs' both psychiatric and physical, adding that 'reducing the extent of drug dependence is one of the major

1

goals of medicine'. For the afflicted individual, Alcoholics Anonymous describes the consequences of addiction as the 'annihilation of all the things worth while in life', the alcoholic illness brings with it 'misunderstanding, fierce resentment, financial insecurity, disgusted friends and employers, warped lives of blameless children, sad wives and parents.'[1]

But the 'wrongs' of addiction clearly vary according to the drug concerned. In Australia, heroin addiction, the 'treacherous road to self-destruction' as one journalist labelled it, attracts the most vivid and wide-ranging descriptions of individual and social harm. Heroin addiction is commonly described as a 'social evil' which spreads serious diseases, causes deaths through overdose and promotes crime, corruption, and prostitution. Nicotine, as a legal drug, is not linked to these kinds of moral and social dangers, but the effects of smoking on health make it an equally powerful example of the tragic costs of addiction. Alcohol abuse is associated with significant health problems too, as well as being linked with violence, family breakdown and traffic accidents.

In one sense it cannot be denied that these are the problems of addiction. But it can be argued that many of these harms, both individual and social, are secondary consequences, rather than essential and inevitable elements of the addictive experience. As commonly observed by supporters of drug law reform, much of the damage associated with heroin and other illicit drugs is caused by their legal status rather than any inherent quality of the drugs.[2]

At a more abstract level, it could also be argued that the problems caused by smoking and drinking to excess are not strictly the results of addiction, but of high levels of consumption of toxic substances. That is, one does not develop cirrhosis because one is an alcoholic, but because one is a heavy drinker, perhaps a heavy drinker who chooses rather than is compelled to continue drinking. This kind of argument presents addiction as a state or condition defined by a compromised will, a condition which is not necessarily defined by the behaviour of excessive consumption. The disassociation of addiction from consumption appears in both medical and popular views. It is expressed most familiarly in the Alcoholics Anonymous view that an alcoholic who has not had a drink for twenty years nevertheless still suffers from the incurable disease of alcoholism.

Considering non-drug-related disorders such as sex addiction and food addiction opens up the enquiry even further. Are the harms of eating and loving too much analogous to the harms of drug addiction? Can food and sex act like psychoactive drugs and alter people's psychological and physiological functioning? Or are these addictions simply moral judgements about 'bad' ways of eating and having sex dressed up in the language of disease? If addiction is not determined by a particular property of the object of addiction, as the recent proliferation of addictions suggests, does this mean that everything is potentially addictive?

There is a view that addiction is intrinsically bad because it destroys the addict's freedom. Philosopher Robert Goodin argues that addictions are 'unambiguously bad, from the point of view of the person addicted' because they deprive her of her capacity for autonomous choice. More floridly, Alcoholics Anonymous and popular therapeutic discourse constructs addiction as the antithesis of freedom. The first step of the twelve steps is to admit powerlessness over alcohol. In *Addiction and Grace,* psychiatrist Gerald May states that addiction is a 'self-defeating force that abuses our freedom and makes us do things we really do not want to do'.[3]

But such claims about freedom are contestable on a range of grounds. It may be extremely difficult for people to change behaviours defined as addictive, but many do, often without any formal treatment. Other habitual and routine patterns of behaviour regarded as benign or positive may well be just as resilient to change; the strength of their hold generally escapes notice because attempts are not made to give them up. Indeed what emerges from the following chapters is that even within the terms of addiction discourse, the distinction between freely chosen and compelled acts is by no means clear-cut. Neither does choice or lack of choice offer a reliable guide to the categorisation of activities as addictive. Moreover, at a more abstract level, constituting addiction as bad because it entails loss of freedom and individual autonomy assumes that these ideals can themselves be taken for granted as innocent. But as critics, including feminists and analysts of neo-liberalism have argued, the production of human beings as autonomous individuals is central to operations of power in modern societies. Certainly, in addiction discourses, the concern for freedom is linked to regimes of control, regulation and surveillance. In this context, as Mariana Valverde notes in her study of the government of alcohol, questions about the maximisation of freedom are less urgent than questions about how we are governed and defined through a certain notion of freedom.[4]

The opposition between autonomy and addiction is also commonly found in the view that the development and encouragement of particular virtues among the citizenry is the key to decreasing the extent and severity of drug problems. For example, psychologist Stanton Peele, an outspoken critic of medical models of addiction, argues vehemently that inculcating values in our children such as self-control, self-direction, autonomy and hard work is the most powerful weapon against drug use and addiction.[5] However, the model of the freely choosing autonomous individual that is championed is deeply implicated in the very problem of addiction. Addiction discourse is driven by a hierarchical and ethically charged dichotomy between rationality and freedom of will as the positive terms, and compulsive desire as the negative which continually threatens them.[6] The valorisation of individual self-control and discipline, promoted as a solution to addiction, is inherent to the concept of addiction and to the troubling experience of 'loss of control' which is at the core of the addictive experience. The addict is someone who has lost control over their desires and thereby over their life, as evidenced in their failure to meet work, family and social expectations. Explaining social deviance as the consequence of a pathological inability to control one's behaviour makes sense to us because of the presumption that people can and should exercise self-control and self-discipline, and that these virtues are the basis of success, achievement and good character.[7]

I will examine why it is bad to be an addict and what the wrongness of addiction is, although my main concern is *how* the problems and experiences we group under the term addiction are wrong. I will not focus on the consequences of drug use, nor attempt to identify the essence of addiction. Instead I will outline the different problems, dilemmas and concerns addressed by contemporary addiction discourses, both medical and popular, and examine how addiction is constituted in these discourses. While there is a pervasive theme of addiction as a disorder marked by physical, psychic and moral pathology, the 'wrongness' of addiction is not fixed nor indeed obvious. It varies according to context: the type of addiction and the type of addicted body, and the type of discourse.

The focus of the book is on both the production of addiction as a disorder located in the individual and on the range of pathological subjects and disordered bodies that are thereby constituted as objects of medical and therapeutic knowledge. Figures as disparate as the desperate young junkie, the respectable but addicted smoker, the habitual overeater and the sexually compulsive married man are constituted in addiction discourse as subjects whose conduct and desires are candidates for rectification and improvement. It is this therapeutic impulse, the will to improve the body and the self of the individual, which unites the medical 'scientific' study of addiction and the burgeoning popular literature of addiction and recovery. Discourses of addiction encourage individuals to scrutinise and interpret their conduct, their experiences, their feelings and their desires and measure them against the goal of physical, psychological, emotional and spiritual health. Specific practices and programs designed to take the individual from addiction to health are promoted as the solution to problems of living ranging from financial woes to low self-esteem.

My interest in addiction emerged out of a fascination with the operations of health and pathology as cultural categories imbued with moral meaning and political significance. The binary oppositions of health and disease, pathology and normality, are amongst the most powerful elements in contemporary regimes of discourse and power, deployed in a wide range of textual and institutional sites to classify bodies, human subjects and modes of existence as more or less worthy of respect and more or less needful of management and control. As early as 1946 the World Health Organization (WHO) defined health as 'a state of complete physical, mental and social well-being and not merely the absence of disease and infirmity'. More recent definitions have added emotional, social, spiritual, sensual and sexual aspects of health as necessary elements of a holistic model.[8] The notion of health as a positive and holistic ideal has been celebrated as a progressive shift from the mechanistic and fragmented view of the body identified with traditional western medicine, but as critics have observed, its effects are heterogeneous.[9] Such an expansive notion of health encourages human beings to understand and judge more and more of themselves in relation to a telos of harmonious and efficient functioning. Desire, discipline and pleasure are appropriated into an economy of health and disease, and distanced from alternative discourses such as those of rights and freedom, sin and salvation or virtue and conduct. As Nikolas Rose puts it, care has become a matter of cure and normalisation. 'All aspects of our care for ourselves are to be judged in terms of a logic of health and reorganized in terms of a quest for normality'.[10]

Addiction, as a discursive and practical meeting place of medical and ethical concerns, presents itself as an ideal site for a deconstructive engagement with health and pathology. Intimately tied up with issues of desire, pleasure, subjectivity and embodiment, addiction discourse necessarily deals in the 'physical, mental and social' elements of the WHO definition. Predictably and perhaps appropriately, my interest in addiction grew from a respectably contained avenue of research to an out-of-control obsession leading me to see everything in terms of addiction—the classic tunnel vision of the addict. In addiction texts, ranging from scientific papers to popular self-help guides for addicted shoppers, workers, lovers and eaters, I found that the dichotomies of health and disease and of the normal and the pathological were only two of many themes which emerged. Cultural anxieties about the boundaries of the body, technology, consumption, pollution and risk, the limits of the natural and the meaning of experience were also reproduced.

As this list suggests and critics have pointed out, addiction is not a universal feature of human existence, but a historically and culturally specific way of understanding, classifying and regulating particular problems of individual conduct. It is tied to modernity, medical rationality and a particular notion of the unique and autonomous individual.[11] Others have noted that the rise of addiction discourse and the emergence of the addict have taken place as part of the development of consumer capitalism, industrial technologies and the modern state. In the context of late capitalism, thinking about addiction segues smoothly into regretful musing on our uncontrollable desire for commodities and the ultimate emptiness of consumption. In Marc Redfield's words, 'the thought of addiction returns us to the West's most ancient topics and texts only to confront us with some of the most prosaic, specific, and in certain cases disastrous characteristics of our own modernity'.[12]

Addiction as an experience, way of life and rhetorical device also seems highly compatible with the cultural patterns, information systems and social relations we have come to classify as post-modern. For David Forbes, the quick and commodified ways of solving problems, producing identity and experiencing pleasure found in post-modern culture produce particular addictive patterns of consumption.[13] While many currently valued processes of identity formation and problem-solving (such as therapy) are in fact painstaking and meticulous rather than quick and easy, Forbes's point about electronic media is suggestive. Television, the internet, virtual reality and personal computers all seem highly amenable to the production of addictive relations with their users as well as being routinely described in the rhetorics of addiction. However, I do wish to guard against a kind of broad historicisation which would read both addiction and addiction discourses as symptoms of a postmodern fragmentation of self, community and identity. In this approach, the popularity of psychological theories such as those of addiction is explained by the need for individuals to 'ground' themselves as society is transformed, social networks unravel, certainties dissolve and traditional values and beliefs lose their authority and relevance. This too easily leads to either a nostalgic and utopian longing for a more innocent time when not only addiction but the regulatory category of addiction did not exist, or a smug reduction of the past to a bland and undifferentiated state where identity was fixed and people were not nearly as inventive, active, questioning and interesting as they are today. It also obscures the specificities of co-existing but distinct and sometimes contradictory discourses and practices, and collapses everything into one explanatory frame. Within this frame, 'the self' is taken to be an entity which is acted upon and influenced by social changes, rather than being a particular way of understanding, organising and describing human beings and being human.[14]

More productively, discourses of addiction can be understood as part of a peculiarly modern regime of disciplinary power and knowledge. Foucault's formulation that there is no power relation without the correlative constitution of a field of knowledge and no knowledge that does not also constitute power relations is useful here.[15] Thinking of the relationship between knowledge, including self-knowledge, and power in these terms enables a critical engagement with processes and programs of normalisation which create rather than constrain individual subjects, which are based on free-dom rather than subjugation. I highlight the operation of such forms of power in discourses and practices of addiction, which are very much engaged in the construction, interpretation and management of individuals and the shaping of their conduct and relationship to themselves.

Discourses of addiction are also engaged in the production of truth about drugs, the body and the processes which occur when they connect. Thus both medical and popular discourses of addic-tion are productive sites for examining what Foucault called 'the general politics of truth': what is accepted and made to function as true, the mechanisms used to distinguish the true from the false, the techniques accorded value in the acquisition of truth and status of those who are charged with saying what counts as true.[16] Following this formulation, this book is not an exercise in challenging addic-tion discourse for its promulgation of 'distorted', 'ideological' or 'false' statements. It is rather interested in the different regimes or economies of knowledge and truth that these discourses produce.

This brings me to the second meaning of the book's title which suggests that there are things that are 'wrong' with contemporary discourses of addiction. Not least, discourses of addiction induce the expansion of both prohibitive and productive forms of power exercised by state agencies, corporations and institutions such as the family, which have very real effects on individual lives. These effects are not universally oppressive or damaging, but neither should they be assumed to be straightforwardly emancipatory or benign. Under the rubric of addiction, certain ways of being are categorised as unnatural, disordered and self-destructive, while others are consti-tuted as natural, healthy and self-enhancing, and these ways of being are regarded as expressions of a totalised self or identity. Moreover their categorisation of bodies and subjects often coincides with existing hierarchies of social value, and reproduces inequalities of race, class, sex and sexuality. To draw on Judith Butler, the domain of addicted, abject and unlivable bodies can be viewed as the necessary, constitutive outside to the domain of the clean, proper and healthy body. Addiction is therefore vital to the regu-latory ideal of rational, autonomous subjectivity; it can be considered one of the 'zones of social life which are ... densely populated by those who do not enjoy the status of the subject, but whose living under the sign of the unlivable is required to circumscribe the domain of the subject'.[17]

In describing the textual production of addiction and addicted subjects I do not wish to deny the destructive effect of drug and alcohol abuse and other compulsions on people's well-being. However, I do think it is possible to criticise the view that drugs are inherently bad and their use is inherently pathological without falling into the trap of romanticising drug use. I also do not wish to diminish the experiences of the many people who have struggled with compulsive behaviours and have found relief and happiness using the language and tools of addiction and recovery. The aim is more to suggest that other ways of approaching ethical self-formation and transformation are possible, outside the demands of normality and the model of disease and health and recovery.

As one reads about addiction in both popular and specialist texts one soon notices the reliance on metaphor, and the use of different metaphors to support different understandings of the phenomena. Is addiction like diabetes or high blood pressure (a chronic disease)? Is it like hunger or thirst (a visceral drive)? Is it like enjoying opera (an acquired taste incomprehensible to non-enthusiasts)? Is it like watching TV in the evening (a routine habit)? Is it like falling in love (an irrational attachment)? The question of identity also haunts the field of addiction studies in a more formal sense. Definitions, concepts and models are constructed, modified, supported and opposed in a sometimes acrimonious, sometimes good-natured debate over the nature of addiction, resulting in a state of 'conceptual chaos', and a 'crisis of categories'.[18]

While this lack of coherence may be frustrating for those directly involved in drug treatment, education and policy, the struggles over the identity of addiction are, to a more distant observer, a fascinating display of language games and truth claims, in which broad issues of scientific authority, disciplinary boundaries, the control of knowledge and the relationship between language and the real are played out. Rather than regarding all the different understandings of addiction as lacking because they fail to grasp the whole or reach consensus, each can be viewed as a suc-cessful construction of a particular object of inquiry and particular problematics of desire and consumption.

Formulating addiction as a disease has been one highly influ-ential way of constituting it as 'real' and distinguishing it from more mundane categories such as bad habits or everyday labels such as heavy drinking. The question of whether or not addiction is a 'pri-mary disease entity' is a perennial theme in addiction texts and a continuing and sometimes heated debate in the field.[19] The more effort is put into finding answers, the more questions keep prolifer-ating. What kind of thing is addiction? Is it a disease or a syndrome or a psychological process? Is it a metaphorical disease or a real one (and what exactly is the difference)? If it is a disease what are its symptoms? How do its physical, psychological and social factors interact and what is their relative importance? The titles of recent articles and commentaries, for example 'Slaying the disease model dragon—again?' adduce a certain weariness with the subject, but the publishing of new insights and evidence 'proving' that addiction is or is not a disease continues unabated.[20] Both medical and popu-lar self-help approaches to addiction are often referred to as employ-ing disease models, although their visions of the disorder are quite divergent, adding to the terminological confusion. Self-help litera-ture proudly asserts its loyalty to a simple and unequivocal disease conception of addiction, while many medical texts do their best to distance themselves from such bold statements, preferring the more cautious and flexible approach summarised in the multifactoral 'dependence syndrome'.

The following three chapters concern the constitution of addic-tion as a disease or at least disorder of the individual. In these chapters the scope is limited to alcohol and drug addiction (as opposed to other 'newer' addictions). Chapter 1 discusses pharma-cological understandings of drugs and their role in producing addic-tive desire, before moving onto neurological models of addiction. Chapter 2 explores the substance dependence syndrome of medical discourse and the problems of diagnosing dependence as a medical disorder. Chapter 3 moves on to popular addiction discourse and its unashamed engagement with issues of selfhood. Connections between addiction, inauthenticity and dishonesty are traced in therapeutic texts and then interrogated through a discussion of the concept of denial. In Chapters 4, 5 and 6 the focus shifts to collections of texts which apply the concept of addiction to substances and behaviours other than drugs or alcohol. Rather than attempting to judge whether smoking, food, sex and love meet the criteria for genuine addictions, the chapters look at what happens, textually speaking, when they are produced as such.

Chapter 7 concerns the promise of happiness and health in addiction discourse and the pleasures of the work on the self required to fulfil this promise. Popular addiction discourse constructs everyday substances and experiences as potentially dangerous, and sees risk, dysfunction and disorder everywhere. But it provides its own antidote to addiction anxiety: a vision of a healthy happy world plus instructions on how to get there. This accounts for the optimistic tone of most of the texts. By constructing health as universally achievable and truth as ultimately knowable they argue for the possibility and desirability of perfection. In the utopia of recovery everything and everyone can be understood and outcomes can be predicted and controlled. Moreover, the practices that lead to physical, psychological and spiritual health can be mastered by anyone, and incorporated into the routines of daily life.

Recovery means wanting what we really want, and these genuine desires are the same for us all. Thus, this model of health presumes a homogeneity underlying people's differences. This is why descriptions of recovery are so often abstract and vague, compared to the specificities of individual addictions. At a broader level the discourse suggests that all problems have an identifiable cause and solution and that all pain can be understood and overcome. This is connected with the proliferation of objects of addiction and the urge to uncover deeper and deeper levels of hidden trauma. If the problem is 'solved' but perfect fulfilment fails to arrive, the identification of another problem is necessary to maintain the viability of the utopian vision. In addition, the techniques of self-surveillance and interrogation promoted as essential to recovery mean the state of recovery is always under threat. The proliferation of potential discourses of addiction means that finding a space of authentic desire is almost impossible, but it also ensures that the pleasures and anxieties of self-problematisation can continue.

1

The Substance of Drugs

Drugs make us ask what it means to consume anything, anything at all.

—Avital Ronell, *Crack Wars*

In 1997 the *Australian Women's Weekly* published the story of the 'almost instantaneous' cure of a young Australian heroin addict who had flown to Israel to undergo a controversial rapid detoxification treatment.[1] During the treatment, naltrexone, an opiate antagonist, is administered to the anaesthetised or deeply sedated patient. The naltrexone speeds up the process of detoxification, which normally takes several days, while the anaesthesia prevents patients from experiencing the distressing symptoms of heroin withdrawal. According to the dramatic story of despair and rebirth told in the magazine, the patient goes to sleep a hopeless addict, then wakes up eight hours later completely cured, all desire for heroin gone.

The article was the catalyst of a heated debate about the benefits of rapid detoxification and naltrexone. At the time, public interest in heroin was high in Australia because a proposed clinical trial in which a small group of addicts would receive prescribed heroin was hanging in the balance. Following the magazine article and television coverage, hundreds of Australian addicts reportedly went to Israel, paying $10 000 each for the treatment. Newspaper articles with headlines like 'Bree's Quick Fix Kills Deadly Habit' appeared, relating amazing success stories. Parents of addicts, newspaper columnists and politicians urged the government to make the 'life-saving' treatment available in Australia. Experts in drug and alcohol rehabilitation called for caution, pointing out that the treatment was expensive, possibly risky and regarded as helpful only for a minority of patients.[2] Stories celebrating the naltrexone cure deployed common beliefs about the power of drugs to transform selves, for better and for worse. The young woman featured in the *Women's Weekly* story was a loving daughter and brilliant student before heroin changed her into a 'dull-eyed' junkie who cared only about her next fix and stole from her devoted family. But the 'heroin-negating' drug naltrexone quickly turned the junkie back into the good girl. On awakening from her treatment she declares that she 'feels new' and her craving for heroin has disappeared. 'My days used to begin and end inside a needle. Now my life's begun again. I am finally free,' she says.[3]

The logic of reversal, from addiction back to normality, allowed the detoxification treatment to be explained in a satisfying narrative of the triumph of good over bad, of disorder restored to order. The pharmacological term opiate antagonist came to be interpreted as anti-opiate in a much broader sense. Naltrexone, the purifying life-saving medication, was constructed as the opposite of heroin, the polluting life-destroying drug. While both drugs were attributed with the power to transform selves and change lives, the power of naltrexone was benevolent and restorative; it returned people to their natural state. In contrast, heroin had a preternatural power of possession.

This view of an illicit drug as an inherently destructive agent of physical disease and moral decline is a staple of addiction discourse. In Australia the evil power of addiction is mostly commonly attributed to heroin. In the United States crack cocaine recently took on this menacing capacity in the most extreme form, as shown in the following passage from a text on drug policy:

> A compulsive crack smoker wants his second pipe more than his first, and his third more than his second. While heroin satisfies the desire for heroin, crack sometimes stimulates the desire for crack. It is as if there were a food that made one hungrier (and kept one awake to experience that hunger).[4]

Here heroin appears as almost benign, compared to crack's ability to produce perpetual craving. As many critics have pointed out, the demonisation of (certain) drugs has significant consequences in terms of public policy and treatment initiatives, justifying a complex system of differential prohibition of recreational drugs. It also encourages a view of drug users as inevitably morally degenerate, neglecting their children, ripping off their friends and quickly resorting to crime to support their habit, as they come under the control of the drug.[5]

In the case of the naltrexone debate, the constitution of heroin and other opiates as universally and innately destructive had the effect of devaluing, if not demonising, strategies which aim to reduce the harmful consequences of heroin addiction. It lent support to opponents of the heroin prescription trial, because if heroin causes an ultimately fatal brain disorder, as the *Women's Weekly* article suggested, then its supply to addicts is surely the antithesis of responsible and humane treatment. Secondly, the Manichean logic of heroin versus naltrexone also positioned methadone treatment on the devalued side of the opposition, although it has been extensively researched and found to be effective in reducing the harms of heroin use.[6] In the rhetoric of naltrexone as miracle cure, methadone was at best a worthless 'substitute addiction', at worst a poison masquerading as a cure. One magazine article stated that to its detractors methadone, 'a synthetic heroin first invented by doctors from the Third Reich', was 'nothing but a legalised form of "genocide"'.[7]

In 'Plato's Pharmacy' Derrida highlights the undecidability and ambiguity of the Greek word pharmakon, which can mean both poison and cure. His concern is with writing as a pharmakon, something that cannot be fixed in oppositions of good/evil, true/false, inside/outside, but rather disrupts these terms.[8] As the story of naltrexone suggests, the concept of the pharmakon, the substance which is both curative and injurious, also illuminates the place of drugs in contemporary western culture. The supply and use of psychoactive drugs such as heroin and cocaine are prohibited and punishable by severe penalties. This is justified by the threat they are seen as posing to individual and social health, which is in turn linked to their addiction-producing potential. On the other hand, the marketing, supply and use of a vast array of therapeutic drugs ranging from simple pain-killers to highly toxic substances and powerful psychoactive agents is central to Western bio-medicine. The development of new and better drugs is celebrated as the key to the conquering of disease and better health for all. The legal (for adults) substances of alcohol and tobacco are located in an interesting intermediate category. Nicotine is recognised as extremely addictive; it is well-known that cigarettes and alcohol account for the majority of drug-related deaths, and excessive drinking is associated with many social ills. Although recent years have seen an increasingly powerful public health discourse which highlights their dangers and urges their strict control, they can be purchased from supermarkets and consumed relatively freely, and regular users are not generally viewed as drug addicts.

The distinctions between medicine and poison, good drug and bad, are unstable and complex, produced as they are by overlapping medical, legal, and cultural discourses which draw on difficult-to-determine criteria such as harmfulness, addictiveness and therapeutic value. The legal and social status of a drug is certainly not determined by inherent qualities in the substance. The widely prescribed anti-depressant Prozac lifts mood by increasing serotonin levels in the brain, a similar action to the illegal street drug ecstasy. Good nicotine in the form of patches and gums is used to treat addiction to the bad nicotine found in cigarettes. Ritalin is an accepted treatment for children with attention deficit disorder, but when diverted to the black market it becomes a dangerous and addictive amphetamine. The distinction between dangerous drug and beneficial medicine is often a question of 'matter out of place', to borrow a phrase from Mary Douglas's classic analysis of purity and pollution.[9] That is, a drug is a chemical which is in the wrong place at the wrong time.

In the face of such complexity, the promise of a rational science of drugs which objectively presents the truth of drugs and addiction, separate from social influences and moral judgements, is enticing. But as I argue in this and the following chapter, there is a tension in medical discourse between the desire to be scrupulously non-judgemental about drugs, to describe them 'objectively' in pharmacological terms, and a therapeutic concern with their destructiveness to health and the dangers they pose to society. The latter concern necessarily involves normative judgements about the way bodies should function and about desirable as opposed to undesirable ways of being, and thereby subverts the ideal of an abstract and pure science of drugs.

Medical and pharmacological discourses often reproduce familiar dichotomies of natural/artificial, inside/outside, self/other and truth/falsity in their accounts of drugs and addiction, despite their desire to simply describe chemical and physiological processes. They can therefore be deployed to support the pathologisation of the addict or drug user as 'other' to the ideal of the healthy and autonomous individual. However, it is also the case that pharmacological accounts, especially those that privilege the brain as the site of addiction, can disrupt easy certainties about the relationship between drugs, bodies, desire, pleasure and truth. Part of my argument is that challenging pharmacological determinism and the often reductive and predictable discourses of drug science does not mean that the things drugs can do to and with bodies and bodily processes should be ignored. Rather, thinking about drug use and abuse in a nuanced way demands that we pay attention to the substance of drugs, their materiality and the physiological microprocesses which occur when they are ingested and absorbed.

Drug Science and Its Limits

Although medically oriented textbooks invariably state that the aetiology of substance dependence is complex and multifactorial, the pharmacology of psychoactive drugs is always an important element. The production of drugs of dependence as a class of substances with peculiarly powerful and universal effects reinforces the idea of addiction as a quality they possess. Their inherent chemical properties are seen as initiating and driving the addictive process, causing the bodily changes which result in dependence and producing a compulsion beyond individual control. Moreover, the pharmacological differences between classes of drugs are used to explain and order the variety of symptoms and behaviours seen in cases of addiction. Focusing on drugs as the agents of addiction seems to offer a way of liberating knowledge about addiction from the ever-shifting and impossible to quantify ground of social meaning and individual subjectivity. The task of understanding addiction becomes the apparently more containable one of delineating the addictive potential of different drugs and understanding their specific actions and their short and long term effects. Thus, in pharmacologically driven understandings of addiction, addicts are not necessarily human. Laboratory rats who will push a lever a hundred times to get a shot of cocaine, losing interest in food, sex, and sleep in their pursuit of its pleasures, are seen as demonstrating the same process as human cocaine addicts. The most salient information about drugs are their various actions in the brain. For instance physician and pharmacologist Sidney Cohen describes cocaine as follows:

> It is believed that the rewarding effects of cocaine are secondary to the availability of large numbers of dopamine [DA] molecules at the postsynaptic receptors in the brain centers that evoke pleasure and elation. These sensations result primarily from cocaine's ability to prevent the reuptake of DA back into the presynaptic neuron, thereby presenting the DA receptor sites with more DA over a longer interval.[10]

This mechanism is the basis of addiction whether the user is a rodent, a Hollywood celebrity or a homeless crack smoker. But on further examination pharmacological description of drugs and their actions raise more questions than they answer. Even defining drugs proves difficult. In contrast to the pejorative and value-laden everyday usage of the term, medical definitions of 'drug' describe a broad category of chemical agents or substances with no reference to questions of harmfulness, patterns and methods of use, legality or social acceptability. These issues are regarded as irrelevant, or even inimical, to the accurate description of a natural category of substances called 'drugs'. The broadest definitions do not distinguish between psychoactive and non-psychoactive substances, describing a drug as 'a chemical other than those required for the maintenance of normal health, which on administration alters biological function' or 'any substance other than food which by its chemical nature affects the structure or function of the living organism'.[11]

Other definitions restrict the category to psychoactive substances, for example the WHO regards a drug as 'any substance that, when taken into a living organism, may modify its perception, mood, cognition, behaviour or motor function'.[12] It is easy enough to find fanciful examples which fulfil the criteria of such definitions and raise questions about their utility. Chocolate, oxygen and water alter mood and brain functioning (not to mention behaviour). A bullet 'alters the structure or functioning of the living organism'.[13] But if these substances are included the sense of drugs as a distinct category bounded by some commonality is lost. The problem is that attempts to distinguish drugs from other things on the grounds of their effects will never completely succeed because 'drug' is not a natural category, but, as Derrida points out, a concept that 'supposes an instituted and an institutional definition' and requires a history and culture of conventions and norms.[14] The difficulty for medical discourse is that its scientific status requires that it distances itself from societal influences to aim for a objective description of physical features, but to make sense and have any utility its definition of drug must fit with medical practice, which is highly institutionalised and embedded in a culture of norms and prohibitions.

In particular, the words 'chemical' and 'substance' cannot be used to avoid the morally and politically loaded cultural category of drugs. The term 'chemical' has its own powerful negative connotations, particularly when juxtaposed with a notion of the body as organic and natural. Natural versus chemical is a central conceptual dichotomy in addiction discourse, both medical and popular, and it can be argued that it provides a new home for the displaced moral dichotomy of good and evil. Defining drugs as substances other than those required for 'normal health' or to maintain 'normal biological processes' is a way of finessing this attribution of unnaturalness. It puts in place a distinction between therapeutic substances like insulin, which work to restore health in cases of disease, and recreational drugs. But identifying normal health and normal biology is based on normative judgements about proper and improper bodies. The assessment of whether a drug is being used to restore or disrupt normal body functions is often as much social and political as physiological. Is pain relief disruption or restoration of normal functioning? Does it depend on whether the analgesic is aspirin or heroin? Prozac can be seen as restoring health because it lifts depression but what if it is used to treat symptoms such as lack of self-esteem, inability to experience pleasure, and sensitivity to criticism? How are such drug therapies different from the routine use of alcohol and cocaine to deal with lack of self-esteem and confidence? Indeed one American drug researcher and commentator has suggested that cocaine and heroin use is self-medication by those who do not have access to psychotherapy or Prozac.[15] For philosopher of medicine Georges Canguilhem, 'normal' in medicine is a highly ambiguous but ultimately normative term, referring both to the habitual state of an individual body and to an ideal type of organic structure. He argues that it is individuals who set their own bodily norms through their habits of life, and therefore normality and pathology can never be objectively and precisely defined.[16] On this view the maintenance of 'a normal state of health', meaning the capacity to continue one's usual activities, could require insulin, Prozac or heroin, and the idea of a group of substances which can be universally and objectively defined as drugs collapses.[17]

The classification of drugs into different categories based on their mechanisms and effects is another fundamental element of drug science which promises to bring rationality to the issue. Many clinical textbooks and general guides on drug use confidently set out straightforward taxonomies of drug types and use these categories to organise their chapters. These taxonomies have the reassuring effect of suggesting there is a natural and orderly system hidden under our confused cultural categories. A typical taxonomy divides drugs into Opioids, Sedatives, Stimulants, Cannabis, Hallucinogens, Volatile Inhalants, and Simple Analgesics. Another textbook develops a more complex categorisation: General Central Nervous System Depressants; Central Nervous System Stimulants; Opiate Analgesics; Cannabinols; Hallucinogens; Glues, Solvents and Aerosols; and, in a category which is unashamedly non-pharmacological, Over the Counter Drugs.[18]

But the difficulties masked by these classificatory schemes are vividly illuminated in a reading of a respected handbook of drug action by critics of 'pharmacological determinism', Richard DeGrandpre and Ed White. DeGrandpre and White highlight the circular journey taken by the handbook's author, pharmacologist and physician Robert Julien, as he considers various ways of classifying drugs and finds problems with them all. Firstly Julien considers classification according to chemical structure—but drugs that look quite different chemically can still behave more alike than drugs that are almost identical. He then turns to mechanisms of action as a way of classifying psychoactive substances. But the problem here is that knowledge of physiology is currently too limited to enable such an approach; moreover drug actions are often not confined to one area of the brain. He ends up observing that classification based on social categories like legality, therapeutic potential and potential for abuse could be considered as legitimate as the scientific categories. DeGrandpre and White observe rather tartly that Julien's account shows drug science verging on 'discovering' the already existing, socially constructed categories of good drugs and evil drugs.[19]

The blurring of the line between pharmacology and normative judgement in drug science is perhaps even more clearly illuminated when the addictive potential of different drugs is directly addressed. The exercise may be presented as straightforward description of chemical properties, but because 'addictive potential' implies the ability to cause individual and social harm, the result is always 'contaminated' by external factors. Because addiction is so strongly marked as a bad thing, addictiveness is not simply a quality inherent to the drug but is connected to perceived dangerousness, legal status and other social historical factors.

E. M. Jellinek's *The Disease Concept of Alcoholism*, a foundational text of modern alcohol studies, provides an interesting illustration of the mutability of addictiveness. Jellinek argued that physical dependence on alcohol, demonstrated by altered physiological responses, was the basis of (some forms of) alcoholism, and that alcoholism was therefore a disease. His argument required the identification of alcohol as a drug that, like morphine and heroin, had the ability to cause addiction through 'grave physiopathologic changes leading to craving'. Nevertheless, he placed alcohol in a different pharmacological category of addictiveness to these drugs, noting that not only were most drinkers not harmed by their habit, but that the amount of alcohol and length of time required for addiction to develop was much greater than was the case with other drugs. He also refers to a 1954 WHO report which noted that a maximum of 10 per cent of drinkers became addicted, while about 70 per cent of morphine users and 'practically' 100 per cent of heroin users were addicted. The historical context of post-prohibition America is evident in these distinctions. Jellinek and his associates at the Yale Center for Alcohol Studies aimed to promote a scientific view of drinking, in opposition to the temperance movement's view of alcohol as universally harmful. They also wished to raise public and medical awareness of the plight of alcoholics and the importance of alcoholism treatment and research. In fact, Blocker argues that Jellinek and Howard Haggard, director of the Yale Center, adopted the disease concept of alcoholism not for scientific reasons, but because it best suited their purposes of promoting moderate drinking habits amongst the general public. Distinguishing alcoholism from other highly stigmatised drug addictions was an important strategy, because it enabled the potentially devastating effects of alcohol for a small minority of drinkers to be highlighted, while also protecting its overall respectability.[20]

More recently, cocaine's ability to cause addiction has undergone re-assessment. In the late 1970s and early 1980s it was commonly accepted that although cocaine was habit-forming, it did not have a well-defined withdrawal syndrome, did not cause physical dependence, and was therefore not genuinely addictive in the way that narcotics and alcohol were. The 3rd edition of the American Psychiatric Association's Diagnostic and Statistical Manual of Mental Disorders (DSM-III), published in 1980, did not include the category cocaine dependence, listing only 'cocaine abuse'. In a 1982 article researchers Van Dyke and Byck compared a cocaine sniffing habit with eating peanuts and potato chips, 'a pattern of continued use while supplies are available and . . . simple abstention when supplies are lacking'. The advent of crack, a cheap smokable form of cocaine accessible to the poor, as well as increasing cocaine use, rendered the snack food analogy obsolete. Crack is regarded as 'extraordinarily addictive' and cocaine itself has been reconstructed in its wake. In a 1993 textbook cocaine is unquestionably an addictive drug with a definite withdrawal syndrome. For Cohen, writing in 1985, it is the addictive substance par excellence: 'If we were to design deliberately a chemical that would lock people into perpetual usage, it would probably resemble the neuropsychological properties of cocaine.[21]

The question of the addictiveness of tranquillisers reveals the problem of medical drugs which are dependence-producing. On one hand it is recognised that benzodiazepams like valium have been overused and that long-term (or even medium-term) use leads to dependence. On the other is their respectability as medically pre-scribed drugs. This conflict raises the alarming possibility that doctors (and medicine) are agents of addiction as well as experts in its cure. The author of an article on addiction in a medical reference volume deals with this tension by stating that it is 'addictive be-haviours' such as compulsive use that define addiction. Therefore, patients who become physically dependent on prescribed drugs are not addicted, even though their 'symptoms of dependence may com-plicate drug discontinuance'.[22] What this seems to suggest is that users of drugs who have access to a steady and legal supply from their doctors are not addicts because they do not behave like junkies. This is hardly a pharmacological distinction, yet it is pre-sented as if it is a consequence of the inherent properties of medical versus illicit drugs. Ironically, the point that it is behaviour rather than physiological dependence which defines addiction is raised by critics as evidence of the inadequacy of medical models of addiction.[23]

Armed with such stories of shifting addictiveness, critics, in-cluding social scientists, drug reformers and clinicians, have been able to mount powerful and sustained challenges to pharmacologi-cal determinism and essentialism. These critics have developed two broad arguments against drug science and medical models of drug use. Firstly, they have argued, as I have done above, that drug science fails to live up to its self-image as objective and rational, unbe-smirched by social and political factors. Secondly, they point out that focusing on the action of drugs on the central nervous system tells us very little about human drug use, which can only be under-stood as a social and cultural practice. A range of evidence is com-monly cited to support this case, much of it attesting to the variability of addictive and drug-related behaviour. Ethnographic comparison demonstrates that intoxicated conduct, rather than being a universal outcome of the effects of alcohol, varies dramati-cally depending on cultural beliefs about the nature of drunkenness. Laboratory experiments have shown that the belief that a drink is alcoholic has a greater effect on behaviour and feelings than drinking alcohol in a disguised form. Most US soldiers who became addicted to heroin in Vietnam gave up without treatment on their return home. Patients on strong medical doses of morphine rarely become addicted, discontinuing drug use without distress when they leave hospital.[24]

Shifting the focus from drug actions to social practices obviously produces very different models of addiction. For social psychologists like Peele and Orford addiction is a learnt behaviour, similar to other habitual behaviours which are necessary for human well-being. From this perspective addictions are determined by a complex interplay of 'reinforcing' and 'restraining' factors in the environment and by powerful cognitive processes. People become addicted not so much to a substance, but to an experience which includes physiological, psychological and social components. Anything which has a powerful effect on mood and perception can be addictive. Thus addiction is a place on a continuum rather than a distinct disease-like entity. Another more sociological approach focuses on the notion of 'addiction' itself as a historically and culturally specific social construction.[25]

The socio-cultural approach to drug use is an extremely productive field of research and analysis, offering insights into how drugs are used in different social locations, the meanings of people's varying experiences with drugs (and other habitual behaviours), and suggesting effective responses to problems associated with drug use. Its challenge to the reductive tendencies of drug science is particularly important at a time when biological and medicalised explanations for social problems are enjoying cultural ascendancy. And its emphasis on the normality of drug use is an important counter to the punitive rhetoric and practices of 'the war against drugs'.

However, cultural accounts of drug use can themselves run the danger of reductiveness if they assume that the materiality of the body and the nature of drugs are a straightforward and fixed substratum to the complex and varied forces of cultural and personal interpretation. For instance Stanton Peele's classic text *The Meaning of Addiction* consistently opposes pharmacology and physiology to 'lived human experience', the latter being the realm of individual beliefs, values, feelings, cognition, interpretation and social relations. It is only this realm of experience which is seen as able to account for the changeable and complicated nature of human drug use. This seems a limiting strategy, as it leaves largely undisturbed the pharmacology of drugs and the processes of brains and bodies.

Pharmacology and physiology are still presumed to be fixed in their mechanisms and uninfluenced by culture, language and history. As Elizabeth Wilson has argued, the assumption that human biology (and I would add drug actions) is 'psychologically inert and politically barren' forecloses some of the most compelling questions about bodies and their capacities.[26] The taxonomic unruliness of drugs discussed earlier could be understood not as purely a cultural phenomenon but as an expression of the slippery and protean networks which emerge when drugs and bodies connect and dis-connect.

For example, it is convincingly argued by supporters of cultural and social models of addiction that withdrawal syndromes are not simple physiological responses to changes in homeostasis. The severity, range and significance of symptoms are highly dependent on contextual and cognitive factors. Even morphine-addicted rats suffer more when deprived of their drug supply in their usual cage than if they are moved to a different cage which has no drug memories or connotations. Peele defines withdrawal as 'a complex self-labelling process that requires users to detect adjustments taking place in their bodies, to note this process as problematic, and to express their discomfort and translate it into a desire for more drugs'.[27] Learning, labelling, detection, interpretation and desiring are here presumed to be extra-biological, and the body is merely the location of the 'adjustments' which seem to require no further investigation. Could it not be that these adjustments are also complex networks of communication and interpretation (and perhaps miscommunication) which are able to offer insights into the experience and meaning of drug use? Moving away from the habit of thought which attributes all complexity and mutability to culture would allow for a fuller and richer view of bodily experiences and their sometimes overwhelming intensity. A shift away from the cultural could in this context enhance rather than threaten a human appreciation of the enticements of drugs and the struggles of addiction.

The Addicted Brain

In recent years neuroscience has become an increasingly authoritative and prolific source of knowledge about addiction. Recognising addiction as a brain disorder is celebrated as the foundation of a bright new era of scientific addiction research and rational drug policy. The United States National Institute on Drug Abuse (NIDA) has adopted the central tenet that drug addiction is primarily a disease of the brain, and is funding extensive neuro-imaging research on addiction. NIDA Director Alan Leshner has stated that the addict's brain is distinctly different from the non-addict's brain. He explains that a metaphorical switch in the brain seems to be thrown as a result of prolonged drug use and at this point the individual moves into the state of addiction, characterised by compulsive drug seeking and use. Previous policy and public health strategies have often been unsuccessful because of the belief that addiction is a social or moral, rather than medical problem.[28]

Neurological models like NIDA's can easily be viewed as extreme examples of the reductive trend in addiction science, for they seem to exclude not only the drug user's subjective experience and social location but also the drug user's non-brain body from the field of concern. However, their insistence that addiction is best understood as a matter of neurotransmitters, neural pathways and receptors is often combined with a robust belief that recreational drugs are inherently dangerous, both to the individual and to society. In scientific papers, government publications and books and articles on neuroscience and addiction for professional and general readers, the addicted brain is commonly figured as a site of disorder, its natural state having been corrupted by the artificial pleasure of drugs. This in turn produces the addict as an individual under the control of a powerful and destructive external force.

But the brain also emerges in these texts as an organ which is not so easily contained in such narratives of purity and pollution, innocence and corruption. Therefore rather than highlighting what is omitted by brain-based models as other critics have done, my concern is with what discourses of the addicted brain already contain in their constitution of desire, pleasure and the boundaries of the natural. It may be that the pathologisation of the addict as 'other' to the ideal of the healthy and autonomous individual can be disrupted from within biological accounts, especially those that privilege the brain as the site of addiction. Elizabeth Wilson has argued that it is productive to approach the brain as the site of an indigenous, although not autonomous, excess which disrupts the presumption of a neurological interior and a cultural exterior.[29] Indeed a striking aspect of the brain as it is constituted in popular and public science is its double identity. In one guise, it is the mysterious seat of human consciousness, 'not only more complex than we imagine but perhaps more complex than we can imagine'.[30] In other sites, including addiction discourse, the brain is presented as a bodily organ like any other. Orderly and neatly contained, its functioning is constituted as a logical and easily represented mechanism of electrochemical cause and effect. This visible and intelligible brain provides the basis for neuroscientific advances in drug and addiction research. Brain imaging techniques such as Positron Emission Tomography and new types of Magnetic Resonance Imaging give researchers what is commonly described as 'a window on the living brain'. It is argued that imaging technology will enable the universal truth of addiction to be revealed, a truth that is presumed to lie hidden beneath the varied and often confusing symptoms and dysfunctions of the individual.

But as feminist historian Barbara Duden has argued in relation to foetal imaging technology, a direct and unmediated view of a hidden object is exactly what such technologies do not provide.[31] These techniques do not simply reveal the hidden reality of the brain, they produce visible entities from invisible phenomena, via specific laboratory procedures and processes of digital coding. When an alcoholic's neurotransmitter activity is translated into a pattern of colour on a computer-generated image, a particular conception of alcoholism as a disease located in and inherent to the individual is made concrete. This materialisation of the formerly invisible allows molecular events to be read as proof that the patient's drinking habits constitute a distinct pathology. Despite the often-mentioned unimaginable complexity of the brain, brain images are often presented in pairs, with one image representing health and normality, the other image whatever disorder is being discussed: schizophrenia, Alzheimer's disease, alcoholism or addiction. Together, the image and the caption telling us what it represents construct a simple and clearcut visual distinction between health and disease, and imply that the assignment of brains and therefore individuals to either category is self-evident. What is not mentioned, perhaps because it is viewed as too banal a point, is that the meanings of these images depend on a prior classification of individuals into healthy and unhealthy, done not on the basis of abstract chemical or biological indicators, but on the assessment of conduct.

Feminist analyses of foetal photography and imaging have made convincing connections between the optical dissection of the body and understandings of subjectivity. The familiar depiction of the foetus as if it is outside the woman's body gives the abstract idea of foetal personhood what Duden calls a 'misplaced concreteness'.[32] Floating in its liquid world, miraculously freed of the maternal body, the foetus has become a symbol of life itself, with significant implications for reproductive politics. If representation produces the real in this way, what kind of reality does the making visible of the brain through scanning technology produce? Certainly, the radical disembodiment of the human as represented by these images is striking. Scanning technology supports an understanding of the self as a matter of electrochemical messages rather than flesh and blood. It also supports the idea of an interior self by depicting a demarcated inner space which is the location of the individual consciousness, separated and distinct from the outer space of the social world. Thus brain scans can be read as representations of the Cartesian model of the autonomous, bounded and disembodied individual.

But these images of the brain also represent the permeability and malleability of the border between what is constituted as the interior space of the brain and the exterior space of the social world. Studies of drug craving commonly exploit the openness of the brain to stimuli by using images and objects as cues to invoke craving. One such study mapped addiction onto the brain by scanning cocaine users' brains as they watched videotapes of people taking cocaine and of drug paraphernalia. The results were compared to scans taken while the subjects viewed 'neutral cues', which were videotapes of art and craft objects such as paintbrushes and clay and of a person handling sea shells. The scans showed that the cocaine video, but not the craft video, sparked increased neural activity in brain regions associated with memory (the amygdala, the cerebellum and the dorsolateral prefrontal cortex).[33]

Moreover, the cocaine users' reports of their craving matched the scans. The greater the reported craving, the greater the brain activity. This impressive concurrence between the subjective and the objective existence of craving, between the responses of the subjects and the colours on the scan, is seen as offering insight into the compulsion that is thought to drive and sustain addiction. The aspect of the study which is emphasised is its support for the idea that a specific form of emotionally loaded memory is critical to craving.[34] It is not surprising that there is a link between memory and desire, in the case of drugs as well as other desires. A common example in addiction literature is of the ex-heroin user who returns to his old neighbourhood after being released from jail, his desire for heroin growing the closer he gets to his old haunts, until by the time he has arrived in his old scoring area, a purchase is irresistible, despite promises he has made to himself and others to stay clean.[35]

But there are other aspects of this study that are equally provocative. Although it is presented as an advance in the objective observation of the physical reality of addiction, the study is a multi-layered confluence of texts and representations. The subjects view video representations of actors simulating drug use, and the resulting electrochemical response in their brains is translated into a pattern of colour. The scientists view these patterns, while also recording the subjects' assessments of their feelings, which are responses to direct questions such as 'how good do you feel?', 'do you have a craving or an urge for cocaine?', 'do you want cocaine?' and 'do you need cocaine?'. This set-up provokes a list of somewhat irreverent questions. What other kinds of images induce such neural activity? What did the scientists' brains look like while they were viewing the scans? How closely does the video of drug-taking have to correspond to the (urban, North American) subjects' own use of cocaine? Would footage of coca-leaf chewing Peruvians have any effect? What if some of the subjects were habitual and passionate art and craft hobbyists? How would their brains respond to the so-called neutral cue of the craft video?

What is most relevant to this discussion, however, is that this intriguing study, which seems to suggest that craving is a type of intense longing, an experience certainly not confined to drug addiction, is incorporated into the binary model of addicted versus non-addicted brains. The study has been reported as the discovery of a fundamental and defining difference between addicted and normal brains.[36] Moreover although the study demonstrates the ability of images and simulations to produce craving, it is interpreted as revealing the pharmacology of cocaine as the source of craving, and therefore of addiction. Thus, it becomes supporting evidence for the National Institute on Drug Abuse's view of addiction as a brain disorder, similar to schizophrenia or Alzheimer's disease. The connection of neuropharmacological models of drug action with ideas about natural and unnatural desires and true and false pleasures produces an authoritative view of addiction as a disorder of the self in which freedom to choose has been lost.

The Addicted Brain and its False Pleasures

Being 'other' to the natural and organic substances of the human body is often seen as the source of drugs' harmfulness. They have been described as toxic pollutants of the internal environment of the body, 'chemical intrusions' into users' central nervous systems.[37] But in the realm of neuroscience, the distinction between the natural and the chemical breaks down, because the brain is itself chemical. Here the power of drugs is not so much their artificiality, but their proximity to the natural. It is their mimicry of naturally occurring brain chemicals which enables them to interact with the nervous system of the drug user. They are, however, not subject to the same control and regulation that endogenous substances are, and their effects are therefore marked by destructive excess and escalation. For example, a guide written by two physicians explains that cocaine causes a massive neurotransmitter overload:

> The stimulation produced by these drugs is qualitatively similar to, but far in excess of, what we normally experience in 'energized' states . . . Instead of these chemicals turning off and resting once their message has been delivered, they continue zinging around the brain, setting off alarms and expending energy stores until the messengers and the energy stores are both exhausted . . .[38]

Here a drug is something that is not the body interacting with the body on false pretences, pretending in fact to be one of the body's natural substances. A drug is something external that becomes internalised, blurring the distinction between not only inside/outside but also self/other, with disastrous, although pleasurable results. A drug is, as Derrida says, the perfect parasite, attacking its host's body from within, 'at once inside and outside—the outside feeding on the inside'.[39] No wonder these substances are attributed with the ability to control their host's behaviour.

The chemical nature of the brain means that in neurological terms, the boundaries between the inside and the outside and the natural and the artificial are unstable and depend on careful conceptual distinctions. The existence of endorphins, which act very much like narcotics, suggests that the brain produces its own drugs. Indeed, compulsive runners and gamblers are diagnosed as hooked on the euphoria caused by endorphin release. This challenge is defused by alluding to the wisdom of nature. To the argument that the existence of internal opiates makes the taboo against similar drugs illogical, pharmacologist Sidney Cohen argues that humans are not wise enough to use narcotics as discriminatingly as the brain uses endorphins. He adds that the artificially sustained ecstasy of the junkie is very different from the pain relief provided by endorphins. The latter promotes survival by allowing enough pain to be felt for remedial action to be taken, while the former is a dangerous state of oblivion. The fine-tuned chemistry of the brain is contrasted to the toxic and crude substances churned out by 'the garage psychochemist'. Distinctions are also maintained between the restorative qualities of medically prescribed drugs and the destructive effects of illicit drugs (even if the drug in question is the same). For example, *Mind Over Matter*, a primer on drugs and the brain for junior high school students produced by NIDA, reassures its young audience that although opiates can 'quickly trigger addiction' when used improperly, 'used as directed by a physician, opiates are safe and generally do not produce addiction'.[40]

Despite these distinctions, the brain does emerge in neuroscientific models of addiction as an organ that has a natural affinity for drugs, for pleasure and for addiction. As well as destabilising oppositional distinctions between normality and pathology, the chemical interaction of drugs and brain challenge fictions of the body as a naturally complete and closed system. In Avital Ronell's words, 'The body of the addict, engendering dependency and the possibility of a *chemical prosthesis*, withdraws from the nostalgia of the body's naturalistic/organic self-sufficiency'. The addicted body can be refigured as a body with something extra, a body that has fabricated a supplementary organ that 'requires absolute attention in the mode of care' rather than a body which has lost an original integrity.[41]

Neurochemistry, by giving pleasure a central role in explanations of drug use, also suggests an alternative to theories of psychological and social lack. The neurotransmitter dopamine is commonly regarded as the link between drugs and pleasure. A *New Scientist* article explains that activities such as eating, sex, mothering infants, even social contact in general are pleasurable because they cause an increase in dopamine levels in the brain, acting at sites on what is called the reward pathway, or more colourfully, 'the pleasure circuit'. The power of drugs lies in their ability to 'hijack' the neural pleasure pathway which evolved to keep us interested in activities necessary to survival of the species. Another report, which argues for an evolutionary perspective on drug use, states that 'Drugs that induce positive emotions give a false signal of a fitness benefit', hijacking 'ancient brain mechanisms' of 'liking' and 'wanting'. Drugs thereby threaten the natural hierarchy of the brain. *Mind Over Matter* explains that they act directly on the 'more evolutionarily primitive' structures which can then 'override the cortex', eliminating 'the most human part of our brain from its role in controlling our behavior'. Here again drugs appear as dangerous border dwellers between the natural and artificial, exploiting their proximity to the natural to deceive the brain, release primitive destructive urges and threaten its (Darwinian) fitness. When we satisfy our hunger by eating, dopamine is released, which gives us a feeling of well-being. This is a genuine or truthful pleasure because it comes from the fulfilment of a need. Drugs provide the pleasure without meeting any needs, but the brain nevertheless registers this pleasure as real. And because the illusory pleasure of drugs is more rapid, predictable and powerful than the well-being gained from daily life and fulfilment of responsibilities, the addict eventually loses interest in the real in favour of the simulacrum. According to Derrida, this attachment to illusory pleasure is what we hold against the drug addict. We do not object to the drug user's pleasure *per se*, he argues, but we cannot abide that his is a pleasure taken in an experience without truth.[42]

Addiction as a state of alienation from truth is central to popular models of addiction, perhaps most obviously in the idea that the addict exists in a state of denial, unable to see the obvious cause of her problems. What the neurological discourse of addiction provides is a scientific basis to the division of pleasures into true and false. The inauthenticity of the addict is constituted as a chemically produced and objectively verifiable state, rather than a normative judgement about a way of being. But while positing a distinction between natural needs and unnatural addictions, these explanations also suggest that for the brain the two are easily, perhaps naturally, substitutable. The fact that eating and sex, which stand for the natural in these accounts, are now accepted as prime candidates for addictive escalation, further complicates the picture. It seems that not only can unnatural desires simulate natural needs, but natural substances and activities can stimulate unnatural desires.

To return finally to the question of drugs, the brain and pleasure, the case of naltrexone reveals that a drug, albeit a good drug, can undo the harm of drugs and liberate the self. The brain dosed with naltrexone is still operating with a chemical prosthesis but one that thwarts rather than produces artificial pleasure. In fact, naltrexone has been described as 'almost a non-drug', distinguished as it is by an absence of discernible effects other than opiate blockade. It is 'neither reinforcing nor addicting and has no potential for abuse or diversion for unprescribed use'.[43] In this sense, it is the perfect anti-addiction drug, and studies have found it successful for maintenance treatment of highly motivated individuals who have much to lose if they continue opiate use. However, its status as 'almost a non-drug' also limits its success; it seems it is too easy to 'just say no' to naltrexone. Poor retention rates and low patient compliance characterise clinical studies of naltrexone maintenance treatment and the accepted explanation is the lack of positive effects when the drug is taken and the absence of negative effects (withdrawal symptoms) when it is discontinued. The ideal anti-addiction drug turns out to be too non-addicting. Without the compulsive drive provided by the craving brain, many fail to comply with the therapeutic regime. In this case, absence of chemical pleasure and the resulting freedom to choose lead back to, not away from, addiction.

The complexities of the neurological and its links with psychoactive substances, both endogenous and exogenous, resist polarised categories of addiction and non-addiction. While the brain provides many insights into compulsion, desire, pleasure and memory, it is not a self-enclosed space that contains the truth of any of these entities. Neither can the different substances we identify as drugs be assumed to be fixed in their actions or abilities. While they are not the all-powerful agents of addiction of popular discourse, nor are they inert objects in a process entirely driven by human actors.

A reformulation of drugs and their relation to the body requires an understanding of corporeality which challenges the conceptualisation of bodies as organic, natural and unified entities. It also needs to be an approach which can recognise that bodies all have a particular sex, race and morphology, and that these specificities encode bodies and subjects, their conduct and habits, with meaning and value.

One promising conceptualisation is of the body as a discontinuous, non-totalisable assemblage, as written by Gilles Deleuze. A Deleuzian understanding of embodied human subjectivity as assemblage enables a refiguration of the encounter between drugs and the body away from the dichotomy of the artificial and the natural. Interpreting and drawing on Spinoza, Deleuze defines the body by what it can do rather than what it is. His concentration on the capacities of a body—more specifically, its capacity to affect and be affected by other bodies—allows a mode of individualisation to be envisaged which is not dependent on the existence of a subject. The affective capacity of a body comprises its power which can be either decreased or increased when it connects with another body. Bodies in this schema include anything that has the capacity to affect or be affected: a human agent, a horse, a piece of music, a grain of sand, a social body or a drug. In the Deleuzian model, there is no ontological essence or stable subject behind a body's actions. A body is essentially active, it cannot be separated from what it can do, how it can be affected, the linkages it can make; and these capacities are always changing, giving rise to a body that is always in a state of becoming rather than being. As a 'becoming' rather than a being it cannot be defined in terms of substance, organs, form or functions.[44]

Writing with Guattari, Deleuze develops a complex model of the body as assemblage, created and connected by flows of desire and intensity. The 'body without organs' (BwO) is the limit point of the body as assemblage; it acts as a powerful reminder that we need not, and should not think of our bodies in terms of their biological organisation. The BwO is not opposed to the organs but to the organism, the organic organisation of the organs. The body without organs is also opposed to the articulation and interpretation of meaning and the formation of the subject. Becoming a BwO is not an ideal state, but something we do every day, at least to some extent.[45]

The BwO is of particular interest to my project in that Deleuze and Guattari specify the drugged body as one of a 'dreary parade' of 'sucked-dry' and empty BwOs, along with the masochist body, the paranoid or schizo body and the hypochondriac body. The empty BwO is a body that has been evacuated of intensities and flows. As Grosz explains:

> This body does not lack; its problem is the opposite: it fills itself to the point where nothing further can circulate. It is empty only in the sense that if a body is made up of proliferations, connections and linkages, the empty BwO has ceased to flow.[46]

But this is not a moral or medical judgement; it does not view the addict body in terms of a pathological ontology or a singular disease. Rather, it is an ethological description of an arrangement of forces. The addicted body has forged a link which has become frozen and fixed, and therefore limiting. A recovering addict body could be viewed as equally frozen, stuck in repetition of a singular truth and blocked to the circulation and proliferation of intensities. Deleuze and Guattari's use of the drugged body as a model of the empty BwO can be distinguished from an attempt to refigure drug use and addiction by using their vision of corporeality. Many of the practices pathologised in contemporary addiction discourse, such as smoking, compulsive eating, devotion to casual sex and heavy drinking are not necessarily productive of an empty BwO. Neither are such attributes as a lack of interest in self-examination, a rejection of the spiritual or a dislike of intimacy (discussed in later chapters). A body that indulges in excess and depends on certain substances and patterns of behaviour to function can still allow for the circulation of intensities and remain open to connections with other bodies.

It is possible to argue that for the 'becoming' body, having abandoned the mythology of organic origins for better or for worse, drugs would not be encountered as radically other and inherently damaging. Rather than alien substances invading a space of natural innocence, the relationship would be between two bodies made up of forces, energies and intensities. Although each body/drug encounter could be judged positive, negative or neutral depending on its specific effects, the encounter between the two bodies itself would not be assumed to be intrinsically bad. Instead of a moral distinction between substances as either good or evil, healthy or unhealthy, the question would be one of either bad or good encounters. This is the realm of Spinozan ethics (as interpreted by Deleuze):

> The good is when a body directly compounds its relation with ours, and, with all or part of its power, increases ours. A food, for example. For us, the bad is when a body decomposes our body's relation, although it still combines with our parts, but in ways that do not correspond to our essence, as when a poison breaks down the blood.[47]

An encounter between a body and a drug could be either a bad poison-like or a good food-like encounter, depending on the specific body, the specific drug and the specific situation. The challenge is to increase the good encounters and limit the bad, just as we do in other relationships. The notion of the encounter seems offers the possibility of an ethics of body practice away from transcendental, universal moral codes and from the categorisation of pleasures into the natural and unnatural, the good and the bad. Instead, it recognises that all pleasures are made, and can therefore be made use of constructively or destructively.

2

Reading the Signs of Disorder: Diagnosing Dependence

The terminology keeps changing, but the basic disorders are the same: alcoholism and drug abuse. One of the problems with substance use has been that because it has been so variously defined (by different writers, for different substances, in different eras), there is substantial disagreement as to exactly what it is and who engages in it. The genius of DSM-IV is to define the disorders related to all the substances more or less uniformly. These definitions replace older terms such as alcoholism, problem drinking, loss of control, physiological dependence, addiction, habituation, and other (often pejorative) terms applied over the years to people who use mind-altering substances.

—James Morrison, *DSM-IV Made Easy*

Safe versus hazardous levels of alcohol consumption, quantified in terms of standard drinks per day, have become a familiar part of public health information on the requirements of a healthy lifestyle. We are urged to judge our drinking habits against the 'low risk' standard of four drinks per day for men and two for women. This level is low risk drinking according to the National Health and Medical Research Council of Australia. US guidelines for moderate drinking stipulate no more than one drink a day for women, two drinks a day for men. Despite these variable standards, it makes sense to distinguish safe from harmful use by the quantity consumed, given that high levels of alcohol intake are associated with numerous health problems. And in everyday life alcoholism is understood as a state marked by excessive and therefore hazardous drinking. But a striking aspect of diagnostic guidelines for alcohol dependence (as alcoholism is called in official classifications of diseases) is the absence of criteria directly addressing quantity consumed. Instead, the focus is on the drinker's feelings and thoughts and on the consequences of her drinking. Is she preoccupied with drinking? Does she feel compelled to drink? Does she continue to drink even though it is causing health, work and social problems? Withdrawal and tolerance, read as evidence of physiological changes arising from long-term and heavy drinking, are also listed, but they are not necessary for a diagnosis of dependence to be made. The criteria for dependence on drugs other than alcohol follow the same pattern.

Subjective experiences are also emphasised by screening tests used to detect drinking problems. The CAGE questionnaire, recognised as one of the most efficient and effective screening devices for alcohol abuse and dependence, does not ask about levels of drinking. Four simple questions make up the test. Have you ever felt you should cut down on your drinking? Have other people annoyed you by criticising your drinking? Have you ever felt guilty about your drinking? Have you ever had a drink first thing in the morning to get rid of a hangover or steady your nerves? Two or three positive answers suggest dependence, a score of four positives is regarded as diagnostic. Self-administered questionnaires published on websites or in self-help texts tend to focus on the drinker's unhappiness and problems relating to others. Mariana Valverde points out that in the US National Council on Alcoholism and Drug Dependence's 26-point alcoholism quiz, feelings of guilt and worry are the most salient signs of trouble. Several of the questions do not mention drinking or sobriety at all. She argues that the test is 'not an inquiry into drinking as much as a test of the soul's relation to itself'.[1]

In broader terms, what these tests and classifications are trying to identify is a particular form of pathological relationship between the subject and the substance. While frequent and excessive consumption may be a sign of such a relationship, the key is the high priority the substance has attained in the person's 'repertoire of choices'. The drug has come to mean too much. Hence the emphasis on subjective states such as preoccupation and guilt, and on secondary outcomes such as employment problems and social difficulties. But as discussed in the previous chapter, the particular properties of psychoactive drugs are viewed as crucial to the development of dependence. The intensity of the relationship between an addict and his drug is explained by the ability of drugs to alter mood and to cause neurological and physiological changes over time. Arguing against including 'nondrug disorders' in the category addiction, physician Norman Miller emphasises the distinct 'foreign' and 'pharmacological' effects drugs have on the brain and behaviour and the ability of drug-brain receptor interactions to produce stereotypical and predictable responses in mood, cognition and behaviour.[2] These effects and changes are taken to confirm the status of addiction as an objective, verifiable medical condition, even though on their own they do not define, describe or explain addiction and its particular subjective and behavioural states of preoccupation and compulsion.

Ultimately it seems that addiction is a state marked by caring too much about the wrong things, and not enough about the right things, and it is unclear why only drugs and alcohol can be genuine objects of dependence. No wonder then that, as Valverde remarks, the irreducibly ethical elements of alcoholism keep emerging despite efforts to confine it to medical terms.[3]

In the context of therapeutic medicine, addiction is a process which takes place over time, observable when the drug interacts with a body, producing a pattern of signs in a bounded space. While subjective factors and patterns of destructive behaviour are recognised as the crucial elements of dependence, the biochemical processes which are believed to underlie the observable changes are an important element in the production of the symptoms into a definable and unified disorder. Not surprisingly one of the continuing preoccupations of addiction medicine is how to conceptualise the link or movement between pharmacological and physiological phenomena and the psychological and behavioural elements of addiction. In its attempts to convey their interconnection, medical discourse is vulnerable to accusations that it psychologises the biological (for example when it writes of 'cells crying out for a drug') or biologises the psychological (for example when craving is read as a result of the physiological processes of withdrawal). Such constructions highlight the problem of addiction as a hybrid experience and concept, and point to the limitations of dominant understandings of psychosomatic processes and experiences.

Dependence Syndrome

When it shifts its gaze to the observable process of addiction in a clinical rather than laboratory context, medical discourse depends on the idea of an organism undergoing a change or alteration from a natural 'normal' state to a disordered, corrupted state. Through concepts such as withdrawal, tolerance, and craving, addiction is internalised in the body of the addict. Binding addiction to the addict's body gives the concept of addiction another form of ontological existence. Unlike neurological markers, bodily and behavioural signs of addiction are visible to the naked eye, their observability apparently unmediated by any interpretative device. The progress of the disorder can be mapped through the signs exhibited by the body, allowing addiction to be constructed as an entity with its own natural history or life cycle. Progressive and orderly development through predictable stages marked by regular patterns of symptoms has been an important element in medical discourse on alcoholism and addiction since E. M. Jellinek first developed the modern disease model. The idea that addiction has a natural history, a 'sequential development of designated biological processes within the individual', provides a satisfying and coherent narrative of decline.[4] It produces a disease which is obedient to its own logic and norms, although it distorts the body's normal and natural functioning. Jellinek numbered the symptoms of alcoholism chronologically from one to forty-three and divided them into three phases of the disease: prodromal, crucial and chronic. The symptoms Jellinek describes are a colourful mixture of the physical, psychological, social and spiritual, setting the trend for future formulations. They include surreptitious drinking, blackouts, preoccupation with alcohol, tremors, indefinable fears and 'vague religious desires'. His sequential model is still presented in medical textbooks, and other chemical dependencies are presumed to follow a similar pattern. Other visions of the disease are more flexible, referring to 'a lawful pattern of signs and symptoms' rather than a chronology of symptoms.[5]

However, the most influential and widespread way of conceptualising addiction as a disorder is synchronic rather than diachronic. In the concept of the dependence syndrome the disorder is presented not so much as a process but as a list of current symptoms to be located in the patient. The notion of temporal development is present, in that the syndrome is described as a pattern of repetitive use and the symptoms do not have to appear simultaneously, only within the same twelve-month period. However, the syndrome in its common tabular presentation appears more as a slice of (a disordered) life than a history or career.

This model of dependence syndrome was first laid out by a World Health Organization (WHO) Working Group in 1980. The definitions of psychoactive substance dependence set out in the two official compendia of disorders, the WHO International Classification of Diseases and the American Psychiatric Association's Diagnostic and Statistical Manual, were developed from this concept. The most recent edition of the International Classification of Diseases (ICD-10) describes dependence syndrome as a 'cluster of behavioural, cognitive and physiological phenomena that develop after repeated substance use'. Diagnosis is made if three of the following criteria are met: (i) a strong desire or sense of compulsion to take the substance; (ii) impaired capacity to control its use; (iii) a physiological withdrawal state; (iv) evidence of tolerance; (v) preoccupation with substance use and decreased interest in other activities; and (vi) persistent use despite clear evidence of harmful consequences. The description in the American Psychiatric Association's most recent diagnostic manual (DSM-IV) is similar, defining substance dependence as a 'maladaptive pattern of substance use, leading to clinically significant impairment or distress'. For a positive diagnosis, three of the following criteria must occur: (i) tolerance (a need for increasing amounts of the drug to achieve the desired effect); (ii) withdrawal; (iii) taking the substance in larger amounts or over a longer period than intended; (iv) a persistent desire or unsuccessful efforts to control use; (v) a great deal of time spent in obtaining, using or recovering from use of the substance; (vi) important social, occupational or recreational activities are given up or reduced because of substance use; and (vii) use continued despite recognition that a physical or psychological problem is caused or exacerbated by the substance. The DSM-IV description also states that tolerance, withdrawal and compulsion are 'usually' experienced, while 'craving', a strong subjective drive to take the substance, occurs in 'most (if not all)' dependent individuals.[6]

The differences between the British-based ICD-10 model of dependence and the American DSM-IV are significant although subtle, reflecting differences in approach between American and British psychiatry. Robin Room notes that British psychiatry has tended to take the view that social consequences do not belong in definitions of diseases or disorders. Differences between American and British and Australian understandings of addiction also demonstrate the much more influential position held by twelve-step models in the United States. American medical texts commonly include twelve-step concepts such as denial, codependence and enabling in their discussions, and are much more likely to support the view of addiction as a progressive disease which can only be halted through the maintenance of complete abstinence. However, these influences from the recovery movement and treatment industry are not apparent in the DSM-IV model of dependence.[7]

Supporters of the dependence syndrome concept stress its flexibility, its inclusion of biological, psychological, and social factors, and its unwillingness to 'assign a weight or special significance to any one factor or interaction'.[8] Indeed as Robin Room has pointed out, one of its most notable characteristics is that despite the sense of a unitary disorder conveyed by the term 'substance dependence', there is no single thing described by this label. The diagnostic criteria are disjunctive, meaning that meeting any three qualifies as dependence; thus one sufferer could have no symptoms in common with another. There are many possible ways of being dependent on a substance, and there is a large number of substances which one could be dependent on in all these various ways, from nicotine to heroin. Moreover, there is no single criterion shared by all who are diagnosed as dependent.[9]

The model is also silent on the aetiology of dependence, aiming only to describe the syndrome as it appears in individuals. This is typical of the ICD-10 and the DSM-IV, which avoid causal explanations in favour of a descriptive and supposedly atheoretical approach to the classification of disease. The move away from psychoanalytic explanations to a supposedly more scientific, modern and reliable nosology has been celebrated by psychiatry as the triumph of fact over theory. But as critics have argued, the notion of an atheoretical classification system presumes the possibility of pure observation free of any interpretative framework. It ignores the presuppositions about the nature of reality, about what counts as evidence, and about the relevance of different events and experiences which structure all scientific observation. As Room has argued, the process of differential diagnosis operationalised in this classification of diseases is a method for comparing competing possibilities. It is therefore not well equipped to deal with the question of whether there is a disease present at all. It also assumes that diseases are either present or absent, rather than existing in degrees of strength or manifestation.[10]

The ideal of atheoretical classification also disavows the role of evaluative judgements in classifying mental disorders. As far as the dependence syndrome goes, there is an obvious aetiological or at least proto-aetiological claim made about the role of drugs in producing unique forms of dependence. The diagnosis requires that the pattern of behaviour be related to the consumption of a psychoactive drug. Similar symptoms of persistent desire, loss of control and preoccupation regarding food, sex or gambling, for example, are located in different categories of disorder.[11]

Despite its broadness and inclusivity, the dependence syndrome concept can be argued to have a definite allegiance to a particular approach to addiction. It constructs addiction as 'a real beast' rather than a stage on a continuum of behaviour.[12] Its reproduction in diagrammatic or tabular form in numerous texts gives the disorder a concrete existence. By constructing addiction as a syndrome or disease, albeit a 'biopsychosocial' one, medical expertise retains its authority over the field. Simultaneously, the knowledge claims of social scientists who view addiction as a socially constructed entity and/or a normal if extreme form of learnt behaviour are marginalised.[13] The incorporation of social factors into the model does not necessarily lessen the degree of medicalisation; the social can instead be formulated in clinical terms. For example, financial problems and the loss of old friends may be described as symptoms of deteriorating 'social health', and lack of joy and intimacy as symptoms of impaired spiritual health, in the same way that liver disease and high blood pressure are the sequelae of alcoholism in the realm of physical health. For those who approach addiction and drug use as primarily social and cultural phenomena, the development of the dependence syndrome concept from clinical observation and research on patients in treatment also limits its usefulness. Anthropologist David Moore points out that most drug use occurs in nonclinical populations and it is unclear whether clinically defined dependence is applicable to community settings. He found that the notion of dependence as 'a measurable psychobiological "it"' made little explanatory sense when applied to the group of young amphetamine users he studied, whose drug use was best understood as part of the fluid and ongoing social action of their lives, and which increased and decreased in relation to cultural, social and economic shifts.[14]

On the other hand, American experts in addiction medicine seem to regard the model as being too vague about the status of addiction as a primary and independent disease defined by specific and predictable symptoms. Miller argues that the shift in terminology from drug addiction to the 'more fashionable' substance dependence obscures the centrality of 'loss of control' as the critical and fundamental component of addiction. The use of the term dependence is also confusing, Miller suggests, because it can be used to refer solely to the physiological processes of adaptation. In this sense it is possible for someone to be dependent on a drug, after medical treatment for pain for example, but not to demonstrate the psychological and behavioural criteria of addiction. For Miller it is clear that addiction is located in the drug-seeking behaviour of the addict, and in particular in the loss of control over her behaviour.[15]

But for others the presence of physical dependence, indicating that the body has adapted physiologically to chronic use of the substance, is the *sine qua non* of addiction. The position that views physical dependence, namely the presence of withdrawal and tolerance as the definitive sign of addictive disease was set out by Jellinek in his 1960 publication *The Disease Concept of Alcoholism*. Here he concluded that physical dependence on alcohol, demonstrated by altered physiological responses, was the basis of (some forms of) alcoholism, and that alcoholism was therefore a disease. The equation of 'altered physiological response' with the 'truth' of addiction was formulated in Jellinek's classification system of five different 'species' of alcoholism, identified by letters of the Greek alphabet. Jellinek stated that only two species, delta and gamma alcoholism, were diseases, because only they demonstrated a 'physio-pathological process' involving adaptation of cell metabolism, acquisition of tissue tolerance and experience of withdrawal symptoms, craving and loss of control or ability to abstain. The notion that a focus on the 'physiopathological process' of addiction is the key to scientific and rational knowledge of the disorder remains a common theme in contemporary texts. Doweiko's textbook for medical students uses 'a demonstrated withdrawal syndrome' as the criterion which indicates whether a user 'actually is addicted to a chemical'. Another textbook for medical professionals remarks that psychological dependence 'is a subjective item that is almost impossible to quantify objectively and thus is of limited usefulness in making a diagnosis'. Instead, the author focuses on the metabolic and pharmacodynamic forms of tolerance and the physiological symptoms of withdrawal syndromes.[16]

In fact, distinguishing between physical dependence and psychological dependence and then formulating their relationship is a continuing problem for addiction discourse, albeit a problem which works to produce drug addiction as a credible 'biospsychosocial' disorder with fluid and undetermined links between the bio, the psycho and the social. Examining the history of the WHO's attempts to define addiction reveals that the seemingly straightforward distinction between physiology and feelings is difficult to maintain. In 1958 the WHO Expert Committee on Addiction-Producing Drugs set out two diagnostic categories, drug addiction and drug habituation, the former signifying the presence of both physical and psychological dependence, the latter 'only' psychological. This distinction was an attempt to justify the subjection of some drugs (the addictive) but not others (the merely habit-forming) to strict international control. It abandoned these terms in 1964, in favour of the supposedly less judgmental term 'drug dependence', but this terminology still implied an important distinction between psychic and physiological dependence. Finally, it developed the idea of a drug dependence syndrome in the late 1970s. Recognising the difficulty of defining physical dependence as a separate component from psychological dependence, it replaced physical dependence with the more specific term 'neuroadaptation' in the early 1980s.[17] By the 1990s ideas of the biological were being expanded: in 1993 the committee stated that the distinction between physical and psychic dependence used in earlier reports 'was not consistent with the view that all drug effects on the individual are potentially understandable in biological terms'. However despite this expansion of the biological it remains the case that drug effects are described in the psychological language of need and desire, for example tolerance is described as a *need* for increased amounts of the substance to achieve the *desired* effect.[18]

Despite the confusion generated by attempts to separate and distinguish between different elements of addiction, the idea that the presence of 'physical dependence' on a drug can be identified, and that it is the sign of genuine addiction, remains in circulation. It operates as an important device in producing substance dependence as a firmly scientific and medical matter, and in refuting arguments that value-laden judgements about conduct and lifestyle are the basis of diagnosis. The problem with this approach is that while physiopathological processes and chemical properties may seem relatively easy to measure and define, they cannot be separated from 'subjective' experiences or cultural interpretations. Indeed, the physiological itself is subject to all the ambiguity and inconsistency commonly attributed to psychosocial phenomena. Moreover, in the absence of any connection with desire, conduct and behaviour, physiological processes cannot sustain a workable or useful model of addiction in the individual.

The Addicted Body: Dependence, Withdrawal and Damage

Despite the official unshackling of physical dependence from addiction in the WHO model, withdrawal symptoms and increasing tolerance still appear in medical discourse as important elements in the charting of the addictive process within the body, providing visible and sometimes dramatic signs of deviation from the physiologically normal. The explanatory narrative is that chronic use causes the brain to adapt to the presence of the drug or drugs, often reducing the production of neurochemicals that are similar to the drug. Tolerance to the drug develops, meaning that more of the drug is required to produce the same effects. Suddenly stopping or reducing drug intake causes distressing 'decompensation' symptoms as the brain readjusts to the absence of the drug. As described in medical textbooks each class of drugs has its own characteristic and recognisable withdrawal syndrome. These tend to be the opposite of the effects of the drug; for instance the drowsiness, relaxation, constipation and analgesia of heroin use is mirrored by the insomnia, anxiety, abdominal pain, nausea and diarrhoea of opiate withdrawal. Heavy cocaine users whose use is interrupted are described as crashing into depression, becoming irritable, fatigued and lethargic. Alcohol withdrawal can be a relatively mild syndrome of anxiety, increased pulse rate and tremor, but the severely affected can have seizures and delirium. The existence of such characteristic syndromes supports the idea that these reactions to the cessation of drug use are not learned responses, but universal processes of biological adjustment.[19]

The dominant conceptualisation of withdrawal constitutes a body which pre-exists culture, complete in its organic and natural unity. It constructs a dynamic and finely tuned state of balance as this body's normal and healthy condition. In its original state, before being polluted by drugs, the body is imagined as uncontaminated by foreign matter and almost effortlessly able to maintain equilibrium. The repeated introduction of an extraneous and toxic chemical disrupts the delicate operation of the system, but it eventually adapts to its presence and indeed comes to expect it. The concept of withdrawal symbolises the conflict between the artificial substance and the natural body. If the drug is suddenly removed from the organism, it has to readjust. Various unpleasant symptoms are experienced, but ultimately the capacity of the body to right itself and its natural wisdom prevail, and balance is restored.

The body producing withdrawal symptoms can also be represented as a machine or collection of mechanical forces. Doweiko uses the metaphor of a car that has been driven with its brakes on to describe an addicted body; you can eventually force the car to drive at normal speed, but if the brakes are then released suddenly it will jump forward because the brakes are no longer fighting the forward motion. This metaphor resonates with the belief that drug-taking 'holds people back' and impedes their progress on the road of life, while simultaneously emphasising the physiological as opposed to psychological and social processes of drug use and withdrawal. More common are organic images of the body as a wise and self-healing entity which, no matter how much it has been abused, retains the ability to detoxify and rebalance itself. Withdrawal then becomes not only a readjustment but a profoundly meaningful process of cleansing and purifying.[20]

But the simple logic of dependence and withdrawal, adaptation and re-adaptation, is muddied by the inconsistencies and unpredictable elements of what one author carefully calls drug 'cessation phenomena', or the events which occur when chronic drug use is halted. He categorises these events into 'true withdrawal symptoms' which 'probably reflect the attempt of the body to maintain pharmacodynamic and pharmacokinetic homeostasis'; rebound symptoms from a pre-existing disorder which become worse when medications are suddenly ceased; and the feelings of frustration, anxiety, discomfort and longing which are experienced when an habitual and rewarding activity is abruptly halted.[21] These three different kinds of symptoms are difficult to distinguish, as they are a unified experience for the individual. And how confidently can symptoms be attributed to one sort of cessation response and not another? Both depression and stomach pains could be explained as either the result of neurotransmitter adjustment or feelings of 'frustrated nonreward'. This seems to suggest that judgements about the presence or absence of physical dependence cannot easily be made.

Indeed the sensitivity of withdrawal symptoms to factors such as memory, experience, anticipation, and environment is evidence of the enmeshment of the pharmacological, the psychological and social contexts and processes. Recent research on the cross-cultural applicability of official alcohol dependence diagnostic criteria such as those in the ICD-10 has found, unsurprisingly, that cultural assumptions about drinking and its effects can have significant impact on results. Perhaps more surprisingly, perspectives on symptoms of physical dependence such as withdrawal varied as much as more supposedly subjective criteria. For example, at cultural sites characterised by generally liberal drinking norms the phenomena of withdrawal was generally regarded with no great concern. In Athens, Greece, for instance, the researchers found there was very little distinction made between withdrawal and the lay concept of a hangover; symptoms such as headaches, anxiety and feelings of shame and regret were emphasised.[22]

Further complication arises from the widespread observation that there is no obvious link between the visibility or seriousness of withdrawal signs and their motivational force. For example, nicotine withdrawal is subtle in physiological terms but has a powerful influence on smokers. Not only do smokers testify to the strength of the distress and craving of withdrawal, but nicotine gum and other replacement therapies have a significant impact on successful quitting rates. The connection between withdrawal phenomena and other signs of dependence is also complex. While Schuckit states that the intensity of withdrawal increases with the usual dose taken and the duration of drug use, he later observes that many alcoholics who have severe medical problems and serious life-impairment never demonstrate signs of physical withdrawal.[23]

Nevertheless the rigours of withdrawal are often invoked in medical texts, perhaps as a way of stressing the seriousness of dependence and its status as a genuine medical condition. Landry states that 'Acute withdrawal from any drug is a particularly intense physical and emotional experience. It is often a medical emergency'.[24] On the other hand, comments about the relative mildness of most withdrawal experiences are also common. The symptoms of opiate withdrawal are routinely compared with the symptoms of 'flu, the most everyday of diseases, the miseries of which we all endure fairly regularly. Asserting the benign nature of most withdrawal symptoms combines easily with judgements about the character of drug addicts:

> Opiate addicts in a medical setting will often emphasize the distress they experience during withdrawal, possibly as a ploy to obtain additional medications. The manipulativeness demonstrated by addicts in maintaining their drug habits has been documented . . . However, while withdrawal from narcotics may be uncomfortable, it is not fatal . . .[25]

The final sentence, coming after the passage on addicts' tendency to exaggerate their symptoms, suggests that because narcotic withdrawal is not fatal the worst it can possibly be is 'uncomfortable'. The fact that addicts complain and ask for medication reinforces the identity of the drug user as a person who is either deceitful and cunning or unable to cope with the normal stresses of life. For Landry the problem is not so much exaggeration, but overinterpretation. He warns readers that people may misdescribe 'normal aches and pains' as withdrawal symptoms, leading to anxiety and fear of further severe symptoms. The anxiety about over-, under- or mis-interpretation suggests that the solidity and reliability of withdrawal symptoms as markers which directly correspond to a disordered physiological or neurological state is at least in part illusory. They are more like complex signs inevitably subject to interpretation, not only by the clinical observer but also by the individual experiencing them. Misreading, including deliberate misreading, at a number of different levels is always possible. And because in this case the existence of the referent, the addicted body, is inferred from the signs, the final truth of dependence remains elusive.[26]

The biology of withdrawal is itself loaded with excess meanings, especially to do with pain and pleasure, which are bound up with the construction of addicted and non-addicted subjects. There is a continuing debate in the field over whether negative or positive reinforcements are more significant in perpetuating drug use. Do people continue to use drugs to avoid negative effects, including withdrawal? Or do they take them because they continue to experience some of the original rewarding effects?[27] Posed like this, the question overlooks the blurred line between avoiding something bad and seeking something good. If one is feeling nauseous and takes a pill which dispels the nausea, how can one separate the pleasure at the shift into non-nauseousness from the 'pure' absence of nausea?

The view that addicts are motivated primarily by the desire to avoid the pain and distress of withdrawal constructs the addict as not so much a reckless hedonist, but a frightened self-medicator. The production of addicts as those who drink or take drugs without obtaining (undeserved) pleasure, but just to maintain normal functioning presents them as more pitiable and less morally objectionable. But the pain-avoidance theory also reinforces the aberrance of the addict body and its occupation of the realm of the monstrous. It is a body which needs a toxic substance to survive and it has a superhuman ability to consume fatal doses without obvious effect, perhaps best symbolised by cocaine users who are reported to take the drug every five minutes, using up to 30 grams a day. The astounding tolerance and resilience of the addict body is the other side of its vulnerability to withdrawal.[28]

There is a satisfying justice in withdrawal symptoms for those who object to the drug user's unearned rewards and escape from the 'real world'. They are the payment for earlier undeserved and excess pleasure, and reassuring proof that there is no such thing as a free lunch, naked or otherwise. They also provide a test of the addict's commitment to quitting and a type of initiation ceremony into the tough world of drug-free living. The effects of withdrawal can be consciously exploited for their punitive potential, a striking example being the 'cold turkey' detoxification in prisons that was once standard treatment for addicts. In its production of withdrawal and the concomitant production of normal and abnormal bodies, medical discourse is involved in a much more subtle way in setting norms and judging bodies against these norms. All bodies interact with the environment, adapt to it, and come to depend on various inputs and stimuli, but this openness to and reliance on the external is only pathologised in some cases. Ultimately, it is evaluative judgement about individual behaviour which enables the progress of addiction to be mapped. For example, in an early article on alcohol dependence syndrome, Edwards and Gross discuss the recognition of withdrawal not only in symptoms such as sweating and tremor, but in the degree of deviation from normative rules of behaviour:

> Clues to the degree of a patient's dependence are often given by the small details he provides on the circumstances and timing of the first drink of the day and his attitudes toward it . . . A housewife who finishes her morning chores before having her first drink is at a different stage of dependence than the woman who is pouring whisky into her first cup of tea.[29]

Of course the chemically dependent can always deny or minimise the extent or nature of their drug use, but signs of pathology on or in their bodies can tell the truth of their condition. The need for medical workers to be ever-vigilant in looking for signs of drug abuse amongst their patients is emphasised by medical texts which focus on the distinctive physical characteristics found in alcohol and drug abusers. According to *Diagnosing Chemical Dependency: A Practical Guide for Health Care Professionals,* physicians may fail to diagnose drug dependence more than 75 per cent of the time. Patients 'seldom offer the information that they are drug/alcohol abusers' and they also tend to understate the amount they use.[30] Thus doctors must learn to identify the health problems which can be signs of drug abuse and dependence, which range from the trivial to the life-threatening. Some are clearly visible on the skin, others are only revealed through laboratory work or X-rays.

The addicted body can be read even more specifically by connecting distinctive signs with the abuse of different substances. The addict body appears as the scene of a crime, the doctor the detective who must deduce the truth beneath the surface. According to an article in *Postgraduate Medicine* clues can be spotted in the skin, the eyes, ears, nose and throat as well as from the 'general appearance'. The authors also stress the importance of first impressions:

> Does the patient appear to be his or her stated age, or has chronic substance abuse and/or life on the street had an aging effect? Is the patient groomed and well dressed or dishevelled and wearing soiled clothes? A lethargic, malodorous patient with alcohol on the breath suggests a far different substance-abuse profile than does a neatly dressed college freshman with reddened eyes and a vivid fear of going crazy.[31]

More specifically, intravenous heroin users are recognised by needle marks and non-reactive pupils while crack smokers exhibit burns on the thumb of the dominant hand. Cocaine users have dilated pupils, irritated nasal mucosa and 'multiple excoriations' on the skin from scratching. Multiple healed and healing forearm burns suggest alcoholism or sedative dependence because they could have been caused by carelessness while cooking.[32]

Diagnosing Chemical Dependency provides an even more vivid picture of the damaged addicted body, combining case studies, photographs, X-rays and typical laboratory profiles. The ravaged body of a severely ill intravenous drug user is presented almost metonymically as a symbol of disease:

> Tracks and abscesses were the words which best described Mr C. His long years of abusing his veins with dirty needles and impure drugs had left his body literally covered with scars. He had tracks between his fingers, down all aspects of his arms and legs. Scars from old abscesses and oozing new lesions dotted his limbs, back and abdomen. In many places the lesions had coalesced and made whole planes of scar tissue and oozing wounds.[33]

Scars and abscesses also dominate the photographs in the text. Indeed the repetitive images of abscesses and scarred skin seem excessive in such a practical and no-nonsense text. Surely such stigmata would not be too difficult for doctors and nurses to recognise? The author says she wanted the book to be accessible 'bath-tub reading' made more interesting by the inclusion of case files from her practice so perhaps the images are there to make the abstract concrete. We are shown 'the hands of a long-time intravenous drug user' marked with tracks and old abscess scars, track marks in an armpit and inner arm, multiple abscesses on a drug user's back in various stages of healing and abscesses on the lower leg and foot of an intravenous drug user. Perhaps the most disturbing complication described is the case of a needle broken off in the arm of a heroin addict, illustrated with an X-ray image of the addict's arm. The needle was discovered to be the cause of an abscess which would not heal; once it was removed the abscess cleared up quickly. In fact, in this case it is the story which carries the impact, not the physical evidence, because despite the addition of an arrow pointing to the bevel, the needle is hardly discernible in the reproduction of the X-ray. Nevertheless, despite its virtual invisibility, the needle lodged inside the addict's arm is the fitting climax to the gallery of bodies that have internalised so much destructive foreign matter that their boundaries are breaking down.[34]

While the signs these texts list and depict have a diagnostic utility, the texts also produce the addict's body as a toxic landscape of destruction and decay, scarred and smelly, marked both by the direct effects of drugs and by the destructiveness of drug-abusing lifestyles. This effect is even more pronounced when linked with case studies describing inexorably escalating drug use and dramatic physical and social decline. Given the concern with missed diagnoses because of the 'hidden' nature of drug abuse and the easily overlooked signs in seemingly normal and respectable patients, the emergence of such a floridly disfigured and deviant body as the image of drug abuse could be counter-productive.

The inside of the addicted body is also presented as similarly disordered. In a popular and often-quoted text on alcoholism, Milam and Ketcham describe electron micrographs of chronic alcoholics' liver cells as a scene of death, mutation, and chaos, 'the mitochondria are scattered haphazardly, some grotesquely misshapen, others with gaping holes in their membranes, and still others white and vacant, bled dry of everything inside'. Continuing their description of the cellular effects of heavy drinking, the authors state that the cell membranes are 'continually battered' by the poisonous after-effects of alcohol; they 'weaken and, in some cases, dissolve. No longer able to function as selective doorways, the membranes now let poisonous substances into the cells while vital fluids and enzymes leak out . . . throughout the body, cells sicken and die'. In these remarks the battered and disoriented cell stands in for the alcoholic. Like the sick cell, the alcoholic's body has leaky boundaries which take in poisons while its 'vital fluids' bleed away.[35]

Addiction, and the diseases and damage caused by addiction, are easily conflated in descriptions laden with connoted meaning. The infections, scars and 'grotesquely misshapen' cells are not only organic lesions, but the appropriate stigmata of a dissolute life, signs of moral as well as physical decay. The sick body of the addict is read as a sign of a self that has a distorted relationship with its self, a self whose internal order has broken down. One of the values of a healthy body in contemporary life is that it demonstrates a proper concern with the self, the correct attitude of care and responsibility. The fact that addicts do not seem to care for themselves or their bodies is evidence of a deeper inner disturbance. The identification of intravenous drug users as a high risk group for HIV infection provides even more opportunity for the conceptual merging of addiction and its associated diseases. In their defence of the disease model of addiction Gold and Miller argue that:

> Addictive people are sick, as is evident in the hundreds of medical, psychiatric and sociological complications from addiction. In New York City, the single, largest risk factor for AIDS is intravenous drug use. AIDS is a medical complication that follows intravenous drug use that in many instances is secondary to addictive use.[36]

Here two categories of corrupted and unnatural bodies are brought together in a vision of sickness, with one disease inexorably arising from another, in a form of spontaneous generation. Injecting drugs can transmit HIV infection because of the exchange of blood that can occur if needles are shared, but Gold and Miller construct AIDS as a medical complication of drug addiction as if the state of being an addict is what causes AIDS. In an all too familiar move, the pathology of HIV infection is used to prove and enhance the pathological status of an 'abnormal' bodily practice associated with the disease.

Addictive Desire

Ultimately however, it is the addict's intense desire for the drug which is at the very heart of the disorder. The production of addictive desire as both quantitatively and qualitatively distinct from normal desires is central to the production of 'dependence' as a pathological state. The disorder is defined by the compulsion of the addict to continue his drug use, even if he desperately wants to stop and even if the costs are severe. The first item in a 1981 WHO checklist of the main criteria of dependence is 'a subjective awareness of compulsion to use a drug or drugs'. And in 1993 the WHO again emphasises the 'strong desire or compulsion to take the drug' and the impaired capacity to control its use, while the American Psychiatric Association's DSM-IV stresses both compulsion and craving.[37] As Griffith Edwards and his colleagues stated in a classic paper on the classification of drug problems, 'Dependence is not dependence if drug-taking, or at least the desire to take drugs, is absent'.[38] Without the presence of intense desire for the substance, it is hard to say that someone is addicted, even though according to the diagnostic criteria it is theoretically possible for a diagnosis of dependence syndrome to be made in its absence. Evidence of tolerance, withdrawal and significant harm arising from drug use would, for example, fulfil the requirement for three of the WHO's diagnostic criteria to be present. But it is difficult to imagine how these three phenomena could exist without a strong desire for the drug also being present. This is in part because craving is often read as a symptom of withdrawal. Indeed, in the case of nicotine withdrawal, the craving for a cigarette is the most consistent and the most severe symptom.[39]

The terms craving, compulsion and loss of control are employed to signify the strength of the forces directing the addict's behaviour. They reinforce the idea that drug dependence is a different order of thing from normal attachment to daily routines and habits, and normal preoccupation with certain activities. By suggesting a will that has been compromised, they explain the addict's seeming irrationality and indifference to the high price of continuing his habit. The connection made between addictive desire and the physiology of addiction highlights the distance between craving and ordinary 'wanting'. One author, who defines compulsion and 'chemical craving' as 'the primary force of the disease' puts it this way:

> what begins with a choice is perpetuated by a physiologic process which the patient is powerless to stop.
>
> Simply put, compulsion is a biological phenomenon. This does not mean that the patient does not have the choice to stop the using behavior; it means he or she does not have the choice of simply saying "No" to the biology of compulsion.[40]

In this passage the desire for the drug is analogous to the physiological need for food or water, and separate from the subjective desires of the individual. Similarly, the representation of craving in the brain scans discussed in the previous chapter produces drug craving as an autonomous, biological phenomena, related to the physiological changes of addiction. Underlying this notion of craving is the presumption that biological needs can be distinguished from mere 'wants', and that the former are much harder to resist than the latter. But the reality of desire is surely more messy than this. When one falls in love it is not only romantic hyperbole that describes the desire to hear the voice of the other as overwhelming and impossible to resist, while the need for food and sleep are experienced as faint and easily ignored sensations. Another characteristic of craving is its double identity as both an aversive and positive state. It is described by some researchers as part of the dysphoria of withdrawal, by others as an expectation of pleasure and enjoyment. Connected to this is the fact that it is variously seen as produced by the absence of the drug, the presence of the drug, or indeed the presence of items, people or places connected with the drug. The term craving also encompasses a physiological state, a subjective experience, and a particular form of behaviour.[41]

In fact, the nature of craving, and its relationship to simple wanting or missing, is subject to continuing debate within addiction research, and confusion surrounding the term has lead to calls to either abandon or severely restrict its use.[42] But its persistence suggests that despite or perhaps because of its ambiguity, it captures an essential and irreducible element of addictive experience. Its suggestion of a desire fuelled by a disordered physiology, which in turn drives drug-seeking, is a causal narrative which explains the irrational and self-destructive behaviour of the addict and expresses the 'biopsychosocial' nature of his addiction. Its ability to emerge from either the presence or absence of the desired object also attests to the peculiar inescapability of addictive desire.

But what is it about a desire that makes it into a craving? On one hand craving implies a particularly powerful or strong desire; this is certainly the case in the everyday meaning of the word. Kozlowski and Wilkinson in their review of the term's use in addiction research argue that it should be reserved for special instances of high intensity urges for drug use. Other researchers have suggested it should refer to urges that are irresistible, pathological, specific to one drug, sudden in onset, inappropriate, induce an urgency to use the drug or are produced by withdrawal.[43] These specifications are to counter the confusing and sometimes misleading tendency to use craving for any form of urge to use a drug, including the mild and trivial. Kozlowski and Wilkinson note, for example, the conflation of 'thinking about cigarettes' and 'wish to smoke' with craving in one study of smoking withdrawal, and remark that it is not surprising that a smoker going without cigarettes would think about cigarettes, but it is uncertain whether these thoughts qualify as 'craving'. In reply, one commentator argued that the problem with restricting to craving to 'a distinct state of especially urgent desire' in this way is that it goes against the empirical evidence in which thinking about, missing and craving are closely correlated in a subject's responses to drug cessation.[44]

The broad question which emerges from this debate seems to be whether craving should be defined by a level of desire (intense) or by the object of desire (a drug). In either case, the deployment of the term constitutes the desire produced by drugs as unique and out of the ordinary, and the slippage between the two meanings has the effect of suggesting that all urges for drugs, even if mild, are pathological and/or inappropriate. However, as suggested in the previous chapter, craving can be conceived of as a form of memory. Rather than a specific type of biologically produced desire, drug craving thus appears as a type of remembering or intense longing based on potent memories of pleasure. This would recognise that powerful and irrational desires are part of human experience, not alien and other to it. As social psychologist John Davies has noted, the idea of craving as memory is not other to pharmacological models, but embedded in them. After reviewing the role of neural reward pathways in producing drug relapse, prominent pharmacologist Roy Wise suggests that one explanation for craving is 'simply that the subject remembers the last reinforcement, and the reactivation of this memory by associated environmental situmuli is sufficient to activate feelings of craving'. He notes that laboratory rats obviously remember rewarding stimulations, and adds that 'Like a cat that has tasted fish, a human that has tasted cocaine may be unwilling to give up the hope of repeating the experience'.[45]

Whatever the role of biology and neural pathways of reward and memory, the way the phenomena of craving and compulsion are actually identified is through the observation of individual conduct. The diagnostic problem is that while the existence of chemical imbalances and altered cell metabolism may be scientifically verified, the presence of 'strong desires' cannot be detected or measured with a laboratory test. Either self-reported experiences or actions observed by others identify an individual as suffering from loss of control and experiencing craving. In the case of medical research on alcoholism, subjects are often asked questions about alcohol use to determine whether they fulfil the criteria of compulsion and impairment of control. Binge drinking, staying drunk for days at time, inability to stop after one or two drinks, neglecting other responsibilities because of drinking, often drinking much more than you intended or expected to when you began are all items read as signifying impairment of control. Linking such experiences with the scientific identification of a disease entity, or even the diagnosis of a syndrome, presents more than minor difficulties. Is it possible to distinguish clearly between not being able to stop drinking until you are drunk and not wanting to stop drinking until you are drunk? Is it possible to decide to not be able to stop drinking? If you intend to have two drinks and end up having four, thereby drinking twice as much as you planned, are you more or less out of control than someone who intended to have ten drinks and had eleven? What if they stopped at ten? The 'intention' question seems to suggest that one way to prevent loss of control is by raising your expected drinking level high enough so that your actual consumption is always less than planned. Using neglect of responsibilities as evidence of loss of control brings more difficulties. The item's utility as a measurement of control is affected by the salience of these responsibilities to the individual. While an ambitious doctor who misses two days of work while on a bender may only be able to interpret such a neglect of duties as a sign that an external force has taken over her will, a worker less attached to and identified with their work may understand it quite differently, judging that because they only took two days off, their use is still under control.

If loss of control is taken to be an absolute measure, then even the hard-core junkie fails to reach it. Addiction can only be recognised by the presence of structure, patterns, and rituals. A total collapse into uncontrolled and meaningless chaos would probably not be able to be interpreted at all, except possibly as psychosis. The parameters of control and rules of consumption followed by the addict may be regarded as negligible or indeed remain invisible to others, but this does not decrease their importance in regulating and structuring behaviour. A relative conception of loss of control is suggested by some as an alternative diagnostic tool, such as, 'Given the opportunity to drink, the alcoholic cannot consistently refrain; once starting to drink, the alcoholic cannot consistently cease before drinking to a state of inebriation'.[46] In this model it is the inconsistency and uncertainty of the alcoholic's behaviour which separates her from the normal drinker rather than an overpowering and constant compulsion. But for others, rigid and predictable drinking patterns are an equally salient sign of alcoholism.[47] The signs of pathology can change, inconsistency and uncertainty or rigidity and predictability, but the determination remains to preserve a qualitative difference between the addicted and the non-addicted through the application of a standard of normal behaviour.

Outside the laboratory, negative social and occupational consequences of drinking or drug use play an important role in the diagnosis of dependence. Not only is continuing drug use in the face of harmful consequences one of the syndrome's diagnostic criteria, but case studies of dependence in medical guides emphasise the patient's social, and indeed moral, regression. The vignette illustrating cocaine dependence in *DSM-IV Made Easy: The Clinician's Guide to Diagnosis* describes a young stockbroker whose life unravels as a result of her crack habit: she loses interest in her work, she calls in sick for days in a row, and is finally fired. She then moves into a smaller apartment, sells her BMW and spends the proceeds plus all her savings on more drugs. It is this conduct and the resulting loss of middle-class lifestyle which makes clear her dependence. This suggests that those with fewer privileges to lose are less vulnerable to the disorder; indeed criteria of harm to occupational and social functioning assumes that without the drug use the subject would not be facing problems such as unemployment, poverty or loneliness. In the diagnosis of substance abuse, a less severe condition than dependence, failure to fill responsibilities and legal and interpersonal problems such as loss of friends are even more prominent. *DSM-IV Made Easy* explains that 'Despite the expectations of others, a substance abuser may be repeatedly late to work or school, show neglect in the care of small children, or repeatedly fail to cook dinner'. As Valverde remarks, these kinds of criteria assume norms of social respectability; for a bartender or sex worker for instance heavy drinking could aid rather than hinder occupational functioning.

And for many people, drinking and drug use facilitate friendship and interpersonal relations; it is quitting that brings about the loss of friends. Valverde concludes that the supposedly objective category of harm cannot do the work assigned to it in producing a medical paradigm of dependence from the moralising category of addiction.[48]

In this context however, I would argue that the ethical *is* the medical, rather than being outside its proper concerns. Compulsion, craving and harm together suggest a conflictual or dissonant state, a state not wanting to want what you want, and not wanting to do what you do. They suggest a distance between the person and their behaviour; the addict is someone whose own behaviour is alien to herself. She is not an autonomous agent, but is controlled by a force that she experiences as external. Importantly these issues, discussed more fully in the following chapter, are issues of meaning rather than objective measures of the strength or quality of different types of desires. As Orford has argued, a diagnosis of addiction or dependence depends on a sense of conflict about the behaviour; the terms have no meaning unless the habit is judged problematic by either the addict or others. As he puts it, an appetite becomes an 'ism' or a 'mania' when 'Either the person or others would like him to do less of it, or do it less often or at different times, in different places, or with different people, or else would like him to give it up altogether'.[49] We do not crave chocolate unless we feel we should not have it. We do not experience our desire for water as a compulsion, unless we cannot get it. The existence of contrary pressures accounts for the force of addictive desires.

Seeing the operation of compulsion in the behaviour of certain individuals is as much an aesthetic exercise of attribution as an observation of reality. It is as if the determination of a person to keep doing what they do despite what appear to be serious negative consequences and very little reward can only be rationally explained by judging them as unable to stop.[50] The need to make sense of the world and view humans as essentially rational creatures makes compulsive desire a more attractive explanatory device than the possibility of a will to annihilation or a passion for the negative. The value placed on the virile healthy body and a harmonious unified self means that suffering and inner conflict cannot be viewed positively, or even neutrally as part of normal existence.

Conclusion

Medical discourse sets itself the task of 'unmasking' addiction and liberating the addict through the application of rational and objective knowledge about drugs and bodies. It regards chemical and physiological understandings as the basis of this knowledge, yet in its perception of substances, bodies and subjects it inevitably engages with questions of individual and societal health, happiness, and harm. In its constructions of the parameters of addictive desire, medical discourse judges different modes of comportment in terms of disease and health. It promotes the translation of the unusual, anomalous or deviant into the abnormal or pathological. The categories of substances and bodies it creates are therefore profoundly normative, structured by hierarchical dichotomies such as natural/chemical, internal/external and order/disorder. The addict is constructed by medicine's evaluative gaze in terms of these dichotomies.

Foucault views modern medicine as fundamentally 'bound up with the delineation of the unique human being, the human person in his or her very individuality and vitality, as a possible object for *positive knowledge*'.[51] This concern with the individual is clearly demonstrated in medical addiction discourse. Rational knowledge about the functioning of addictive desire depends very much on careful observation of individual conduct and attention to subjective states. It also entails engagement with broad questions of free will and the limits of personal identity. The point is not to chastise medicine for its lack of scientific objectivity; therapeutic concern, that is concern with improving and curing, necessarily involves normative judgements about some states being more desirable than others. But understanding addiction in terms of health and disease rather than good and evil is no liberation from disciplinary regimes of power; rather it is the expansion of one form of power against another. As Rose has argued, the medical demythologising of suffering has brought with it an anxious search for normality and health, and an organisation of human experience in fundamentally medical terms.[52]

That medicine is inevitably concerned with ethical and political questions about styles of life affects the nature of the connection between medical addiction discourse and popular addiction discourse. Medical experts are keen to distance their enterprise from the unscientific and explicitly value-laden approaches of self-help authors and therapists. Psychiatrist Jerome Jaffe, commenting on the 'fashion' of describing all sorts of behaviours as addictions, states that:

> While journalists and popular writers have every right to use words like 'addiction' and 'dependence' metaphorically, when these words are used by the helping professions with the implication that there are valid and reliable diagnostic entities to be treated by some equally scientifically validated methods, they cease to be metaphors. Metaphorical usage increases the risk that many diagnoses will be seen as self-serving medicalizations of undesirable behaviours.[53]

In this passage Jaffe contrasts the reliability and validity of medical knowledge with the sloppiness and lack of authority of popular discourse. It is indeed the case that the processes and traditions through which medical knowledge is constructed are unique, and do give medical knowledge a particular value and status. However, by making a distinction in terms of metaphoricity, Jaffe makes an untenable claim for the possibility of purely descriptive language. He also obscures the similarity of the medical and popular therapeutic enterprises. The efforts of medical science to understand and ameliorate problems of drug dependence and alcoholism, and the general proliferation of addiction discourse as a way of thinking about how to be a good person and live a good life, are connected by their understanding of an individual who can be improved through rational management. The retreat from a clearcut notion of physical dependence seen in the dependence syndrome concept also makes the notion of addiction to non-drug activities such as eating, gambling, work and sex more credible. If withdrawal and tolerance as signs of physiological alteration caused by drugs are no longer essential to addiction, and if craving is understood largely as a subjective and cognitive phenomena, then drugs no longer seem to be necessary components of the syndrome. As becomes clear in later chapters, strong attachments, powerful urges, preoccupation and social harms can all be found without drugs as the source.

It is not so much that popular writers have departed from the medical enterprise by applying the language of addiction to a diverse range of dissatisfactions, but that they have appropriated and continued its construction of human beings and human desire as objects of knowledge. Both are engaged in producing the individual as a free subject, but one whose freedom consists of choosing to be autonomous and productive, one who is, in Rose's phrase, 'obliged to be free'.[54]

3

Further and Further
from the Normal World:
The Addicted Self

In the taxonomic re-framing of a drug-user as an addict, what changes are the most basic terms about her. From a situation of relative homeostatic stability and control, she is propelled into a narrative of inexorable decline and fatality, from which she cannot dis-implicate herself except by leaping into that other, even more pathos-ridden narrative called 'kicking the habit'.

—Eve Sedgwick, 'Epidemics of the Will'

The disease of addiction found in self-help literature is a very different order of disturbance from the 'drug dependence syndrome' of clinical medicine. In these texts addiction in its many forms is virulent, destructive and contagious, affecting a sizeable and growing percentage of the population. Best-selling self-help author Anne Wilson Schaef identifies addiction as 'any process over which we are powerless', then adds that 'Like any serious disease, an addiction is progressive, and it will lead to death unless we actively recover from it'.[1] Rather than careful classificatory schemes which limit the diagnosis of addiction to those who fulfil certain criteria, the category of addiction is opened up to anyone who feels they belong, and many who would strongly assert that they do not. After the punctiliousness of the debates which mark scientific and medical discourse, this broad perspective and inclusivity is refreshing, even though it is often expressed in hyperbole and the banal truisms of popular psychology.

Self-help texts, especially those drawing on the ideas and practices of Alcoholics Anonymous, generally proclaim the disease nature of addiction as a foundational and universal truth, rather than a proposition to be tested or a heuristic diagnostic device. In AA theory alcoholism is, by definition, a pernicious, progressive, and irreversible disease. Not surprisingly, the disease found in popular texts tends to be dismissed by medical science as a crude and/or vague formulation 'unsupported either by clinical evidence or research findings'.[2] Self-help texts slip back and forth freely between metaphoric and literal usages of the term disease, so that at times a physical illness is being denoted, at other times a spiritual 'dis-ease', and sometimes both at once. This description, from an AA pamphlet, captures the sense of simultaneous physical and moral decline invoked by the popular disease model:

> Alcoholism is a disease, which manifests itself chiefly by the uncontrollable drinking of the victim, who is known as an alcoholic. It is a progressive disease, which, if left untreated, grows more virulent year by year, driving its victims further and further from the normal world, and deeper into an abyss which has only two outlets—insanity or death.[3]

Given the hybridity of popular addiction discourse, these shifts of meaning are not surprising. AA theory, for instance, combines elements of Christian revivalism, temperance doctrine and Jellinek's disease model of alcoholism, plus more pragmatic ideas about habit and behaviour modification. Contemporary addiction and recovery discourse shows the influence of New Age spirituality, growth psychology and feminism, as well as recent theories about genetic predisposition and neurological function.

It is easy to label this popular discourse banal and incoherent, but this fails to recognise its productive power and its engagement with compelling questions of self-management and self-production. Popular addiction texts produce the inner self as an object for inspection and rectification. They offer practical solutions to predicaments about consumption and ingestion, while simultaneously reinforcing the idea that what you consume and how you consume are the keys to physical and moral fitness. They deploy binarisms such as internal/external, free will/compulsion, natural/artificial, authenticity/falsity and health/illness to produce addiction as a disease of self, but at the same time reassure readers that the infection of the positive element by the devalued element in each pair can be overcome through improved hygiene of the self and the body.

While there are significant differences between popular and medical discourses of addiction, and recovery experts do challenge medical authority, self-help can usefully be read as a continuation and expansion of the medical concern with the addict. In common with medical science, self-help discourse demonstrates a will to truth, although the truth of its discourse is supported not so much by science but by its virtues of sincerity and accessibility, the personal experiences of the authors and their experiences of helping others. It produces systematic and authoritative knowledge about individuals, organised around evaluations of health and disease, function and dysfunction. It offers remedies based on rational and technical programs of management.

Anyone who ever browses in book stores will be aware of the vast quantity of books that exists in the popular addiction and recovery genre. Written by therapists, counsellors, psychologists, doctors and recovering addicts (especially recovering addicts who have become therapists in the course of their recovery), the flood of self-help and health information literature shows no sign of abating. There are many variations on the 'disease of self' theme: some texts emphasise the addict's lack of self-esteem, others the role of fear, or perhaps the need for spiritual growth. Some focus on special groups: women, men, adolescents, and lesbians and gays. Some, particularly those written from a feminist perspective, contain social criticism; others are much more concerned with restoring family relationships; others with spiritual enlightenment.

However, general remarks can be made about the genre. A common influence is the US-based humanistic or growth psychology movement of the 1960s and 1970s. Opposing the mechanistic and reductive anti-humanism of behaviourism, growth psychology flourished at a time when liberation and self-expression were dominant cultural themes. Encouraging individuals to tap and release their full potential, growth psychology promoted the now taken-for-granted belief that merely being free from psychological illness was not equivalent to a positive state of psychological health. As Elayne Rapping has argued, the self-help movement also owes a

great deal to second wave feminism, especially the theory and practice of consciousness raising.⁴ From both these traditions, as well as
a Christian tradition of bearing witness, comes a belief in the value
of individual experience as a basis for knowledge. Although the
expertise of the author—often signified by a prominent 'PhD' after
their name on the cover—is vital to the marketing to self-help texts,
they are at the same time often suspicious of scientific expertise.
Much store is placed on experiential knowledge and empathy: the
recovering addict who has emerged from denial is regarded as having
an insight the most eminent researcher lacks. Indeed, the privileged
relationship that the recovering addict has to the truth of addiction
is almost the inverse of the active addict's state of denial. And while
medical treatment may be necessary, it represents only the beginning
of a genuine recovery. Interwoven with these threads is the health
promotion approach to 'lifestyle' and individual responsibility for
well-being. Despite the elaboration of an incurable disease which
controls people's behaviour, it is assumed in self-help discourse that
individuals can create their own destiny and make healthy choices,
whatever their social and economic situation.

The risk in interrogating self-help discourse, as I do in this
chapter, is that it can appear to deny or minimise both the suffering
and the achievements of those who have struggled with problems of
addiction and found practical help and inspiration in self-help
recovery programs. There is no doubt that AA and other twelve-
step groups have helped many people transform their lives, but in
this critical exercise my concern is not with the experiences of individuals. In her historical study of the governance of alcohol and
alcoholism, Mariana Valverde makes an important distinction
between the theoretical claims made in AA literature and the actual
practices and techniques used by AA groups. She argues that focusing on the latter reveals AA to be much more pragmatic and hybrid
in its approach to managing alcoholism than is usually apparent in
sociological and critical studies.⁵ While my project could be criti-
cised for continuing the emphasis on ideas, ideals, texts and theory
rather than practice, it is the case that the reading and writing of
texts are a major part of the self-help and recovery movement. For
many, reading texts by various experts is their primary form of par-
ticipation in the movement, and a major source of not only theories

and frameworks for thinking about the self but of techniques of self-government.

Self-help addiction discourse and practice promotes the ideals of the self—autonomy, responsibility, individual fulfilment and happiness—which are the fundamental to the 'enterprise culture' of contemporary liberal societies. As Nikolas Rose has observed, self-help displays a potent and seductive way of thinking about, judging and acting upon selves which has become pervasive in the modern West: 'The self is to be a subjective being, it is to aspire to autonomy, it is to strive for personal fulfilment in its earthly life, it is to interpret reality and destiny as matters of individual responsibility, it is to find meaning in existence by shaping its life through acts of choice'.[6] This image of the self, and the therapeutic domain which addresses itself to the development of this ideal, are not antidotes to the demands of economic, social and public life as is often suggested in self-help texts. They rather act as a medium for and justification of the regulatory programs and operations of power which characterise modern government, including self-government. Therefore, without denying the therapeutic value of self-help for individuals, it is worthwhile to examine and denaturalise their models of healthy and unhealthy selves.

Sick Body Sick Self

It is the connection made between a disordered body and a disordered self which gives the popular notion of addictive disease its explanatory and descriptive power. On one hand, it regards alcoholism (or addiction) as a bio-medical disease entity with specific predictable symptoms and a predictable natural course. Comparisons with cancer, heart disease, and most commonly diabetes, are drawn to reinforce its identity as a genuine disease and not a matter of moral weakness. But its symptoms, physical and behavioural, are nourished by a profound existential malaise. Self-pity, self-loathing, self-centredness, and the absence of hope are viewed as the bedrock of the addict's existence, at the same time that the addict is being produced as the victim of a physical disorder. Unlike most diseases, therefore, recovery from addiction requires spiritual renewal and personal transformation, encompassing changes in behaviour, thinking, values and beliefs, relationships and lifestyle.[7]

The productive slippage between the physical and the moral is illustrated in the personal accounts contained in *The Big Book*, the basic text of AA. These accounts feature many vivid signs of physical decline: loss of appetite, withdrawal shakes, enlarged livers, monstrous hangovers, vomiting of blood, delirium tremens, and blackouts. But these symptoms are not merely signs of physiological processes, they symbolise the falling apart of the alcoholic's life, the all-encompassing desperation and pain of alcoholic existence. In these personal stories, the body of the alcoholic is a crucial site of decay, demonstrating the undeniable truth of a sick life. Significantly, once the protagonist joins AA and order is restored in the soul, his physical problems fade out of the picture, even though their effects would surely continue to be felt.

The AA story follows a predictable structure: a downward spiral of substance abuse, the reaching of a crisis point which is the catalyst for epiphany, then the upward climb of recovery. Or as Alcoholics Anonymous puts it, 'what we used to be like, what happened, and what we are like now'.[8] Not only are these stories central to recovery in twelve-step programs; the narrative of addiction and recovery has become one of the more familiar forms of life story appearing in the mass media. As Warhol and Michie observe, it is a conversion narrative, a retrospective reinterpretation of the past in the light of a more enlightened present identity. The discursive form of the AA story enables the teller to construct 'a new referent for the word "I"', a new self invoked, produced and performed in the deceptively simple phrase, 'My name is _____ and I am an alcoholic'.[9]

Even without the significant role of personal narrative in twelve-step programs, the concept of addiction is itself inseparable from what Pertti Alasuutari calls 'biographical reasoning'.[10] Addiction discourse both reflects and supports a model of personal identity based on a bounded, singular individual who exists over time, and whose experiences and actions can also be understood as having a measure of continuity. A diagnosis of addiction requires that acts be understood not in the specific contexts in which they took place, but as recurrent expressions of a single ongoing pathology located in the self.

The repetition of the formulaic alcoholic life story produces an individual defined by collective identity with other alcoholics and difference from 'normal drinkers'. The idea of a physiological anomaly which marks the addicted body is also used in a character-istically metaphoric manner to construct the addict as inherently and unchangeably different from the rest of the population. Alcoholics Anonymous identifies this crucial difference as the alcoholic's 'powerlessness' over alcohol. As opposed to normal drinkers, even those who drink to excess, the 'real alcoholic' has lost 'the power of choice in drink'. Early AA literature relates this powerlessness to an allergy to alcohol, drawing on the theories of Dr William Silkworth. The importance of the allergy theory is not its scientific validity, but its resonance with the AA belief in the unique identity of the 'real alcoholic' and the concomitant belief in absti-nence as the only way out of alcoholism. The allergy theory has been superseded by theories of genetic predisposition, and self-help texts now appropriate the notion of a genetic marker into their model of the addict as physically different from the 'normal' drinker.[11]

However, there is a tension in understanding a problem as simultaneously medical and spiritual. How can a disease compar-able to diabetes be alleviated through spiritual awakening? Some commentators argue that popular discourse simply uses the lexicon of disease to label what are in fact profoundly moral judgements.[12] But while both medical and moral elements can be identified in self-help discourse, much more is going on than the use of medical metaphors to dress up old-fashioned moralising. A concept of dis-ease, no matter how broad, classifies modes of being and habits of thought not as virtuous versus wicked, but normal versus pathologi-cal. It implies that the correct response to the predicament of the individual is therapeutic. In the case of addiction, individuals them-selves are urged to examine themselves for signs of disease, they become both the subjects and the objects of an evaluative and nor-malising gaze. This is not 'just' a matter of usage, but represents a further step in the formulation of the individual as object of medical and rational knowledge. Health comes to require not only a clean body but an authentic, orderly and autonomous self.

The concept of a disease of self enables addiction discourse to expand beyond the relationship between a drug user and his drug, while still maintaining a medical model of disorder, diagnosis and treatment. Because it locates addiction in the inner self, the chemical properties of drugs and alcohol are not an indispensable element of the addictive process. The symptoms of addictive disease can be discerned in individuals whose inner self is distorted not by obsession with a drug, but by obsession with a person who is obsessed with a drug, giving rise to the subjectivities of the codependent or co-addict, the enabler and the adult child of the alcoholic. These identities have their own sizeable collections of therapeutic and recovery literature and their own twelve-step groups.[13] And beyond the confines of the individual human being, the disease can be diagnosed in the pathological systems of the dysfunctional family and the workaholic organisation, not to mention what happens 'when society becomes an addict'.[14] The disease of self concept also opens up the category of potentially addictive substances and processes. The idea that people can become addicted to food, shopping, sex, emotions or religion becomes plausible, indeed almost logically necessary. Regulation of such activities is thus added to the expanding demands of healthy living. This does not mean however that the body and its pollution by drugs is excluded from concern; in fact the correlation made between abstinence from drugs, the health of the body and the health of the self is part of this discourse's power and appeal.

In self-help discourse, the chaos and despair of the addict's life is sustained not so much by drug use and its harms, but by inner conflict and alienation from reality. Vows to stop are repeatedly made and repeatedly broken. Delusional beliefs are clung to. For 'secret addicts', like the yoga teacher dependent on diet pills whose story appears in a text on women and drugs, there is an extreme discordance between public persona and private self. 'I sat there, flying on speed, saying, "Close your eyes, relax, be aware of your breathing, go deep within, feel the inner peace." Everyone said I was the best teacher in the yoga institute, which underlined the sense I had of myself as a fraud'. In the same text another woman tells of the delusional beliefs she held on to during years of daily marijuana smoking:

> It was so much a part of everyday life that it wasn't like using a drug. It was just part of what I did. And it made everything nice. It relaxed me. It took away my problems. I didn't think I had problems. It somehow made me feel at peace.[15]

She exists in a topsy-turvy state where the substance that is causing her problems is perceived as the solution to these problems. She even loses sight of the fact that her drug of choice is a drug. These passages suggest the addict is someone who does not and cannot know herself, and cannot perceive the truth of her own situation. The acute anxiety suffered by addicts can be partly attributed to their awkward position of being simultaneously deceiver and deceived, vividly captured in Sartre's description of self-deception:

> We can hide an external object because it exists independently of us . . . But if I *am* what I wish to veil, the question takes on quite another aspect. I can in fact wish 'not to see' a certain aspect of my state of being only if I *am* acquainted with the aspect that I do not wish to see . . . In a word, I flee in order not to know, but I can not avoid knowing that I am fleeing; and the flight from anguish is only a mode of becoming conscious of anguish.[16]

The diet pill addict/yoga teacher exists in exactly this state of bad faith. She hides the truth of her chemical dependency from herself, managing to disconnect her two selves, but only because she knows her chemical dependency makes her a fraud. It is this idea of the addict as an individual trapped in self-deception which makes her so suitable for projects of (self) improvement. Unlike some other more fixed conditions of mental disability, the identity 'addict' implies an obligation to make an effort to recover. The developmental aspect of addiction means that inherent to the identity of addict is the sense of someone who was once not addicted, and could be free from active addiction in the future, if only her attachment to the 'delusional belief system' of addiction could be loosened.[17] And because hiding from yourself can never be completely successful, as Sartre conveys, there is always the potential for the wall of denial to be broken down.

Deceit, Authenticity and The Addicted Self

Deceit dominates the addict psyche as constructed by self-help discourse. Addicts are 'consummate liars' and 'terrific cons'. They use 'outrage, tears, accusations of abandonment, abject pleading, promises of cooperation and seduction' to get what they want.[18] They fake symptoms to obtain prescriptions for the drug they desire. They convince therapists to keep their supplies of drugs for them. They make a show of overtly complying with treatment in order to avoid further confrontation.[19] But their deceitfulness is much more than a tool to get them what they want. They lie to themselves as much as to others. The flaw in the addict's being is not so much dishonesty as inauthenticity, an inability to be true to oneself; in Schaef's words: 'They are particularly good at figuring out what is appropriate, expected behaviour and behaving that way, even when it has nothing to do with who or what they are'.[20] Thus while the lying and deceptions of the addict can be read as an expression of the disease and separated from the individual's true self, the state of inauthenticity which underlies this separation places the individual in a much more compromised category of subjectivity. As Charles Taylor has argued, authenticity is a potent modern ideal. Taylor contrasts an earlier belief that being in touch with one's inner voice was important because it told us the right thing to do, with a later view in which being in touch takes on its own independent moral significance. Taylor summarises the modern ideal of authenticity and its implications when he says:

> There is a certain way of being human that is *my* way. I am called upon to live my life in this way, and not in imitation of anyone else's. But this gives a new importance to being true to myself. If I am not, I miss the point of my life, I miss what being human is for *me*.[21]

The addict is not true to himself even if he appears to be living his life in his own way, unbound by social conventions. He cannot hear his inner voice, what Rousseau calls 'a voice of nature', because he is deafened by the clamouring of his cravings for the drug, cravings which are external to his inner self. His inauthenticity is thus closely linked with the loss of the power of choice which defines his relationship with the substance. Addiction has been explicitly constructed by some authors as a battle between the true self and a false self, fuelled by the power of the drug and the disease, the latter overcoming the former, but never quite destroying it completely.[22] This understanding of addiction as possession by an external force or being captures the sense of not being oneself which is at times the only way we can explain irrational, irresponsible or

egregious behaviour in ourselves or others. It can lift a great burden
from victims and their friends and families as it leads away from the
view of the addict as a weak, selfish and uncaring person. But while
models of true and false selves eloquently express a common human
experience of internal conflict, they also justify coercive practices as
endeavours to assist the true self and respect its genuine desires. In
the case of the addict, any desires or beliefs she expresses contrary
to the truth of addiction and recovery discourse can be dismissed
as an expression of the disease. As Eve Sedgwick has remarked, the
re-framing of a drug user as an addict marks a profound shift in
subjectivity. 'From being the *subject* of her own perceptual manipu-
lations she is installed as the proper *object* of compulsory institutional disciplines, legal and medical, which, without actually being
able to do anything to "help" her, nonetheless presume to know her
better than she can know herself . . .'.[23]

Sedgwick's brilliant article on addiction and the will also speaks
to the relationship between authenticity and freedom. Noting the
contemporary fact that 'any substance, any behavior, even any affect
may be pathologized as addictive', she argues that the locus of addiction can no longer be a problematic substance, nor a problematic
body, but must be an abstract space connecting the two, the space
of healthy free will. She says, 'Addiction, under this definition,
resides only in the *structure* of a will that is always somehow insufficiently free, a choice whose volition is insufficiently pure'. In
her account, addiction discourse becomes intimately connected with
both the circulation and the disruption of the concept of free will.
Addiction discourses identify and reveal the compulsion that lies
in our everyday choices and most mundane volitional acts, while at
the same time holding out the promise of 'some new, receding but
absolutized space of *pure* voluntarity'.[24]

The 'space of pure voluntarity' from which free choices emerge
is coextensive with the space of the authentic inner voice valorised
in self-help discourse. In fact, Sedgwick has isolated the anxiety of
desire and selfhood central to addiction discourse. To be self-willing
individuals, moving toward a telos of self-fulfilment, we must subject
our desires to scrutiny and reflection, we must want what we want,
and our wants must issue from some inner place or thing that we
can identify as truly our own. But so often our desires fail to meet
this standard, we want a second piece of cake but we wish we didn't

want it, we feel that powerful corrupting forces—advertising, socialisation, the influence of others, our own base appetites—pollute the purity of our will. Compulsive and obsessive attachment, even to things that are good (such as exercise and work), is bad because it makes us slaves to an external force, the process of addiction and prevents development of the authentic self.

The notion of addiction gives the individual a formal device for distancing himself from the actions he feels are alien to his self. But the cost of adopting an addict identity is that the competition between desires, the feeling of not wanting what I want, or the sense that 'I was not myself when I did that', becomes a pathology that organises the whole self. The issue is shifted from that of an individual who has some troubling and self-destructive desires, to the much more serious problem of a radically inauthentic individual. But it is important to qualify Sedgwick's claim that addiction resides *only* in the structure of the individual will. As we saw in Chapter 1, the status of drugs as a special category of substance—powerful, artificial, and foreign (to the body and often to the culture)—is an important part of the compromised authenticity of the addict. The following passage from a text called *Drugfree: A Unique, Positive Approach to Staying Off Alcohol and Other Drugs* constructs the falsity of the addict's being as the logical result of 'chemical' brainwashing:

> Because of the unique reaction that the genetically addiction-prone individual experiences to his drug of choice, he or she programs his or her belief system with the deep conviction that the substance is 'good' and that similar substances are 'good'.

The implication is that the substance is actually bad: it lies to the brain, programs the belief system like a cult leader indoctrinating an innocent follower. Similarly, the authors talk about the effect of drugs on the mind as a form of deception; drugs gain a hold on us by 'clouding our ability to see or to believe that their use is against our own best interests'. By using artificial means to feel artificial pleasure, the addict is already in the realm of untruth, even before any statements are made about his interior being.[25]

As noted earlier, in some texts the category of artificial mood-altering agent is expanded from drugs and alcohol to just about any mood-altering activity. However, the natural/artificial and true/false dichotomies of the body–drug encounter remain in force. Nakken, for example, distinguishes between the 'natural relationships' which people turn to for support, love and growth, and addictive relationships in which people rely on objects such as drugs, money or food, or events such as sex, shopping and gambling to meet their emotional needs. He defines natural relationships as those a person has with family and friends, with a spiritual power, with the self and with communities. The problem for Nakken is that it is not clear why getting fulfilment from family life, religion or community involvement is any more natural than finding fulfilment in food or sex. He responds by arguing that 'normal' relationships with objects and events do not involve 'emotional bonding or illusion of intimacy'. All objects have their own normal and 'socially acceptable' function: 'Food is to nourish; gambling is for fun and excitement; drugs are to help overcome illness'. The addict turns to these objects for the wrong reasons, and is thereby seduced into a state of false consciousness:

> Addiction is a process of buying into false and empty promises: the promise of relief, the promise of emotional security, the false sense of fulfillment, and the false sense of intimacy with the world . . .
>
> Finding emotional fulfillment through an object or event is an illusion.[26]

Nakken's model of natural versus false relationships works by combining ideas about the artificial mood alteration of drug use with normative and prescriptive views about appropriate behaviour. This juxtaposition, which is discussed in more detail in later chapters about sex and food, allows a broad territory of social life to be colonised by addiction discourse.

Denial and Disorder

It is a central tenet of popular addiction discourse that the denial of the existence of addiction is one of the surest signs of addiction. Denial is argued to be the most damaging and insidious symptom of addictive disease, perpetuating the addiction by causing the addict to blame everything for her problems except the actual culprit.[27] The concept of denial deserves close scrutiny because it justifies, even requires, overriding the addict's expressed wishes and ignoring his version of reality, in the name of his genuine needs and desires. The most formal expression of this logic is the process known as intervention, an orchestrated confrontation aimed at obtaining an individual's agreement to undergo treatment. It should be noted that the concept of denial is not part of traditional Alcoholics Anonymous doctrine; nor is the practice of intervention. In fact AA cautions against the use of threats and force because the desire for change must come from within the affected individual. As Miller and Kurtz observe, a number of AA tenets have been abandoned or significantly altered in contemporary interpretations of the disease model, and with the rise of the treatment industry confrontational and coercive practices have become more acceptable.[28]

The model of denial and intervention on which I base the following discussion is largely, although not exclusively, drawn from veteran drug educator Vernon Johnson's 'complete guide for families', *Everything You Need to Know About Chemical Dependence*. It contains extensive coverage of these topics, including information on how to carry out an intervention and a dramatised account of a fictional intervention.

In standard psychological terms, denial is a process by which painful realities are disavowed and kept out of consciousness. It is distinguished from repression by its focus on external rather than internal conditions. Despite the popular belief that facing reality and being honest with oneself are necessary for mental health, contemporary psychology views denial processes as having positive as well as negative consequences. Indeed, it is possible to argue that mental health and social functioning demand self-deception and at least some collusion in shared cultural deceptions. Denial is taken to be a normal and healthy coping response in patients with serious illnesses, and has been associated with better survival rates.[29] In other contexts it receives societal approbation under the labels of optimism, positive thinking or perseverance, such as the heroic refusal of the sailor lost at sea to give up hope of rescue.

In addiction discourse, however, denial is a bad thing. Rather than a fluid set of ongoing processes, it is produced as a static and monolithic state of delusion. In its most extreme form it is regarded as a type of insanity whose victims cannot tell reality from fiction or truth from falsity. Its lesser forms are seen in everyday rationalis-ations and half truths. The alcoholic drinks her wine out of an over-sized glass so she can tell herself that she has only a couple of glasses a night. She reassures herself that anyone would drink if they had such a stressful job. In short, she hides unpleasant realities from her-self to maintain her sense of herself as normal. It is the operation of denial which makes addiction the most cunning of diseases, like a parasite which masks its own presence in the host's body. In Johnson's words:

> Most people, when they come down with a disease, will set about trying to find treatment for it . . . Here is where chemical dependence distinguishes itself as a disease unlike any other. *The people who have it generally do not seek treatment of their own volition because they are not aware that they have it.*[30]

It is not just that they are not aware they have it, but that they refuse to accept that they have it no matter how strong the evidence. And because denial of the disease is a universal symptom of the dis-ease, the stronger their insistence that they are fine, the stronger the proof that the disease has them in its grip. Another inimical aspect of denial is what Johnson calls a delusional or 'faulty memory system', made up of a pattern of blackouts, repression and euphoric recall. Working in concert, this trio of memory disorders destroy the addict's ability to remember what happened while she was drunk or high, and therefore ensures the uninterrupted progress of the dis-ease. During blackouts the person continues to behave as if she is fully conscious, but is later unable to recall anything about that period of time. She is therefore denied access to the reactions her 'bizarre, antisocial' behaviour has caused. Repression refers to the ability to shut unwanted and shameful memories out of their minds until the truth becomes 'virtually unattainable'. Finally, euphoric recall, the most devastating component in the system, replaces the truthful, shameful memories with rosy recollections of bonhomie. Euphoric recall convinces addicts that they remember a drinking or using episode perfectly. But rather than remembering how they behaved—talking incoherently, stumbling, becoming aggressive—they remember how they felt: brilliant, witty, and sexy. These are serious claims about the status of addicts as individuals. As Ian Hacking has stated, in the nominalist tradition personal identity is constituted by memory. To be someone who consistently cannot remember, or even worse remembers falsely, is to lose the continuity of experience which défines the life of an individual.[31]

These mechanisms of denial are presented as descriptions of disease, caused by the chemical actions of drugs in the brain and exercising a global effect on the whole existence of the addict. Connecting denial with a disease process overcomes the tendency to view it as intentional self-deception, which would reduce it to a type of bad behaviour. If denial is read simply as the addict pretending not to know she is addicted so she can keep on drinking, then it follows that she does know she is addicted. She is cynical rather than deluded. But classifying denial as a symptom of a disease lifts it from the status of dishonesty. It instead operates as a type of Sartrean bad faith with a similar self-perpetuating quality. As Sartre says of bad faith, the problem is that it is *faith*. There is no reflective or voluntary decision, rather 'One *puts oneself* in bad faith as one goes to sleep and one is in bad faith as one dreams. Once this mode of being has been realized, it is as difficult to get out of it as to wake oneself up'.[32] The heavy sleeper needs to be woken by others because she cannot do it herself. Although this may be an unpleasant experience, once awake she recognises the awakening was for her own good.

The practice of intervention, developed by Vernon Johnson and his colleagues in the 1960s, demonstrates the implications of being viewed as being in denial. Intervention is the equivalent of a rude but necessary awakening for the chemically dependent individual. An intervention is a carefully prepared and rehearsed confrontation of the alcoholic or addict, which aims to break through his denial and get him to accept that he is addicted and needs help. Johnson calls it 'presenting reality to a person out of touch with it in a receivable way'. It is carried out by a group of people who have significant relationships with the addict and who have witnessed his behaviour while under the influence of alcohol or drugs, the most common participants being his spouse or partner, children, close friends, employer and work colleagues. Each member of the team prepares for the intervention by compiling lists of specific incidents or situations related to the addict's drinking or using, which must be described with 'unsparing detail'. The use of videotaped evidence of humiliating moments is also recommended. Rehearsals are held and a chairperson is appointed to direct the proceedings. At the conclusion of the intervention the addict is told that he must accept help and a list of treatment options is presented.[33]

Johnson argues that a properly executed intervention can save the life of the subject, and many self-help texts support intervention as a way of convincing addicts that they need help before they 'hit bottom', that is, before they reach the point where they cannot go on.[34] It is hardly surprising that intervention is a powerful tool for gaining someone's agreement to treatment. The thought of being faced with one's employer, spouse, parents, and children, closest friends and perhaps even one's work colleagues, gathered with the explicit purpose of telling you the truth about yourself, is bound to make even the most virtuous or thick-skinned person uneasy. Johnson rather blithely states that the essence of the successful intervention is its nonjudgmental and objective nature; it is an act based on empathy and care. But his very insistence that these confrontations are not punitive, cruel, secretive or invasive highlights how vulnerable they are to interpretation as all of those things, as orchestrated acts of pre-meditated bullying, or at least as exercises in coercion and threat. The necessary coercive force of intervention, according to one therapist, can be thought of as 'therapeutic leverage', the forcing of 'a small degree of self-awareness' on the alcoholic or addict. In Landry's guide to intervention, leverage is what the intervention team must turn to if the addict rejects its recommendation for treatment; 'Although leverages might diplomatically be described as contingencies, they are in fact threats'.[35] Examples are a wife threatening divorce and business partners demanding resignation.

Intervention is presented as a straightforward confrontation between truth and falsity. It is assumed that the real exists independent of perception, and that the members of the intervention team have access to it and can present it objectively. The effects of codependence which, Johnson himself argues, supposedly makes the addict's significant others and close family members as obsessive and disturbed as the addict, are here conspicuous by their absence. They are simply 'presenting reality to someone out of touch with it', to use Johnson's phrase. But the process is surely a much more creative form of labour than this description suggests. In both the intervention itself and in the description of intervention in addiction texts, the addict and the truth are being constructed in such a way that they cannot coincide. The discourse and structure of intervention produces the addict as a subject excluded from the truth, because the truth resides in the story of disease and loss of control summarised in the lists prepared by the others without her knowledge. Any alternative story with which the addict might understand her actions is, by virtue of her position, not the truth. Like Foucault's madman, whose words were considered null and void, 'mere noise' without truth or significance, worthless as evidence, 'rejected the moment they were proffered', the addict is placed in an oppositional relation to truth and reality.[36] Even the most functional of families is likely to have an array of contradictory and conflicting versions of reality operating simultaneously, interwoven with webs of power, resentment and love. But the intervention process removes all such complicating factors from the scene, leaving behind a manichean encounter between the addict and the truth.

Thinking about 'truth' as something produced in the intervention process puts the strongly asserted need for careful and painstaking preparation in a new light. Members of the team must all agree to all of the items being presented, the whole presentation is a tightly constructed performance.[37] Johnson argues that all this effort is necessary to maximise the impact on the addict, but it also demonstrates the hard work involved in constructing a robust and seamless collective reality, with no anomalies or contradictions. The interveners' work involves extracting material from their own memories and shaping it into discrete items which suit the purpose of the intervention. Some memories are included, others are excluded. The addict will have her own versions of past events with different inclusions and exclusions, but in her case the gaps are read as the product of denial and faulty memory systems.

From a critical perspective, keeping in mind the agonistic set up of intervention, denial can be read as a conceptual device that guarantees the impermeability of addiction logic to refutation. If it is the case that 'a patient's resistance to accepting a diagnosis of alcohol or drug dependency, and continuing to think and act in ways that promote the illusion of self-control, are themselves aspects of alcoholism and addiction, just as surely as physical tolerance is', then the more vehemently a person insists that they are not addicted, the more it proves they are.[38] It works like a noose which tightens if the prisoner struggles. Perhaps individuals who feel that they have been wrongly categorised as addicts would be wise to insist that they *are* chemically dependent and need help; such insight and honesty would surely argue against their classification as addicted. The problem with this tactic is that being worried that one is addicted is also read as a sign of addiction. As an appendix to her book on Alcoholics Anonymous, journalist and AA member Nan Robertson reproduces a National Council on Alcoholism questionnaire, introducing it by talking about the power of denial. She then adds that readers should ask themselves if they are worried about their drinking. 'If you are, chances are you have reason and do have a drinking problem'.[39] Both being worried and not being worried are signs that there is really something to worry about.

The prevalence of 'Are you an Alcoholic/Addict?' or 'Do you have a drinking problem?' questionnaires in self-help texts suggests that auto-intervention is possible if the disease or disorder is not too advanced. Again, this possibility is due to the authentic self that is lying dormant behind the addicted self. The individual can be both examiner and examined, the core of the self can be mobilised against the disease. A similar emergence of the true self occurs at the close of a successful intervention when the subject breaks down, and admits his accusers are right. 'I can't believe this is happening. Why didn't anybody say anything about this earlier? Why didn't anybody tell me what I was doing to you?' are the words Johnson puts in the mouth of the alcoholic at the end of his fictional example of a successful intervention.[40] Sometimes this acceptance of the truth and expression of gratitude does not occur until after some period of treatment. But it is the necessary conclusion to the successful intervention, it demonstrates that one version of reality, the story of disease and delusion, has been installed as 'what really happened'.

If an intervention is refigured as the construction of a particular discursive reality, and the simultaneous production of an individual at odds with that reality and with the reality of their authentic being, the possibilities that are being silenced become easier to identify. Looking at an account of a specific intervention illuminates this process. In her book Robertson describes the intervention which succeeded in beginning the recovery process of one of America's most famous addicts. She relates how Betty Ford's husband and children, accompanied by the head of a naval hospital's rehabilitation service, confronted her about her drug and alcohol use just before her sixtieth birthday:

> The President recalled times she had fallen asleep in a chair, her blurry speech, her memory lapses. Her son Mike and his wife told her why they hadn't wanted to have a child—because they didn't want it to have a grandmother who was not there for the baby. Another son, Steve, remembered bringing a new girlfriend home and cooking dinner for his mother while Mrs. Ford slipped into a haze in front of the TV with one drink, two drinks, three.[41]

Mrs Ford breaks down weeping and agrees to enter treatment, issues a statement to 'a stunned nation' and eventually goes on to found the Betty Ford Clinic to help other addicts. Robertson presents the confrontation and its consequences as proof of the possibility of recovery and a testimony to family love. But the encounter could also be described as four powerful men (plus the unnamed wife of one of the men) presenting a woman with examples of her failure to conform to the role of devoted wife and mother. The script does not allow for Mrs Ford to reply with a rejection of the behaviour and demeanour expected of her or with a challenge to the authority of her accusers. The form and content of the intervention does not allow the accusations to be false or the subject of the intervention to have her own equally true stories to tell about betrayals, disappointments and bad behaviour. Her reliance on drugs could be viewed as one of the many prices she has paid in supporting her husband's political ambitions. The pills she became dependent on enabled her to be a smiling and gracious political wife, despite severe pain from arthritis. The irony is that in spite of the concern with the authentic inner self and its destruction by addiction, this intervention is largely about Mrs Ford's failure to keep up appearances and meet her maternal and wifely duties. The Ford family seem to be accusing her not so much of being an addict, but of letting her addiction show and interfere with the smooth running of their lives.

Questions of gender and sexual politics, of marriage and families as social and economic institutions and of relations of power in general are even further from consideration, even though they would seem to be of great pertinence in the Ford case. The network of dependence revealed in this encounter is not confined to the reliance Mrs Ford has on psychoactive substances. Feminist sociologist Elizabeth Ettorre points out that two forms of dependency, 'dependency of the addiction kind' and 'dependency of the subordinate thing kind' are often intimately connected in women's lives. But because the former is socially unacceptable and the latter is regarded as a natural and beneficial state for women (when it involves being dependent on a husband, male protection or male superiors for financial support or aid), the links between them are mystified. Also obscured in dominant notions of dependency is the reliance of apparently independent men on women and on various forms of female labour.[42] In the Ford intervention, Mrs Ford's dependency on pills and alcohol is in the spotlight, but her dependence on powerful male figures and her husband and family's dependence on her continued functioning provide the context.

Addiction discourse is ever-vigilant in its desire to expose the mechanisms of addictive denial wherever they occur. Taking a stand against selective perceptions of reality, particularly the concealment of ugly and inconvenient truths, it promotes the health-giving properties of total honesty and the vital importance of seeing things as they are. But what if we think of denial as a device which operates in discursive fields, setting limits and boundaries to what can be known and can be recognised as true? Then the accusation that the heavy drinker or drug user is in denial because of the disease of addiction appears as an attempt to resolve a clash between different discursive constructions of reality. And it becomes clear that addiction discourse itself is 'in denial', depending as it does on certain exclusions to maintain its integrity.

Most obviously, addiction discourse could be argued to be in denial about the usefulness and pleasure of drugs, both licit and illicit. As anthropological and sociological studies, as well as everyday experience, make clear, psychoactive drugs make significant and varied contributions to human cultures and social relations. Their use is pervasive and widespread, and large numbers of people who drink and take drugs enjoy these experiences, without suffering significant harm or becoming dependent.[43] The orientation toward drug use as a problem in self-help texts is of course not surprising, because the intended audience is those who are in trouble with substances. But a common stance in contemporary self-help discourse is to interpret all substance use as harmful and as infallible evidence of inner disturbance.

Typical is Charlotte Davis Kasl's interpretation of moderate drinking as indicative of deep psychological problems. She describes two categories of habitual alcohol use which are especially damaging. The first is 'robot drinking', defined as the daily, almost automatic use of alcohol 'to escape the world'. Even if robot drinkers only drink one glass of wine a day, they will not grow or mature until they give up drinking, according to Kasl. 'Escape-hatch drinking', the second category, is demonstrated by those who do not drink every day but nevertheless use alcohol as a way of reducing tension and taking the edge off their emotions. They therefore 'never quite face life'. 'Escape-hatch drinking' is related to an inability to genuinely connect or commit to others, a lack of awareness of the self and a generally superficial way of being. Kasl therefore insists that her therapy clients abstain from all drugs including alcohol, even if they insist they have no problems with their use. Reducing tension, taking the edge off emotions and even escaping the world could all be argued to be amongst alcohol's dearly loved effects for social drinkers. The drinking described by Kasl reflects the role of alcohol consumption in demarcating leisure time, enabling release from constraints of work and duty and mediating social interaction, but her interpretation locates the cause of these socially constituted patterns in the neuroses of unhealthy individuals.[44]

In contemporary self-help and recovery literature, especially texts influenced by new age spirituality and alternative health philosophies, the distrust of moderate drinking is often part of a view that all 'artificial' substances are inherently harmful. Cigarettes, coffee, sugar and refined carbohydrates are all classified as mood-altering substances inimical to the achievement of health, clarity and autonomy. Hence Kasl tells of her struggle to overcome her caffeine addiction, and Richard Seymour, co-author of *Drugfree*, says he felt he could only write the book in good faith after giving up his substances of choice: sugar and caffeine.[45] Here a perfectionist ideal of an uncontaminated and autonomous body and self is the goal, quite different from the AA approach, which identifies one substance, alcohol, as harmful to particular vulnerable people. Tra-ditional Alcoholics Anonymous literature makes no comment about the use of drugs such as nicotine or caffeine. In fact, the amount of coffee drinking and cigarette smoking which goes on in meetings and conventions is a common source of AA humour. It also advises members never to show intolerance for drinking as an institution, stating, 'For most normal folks, drinking means conviviality, com-panionship and colorful imagination. It means release from care, boredom and worry. It is joyous intimacy with friends and a feeling that life is good'. This was written in the 1930s, although it con-tinues to be published in revised editions of *The Big Book*.[46]

Another symptom of denial in contemporary self-help dis-course is the insistence that healthful and wholesome activities can provide all the rewards of drug use with none of the costs, and that sobriety is therefore no less rich, pleasurable and exciting than one's life with alcohol and drugs. Yoga, meditation and exercise fulfil the desire for altered states of consciousness and reduce stress, new hobbies, sports and outings with friends offer adventure and relax-ation. But is it always the case that nothing of value is lost when individuals (or societies) renounce the use of drugs? Other enjoyable and productive pastimes and habits can be embraced; but is it necessary to insist that they can completely replace the particular attractions and benefits of mood-altering substances and seamlessly fulfil their functions? Allowing mourning for the renounced sub-stance or activity might help rather than hinder recovery, especially if it enables 'relapses' to be viewed as understandable returns to familiar pleasures, rather than the re-emergence of a pathological identity.

A different kind of denial is seen in what might be called the dysphoric recall which operates in personal accounts of recovering addicts (as opposed to the euphoric recall of the active addict dis-cussed earlier). The past is reconstructed as uniformly unhappy, and the effects of drug use entirely negative. Times of apparent happiness or moments of pleasure are presented as illusory, hiding the grim reality of loneliness and fear. Earlier selves are unceremoniously cast aside as of no worth. A compelling example is the story of Jane, a writer who had been sober for more than twenty-five years when she was interviewed for a book of women's recovery stories. Her tale is dramatic and grim; by the end of her drinking career she is a suicidal physical wreck, with no money, no friends and nowhere to go, except the local AA meeting. But before getting to this part of her story she describes the adventurous life she led in New York in the 1920s. Still only in her twenties, she was drinking heavily but also 'working with some truly remarkable people' in the theatre and mixing with politicians and celebrities. She becomes a playreader for a major Broadway producer, 'Mr Z', reading scripts with a bottle of Jack Daniels open on her desk. She meets and works with Elia Kazan, Marilyn Monroe, Robert Kennedy, Lee Strasburg and Stella Adler, among others. One day she goes out drinking with Mr Z, an occasion she has no memory of, but 'somehow, during the course of this dinner, he heard my life story . . . because within a week he had arranged for me to be appointed to the National Cultural Center'. Despite these experiences her assessment of this phase in her life concentrates on her drinking and its negative effects—the hangovers, the anxiety, the exhaustion:

> So I was running as any alcoholic will, people-pleasing all over the place, covering up the fact that I didn't know what I was doing and drinking more to relieve the anxiety, the fear and the pain. Just getting caught in the vortex.[47]

To make sense as a story of recovery, Jane's account has to follow the narrative of degradation and redemption common to AA stories and other conversion narratives. Norman Denzin observes in his ethnographic study of AA that the radical restructuring of a drinking self into a recovering self requires the adoption of a particular reflexive stance towards the past. The old self must be distanced from the new, but must be kept alive to maintain the precarious existence of a sober alcoholic. The old alcoholic self becomes the subject of stories related at meetings, and through this the teller defines themselves by who they no longer are and no longer want to be.[48] This process could be seen as the disciplining of the past in the service of the present. But when the story appears as a text, it has an excess which cannot be controlled by the narrator. Jane's New York life could just as convincingly be interpreted positively, as a time of excitement and opportunities, in which drinking played a vital part. My point is not that Jane's drinking was without damaging effects, nor that her suffering was not genuine, nor that mixing with celebrities is the source of true happiness. But if she had been going to five AA meetings a week in those days, as she is now, would she be the writer she is today? The 'dysphoric recall' which characterises the genre of addiction/recovery story makes such a version impossible, yet it cannot be completely silenced.

Addiction texts bring together a concern for the healthy body with a concern for an authentic and well-ordered self. The special quality of addiction discourse is its ability to promote authenticity and autonomy as public health goals in service of the healthy body, as well as abstract moral ideals. Substances, pursuits, attitudes and feelings are classified as natural or artificial, with the former being healthy, therefore good, and the latter being damaging, therefore bad, in a blurring of biological and ethical categories. In addition to the body and the conduct of the individual, the interior world of the addict's self, and of other selves associated with the addict, are opened up for judgement and marked for therapeutic intervention.

4

Smoking, Addiction and Time

A cigarette is the perfect type of a perfect pleasure. It is exquisite, and it leaves one unsatisfied. What more can one want?
—Oscar Wilde, *The Picture of Dorian Gray.*

Smoking may seem to fit into the well-established category of drug addiction; after all nicotine is an addictive drug, even the tobacco companies have admitted it. But the unique cultural location inhabited by cigarettes means that smoking is constructed and experienced quite differently from addiction to illegal drugs or from alcoholism. The status of smoking as an everyday and normal practice is under threat, but still retains significant currency. In spite of the steady decrease in the number of smokers in western countries, about a quarter of adults in the United States, Australia and Britain still smoke.[1] Because the notion of addiction is generally constructed against the idea of normality, the discourse of smoking as a drug addiction contains significant moments of ambiguity and contradiction. This chapter examines some of the tensions present in contemporary understandings of smoking as an addictive disorder, focusing particularly on the issues of time and pleasure.

In anti-smoking discourse the smoker often appears as a squanderer of the precious and scarce resource of time. Not only does the purchase and consumption of the drug take up time in the smoker's daily routine, but her attachment to its dubious pleasures is steadily subtracting time from the future. The rate of loss has been quite precisely calculated—about $5\frac{1}{2}$ minutes of life per cigarette, according to one source. No wonder troubled smokers think of their habit as 'an insidious slow form of suicide'; each cigarette consumes energy and income and brings illness and death one step closer. Images of smokers as prisoners of time, unable to break free from the chains of their past actions, appear most vividly in texts which understand smoking in terms of a powerful physical addiction to nicotine. In this model, nicotine addiction is an alien and malign force which takes over the life of its victims, compelling them to continue no matter how strong their desire to stop.[2]

However, even in texts devoted to the dangers and despair of nicotine addiction, the multifaceted and autoerotic pleasures of smoking keep emerging, polluting the apparent purity and transparency of the anti-smoking case. One common response to this tension is to emphasise the serious future consequences of smoking. But once the pleasures of cigarettes are taken as seriously as their dangers, the relationship between smoking and time becomes more complex than the rhetoric of future risk can admit. Not only is confining the meaning of smoking to the pathology of addiction not possible; but the move to reduce smoking to these terms has a quite different effect from the one intended. It stretches and weakens the boundaries of the category of addiction, blurring distinctions between health and pathology, order and disorder, production and destruction, present and future, in the process advertising the attractions of addictive desire itself.

Richard Klein has written eloquently on the philosophical and cultural significance of cigarettes, and his work has informed my discussion, especially his theme of the temporal productivity of smoking, and the alluring repetition and brevity of the act. But whereas Klein's main thesis is that the sublime beauty of cigarettes has been forgotten and repressed in an era of puritanical healthism, my argument is more that the virtues of cigarettes and the appeal of addiction *cannot* be excluded, even from the discourse of nicotine addiction.[3]

Nicotine Addiction

In 1988 the United States Surgeon General's report on the health consequences of smoking was devoted to an extended discussion of nicotine addiction. The report concluded that cigarettes are addicting, that nicotine is the drug in tobacco that causes addiction, and that the processes of tobacco addiction are similar to those of heroin and cocaine addiction. It termed tobacco use 'a disorder which can be remedied through medical attention' and wrote of the achievement and maintenance of 'tobacco abstinence'. Not too many decades ago, such statements would have been regarded as risible if not deranged. In 1926, the president of the Royal College of Physicians, Sir Humphrey Rolleston, observed that tobacco could only be regarded as an addictive drug 'in a humorous sense'.[4]

Widespread knowledge about the serious health consequences of smoking, beginning with the first US Surgeon General's report in 1964 which linked smoking with several forms of cancer, have made humour on the topic unlikely, at least from government officials and medical experts. As the serious risks associated with smoking became well-known, the idea that people who smoked were compelled to continue gained greater logical force. Increased regulation of smoking, in particular the enforcement of smoke-free work and public places, has also had the effect of highlighting the addictive nature of the habit. One recent text on smoking remarks that anyone who doubts that smoking is an addiction should look outside an office building on a freezing winter's day and observe what smokers are prepared to endure in order to have a cigarette.[5]

The pharmacological/medical approach of the 1988 report has become widespread in popular literature on smoking, particularly in how-to-quit guides. According to one recent text, smokers who cannot quit are 'enslaved not by cigarettes but by a single chemical, $C_{10}H_{14}N_2$, or nicotine'. Another claims that 'If you take people who are smokers and withhold cigarettes from them but give them syringes containing nicotine, they will inject nicotine into their veins, exactly like heroin addicts'. The language of drug addiction is also routinely adopted in smokers' self-presentations. Actor Mel Gibson, referring to his 26-year smoking career in a recent interview

('His right hand plays with a cigarette, despite the fact that only months ago he was celebrating kicking the habit'), is reported as saying that nicotine is harder to get out of the system than heroin. In addition, the addictive power of nicotine has featured prominently in recent litigation against tobacco companies, both in damages claims brought by former smokers and their families and in government lawsuits.[6]

Whatever nicotine's particular pharmacology, reducing the meaning of smoking to 'enslavement to a chemical' and insisting on its identity as a drug addiction are discursive events which produce the smoker as a pathological subject. The smoker's problem is transformed from a (bad) habit into an addictive disease, and, as I go on to describe, his disordered inner being becomes the proper object of rehabilitative self-discipline. At a broader level, the discourse of nicotine addiction can be located within a trajectory of medicalisation in which human conduct and experiences are increasingly understood and explained in medical terms.

At first glance, the construction of 'the smoker' from the template of 'the heroin addict' would seem to further the status of smokers as weak and immoral deviants. But to its proponents, the discourse of smoking as addiction is both scientific and humane, an alternative to old-fashioned moralising about bad habits and lack of self-discipline. It argues that overcoming dependence on 'one of the most addictive substances known to man' is much more than a matter of will power, and that smokers should not be blamed for their addictive disorder.[7] In this context, the smoker is often presented as an innocent victim of evil and rapacious tobacco companies. All smokers are regarded as passive, whether first- or second-hand inhalers, while the tobacco industry fills the role of active agent of disease and death. One of the conditions of this benevolence is, however, the embracing of an identity based on pathology. The discourse of nicotine addiction suggests that smokers are fundamentally different from non-smokers at a physiological level. Their bodies not only tolerate but require a poison to function. In this context of identity production it comes as no surprise to find that twin studies have supported the existence of 'smoking genes' which control susceptibility to nicotine addiction. This suggests the smoker/addict identity is encoded at the deepest and most immutable level of personal identity, that is, on the DNA. According to smoking cessation expert Renée Bittoun, there is mounting evidence that individual reaction to nicotine and even difficulty in quitting may be inherited.[8]

Viewing smoking as a symptom of affliction, rather than a cultural practice or individual choice, transforms the political landscape of tobacco use. Arguments based on rights and freedom are disarmed in the face of biology and the absence of choice it implies. For example, Bittoun suggests that children may become addicted to nicotine before they can speak, from inhaling parents' smoke. She also argues that passive smoking is a crucial issue for ex-smokers, because they can be so sensitised to nicotine that inhaling secondhand smoke triggers 'a neurological reaction'.[9] Smoking is seen as an irrational behaviour that serves no useful purpose and can only be explained in terms of pathology. If smokers are not suffering from a disorder, why do they continue a dangerous habit which they do not really enjoy? It is no coincidence that a counter-discourse of smokers' rights has gained prominence at the same time that the smoker as addict has become a common figure. This discourse constitutes smoking as a matter of choice and freedom—the very terms the notion of addiction undermines. In rights discourse, smokers' freedom is threatened not by the tyranny of addiction, but by the puritanical and fascistic forces of anti-smoking.

The move to refigure smokers as powerless victims of an addictive drug does not remove the debate from the realm of ethical and moral judgement. Rather, it widens the scope of normalisation and imbues it with the authority and familiar appeal of medical discourse. True, the discourse of nicotine addiction constructs addicted smokers as sick not bad, but it assumes that the only way to live a meaningful, productive, and happy life is to adopt a healthy non-smoking lifestyle.

The ethical dimensions of addiction discourse are made obvious in the theories of Nicotine Anonymous (NA). Basing its twelve-step program on that of Alcoholics Anonymous, NA is a relatively small organisation, but a visit to its internet web site suggests that it is experiencing some success. Regular meetings throughout North America are listed, with more than one hundred established in California alone. Australia, the United Kingdom, the Netherlands,

Spain, Sweden, Brazil and Argentina are among the other countries in which NA has a presence, albeit a limited one. NA combines a notion of physical addiction with an explicit moral stance. For NA, smoking is a physical, emotional, and spiritual disease with 'deep-seated origins and symptoms that pervade every aspect of the addict's waking and sleeping life'.[10] In the familiar words of the first step, addicts are powerless over the drug and their lives become unmanageable. What is required is not merely cessation but re-covery, involving a process of 'thorough moral housecleaning'.[11] The smoker–nicotine relationship is much more than a physical dependency in this model; 'smoker' becomes a subjectivity defined by reliance on a drug and marked by a deep and pervasive emo-tional impairment. *Recovery from Smoking*, a twelve-step guide to quitting, devotes fifty-two pages to the process of emotional recov-ery, more than twice as many as it uses to discuss the physical prob-lems faced by quitters. In this text, the nicotine addict's smoking habit is the exterior sign of a deep inner anguish, which the smoker attempts to mask and control with the compulsive use of cigarettes. Beneath their generally competent and rational demeanours smokers are intensely lonely, controlled by fear (ranging from the fear of gaining weight to the fear of abandonment), suffused with shame and, most tragically, emotionally numb. They have used the power-ful effects of nicotine and the rituals of smoking to hide their feelings, not only from others but from themselves, and to success-fully recover they must embark on a long and painful journey of emotional re-education, learning to 'identify, accept, and express feelings of shame, fear, sadness, loneliness, grief, depression, and anger'. In a move that will be greeted sceptically by some non-smokers, the author argues that because smokers exist in a state of emotional anaesthesia they tend to be more aware of others' feelings than their own. Therefore, they often lack assertiveness skills, and are frequently taken advantage of by other people.[12]

A smoker, then, becomes a subject requiring self-improvement, and *Recovery from Smoking* offers a series of exercises to help the reader on the path to healthy living. The tasks for the recovery of emotional well-being are varied: completing charts, answering ques-tions and making lists on topics such as feelings, boundaries, and intimacy; recalling childhood memories of loneliness and parental substance use; repeating affirmations such as, 'I can play and have fun without being self-destructive' and 'Accepting my sadness heals my pain and helps it pass';[13] and visualising and drawing pictures of different emotions. Together, they provide training in a regularised discipline of self-examination, self-interpretation, and self-expression, through which an accessible, orderly, and balanced inner self is produced.

Portrait of the Smoker as a Drug Addict

An engrossing and affecting portrait of one smoker/addict subject is presented in *Smoker: Self Portrait of a Nicotine Addict* by Ellen Walker, a fervent champion of the NA model. Walker's story has many of the elements of classic addiction narratives: obsession with the drug, secrecy and shame, failed attempts to quit, and despair and self-hatred. But her account, nevertheless, undermines as well as supports the case for the pathological power of nicotine, and the aberrancy of its devotees. The very fact that she is still an active nicotine addict at the time of writing the book distinguishes her addiction from the more flamboyant and dramatic addictions, which only allow their stories to be told once they have been conquered.

Walker presents her personal story as representative of the stories of millions of other smokers whose lives are delineated by the most insidious of addictive desires. A long-term smoker who watched her father die of lung cancer, she is desperate but unable to give up. She presents herself as suffering from an incurable disease, forced to continue smoking by an addiction to a powerful drug which controls her life. She insists that just like other drugs nicotine becomes the centre of the addict's existence, leading to reprehensible behaviour, abdication of responsibility, and a pervasive 'spiritual bankruptcy'. Adopting a familiar addict identity, she states, 'As with other addictions a drug often dictates where I go, which people I associate with, even where I will work'.[14]

But the stubborn ordinariness of smoking and smokers undermines her attempts to inhabit the junkie persona. As Walker herself states, most smokers' lives appear relatively orderly, autonomous, and productive. To prove this is an illusion, she relates the low points of her own smoking career: drying out old butts from the rubbish with a hairdryer; refusing to go on church trips with her children because they entail two smoke-free hours; spending her honeymoon sneaking cigarettes in the bathroom; and risking her life smoking outside in a snowstorm. Her confessions are touching because of the strength of her self-directed frustration and shame, but as a portrait of the degradation of addiction the effect is less than dramatic. The fact that she finds these incidents so horrifying and alienating emphasises, rather than casts doubts on, her general probity and sense of responsibility.

Since a steady supply of high quality nicotine can still be relatively easily maintained, smokers are not generally desperate junkies controlled by an unmanageable, compulsive desire—at least until they attempt to stop. When she writes about her own longest period of abstinence, Walker unintentionally but eloquently suggests that smokers only become addicts when they quit. After a week without cigarettes she is 'a useless lump'.[15] She gains forty pounds, she develops high blood pressure, a stiff neck, a painful rash and aching joints, and she becomes a depressed recluse unable to concentrate, work, sleep, or stop crying. After eight months of torment, and partly at her husband's request, she starts smoking again. She ironically notes that having recommenced her unhealthy habit, she becomes healthier and more optimistic every day. All her symptoms gradually disappear and she is able to resume her normal busy life.

The dichotomies of addiction and normality, and disease and health, central to disease models of addiction, are unstable in the case of smoking, despite the spectres of cancer, emphysema, and heart disease. Part of the reason why the disease and disorder of addiction remain remote is that for Walker, like many quitters, the serious consequences of smoking are yet to become manifest. They exist as abstract possibilities, while the distress of giving up is corporeal and immediate. Doing the healthy thing makes Walker unhealthy. Nicotine is the pharmakon in her narrative, both poison and medicine. It is killing her but can also cure her.

The very existence of *Smoker* is testimony to the peculiar status of smoking among drug addictions. The book's publisher is the Hazelden Foundation, a major US provider of drug rehabilitation services, whose publishing mission is to provide literature and material to inspire and assist readers in their own twelve-step recovery programs. In view of this aim, its policy is to publish books by people who are successfully 'in recovery' from the addiction they are writing about, *Smoker* being the first exception to this policy. According to editor Sid Farrar, the prevalence of nicotine use among members of the recovery community who are otherwise abstinent, and the damage it causes, makes smoking a unique case which is worthy of such an exception.[16] What he does not mention is that the acceptability of a still-smoking smoker writing about her addiction also depends on the incongruity between smokers and other drug addicts. Despite their inability to control their drug use, smokers are regarded as capable of rational thinking and realistic assessment of their situation. In marked contrast to an active alcoholic locked in denial and self-delusion, Walker has insight into her addictive disease and can describe it clearly and honestly. The text argues that smoking is an addiction as destructive as all others, but the fact that the book exists suggests otherwise.

Another unacknowledged paradox in anti-smoking discourse is that the 'uniquely cunning' drug Walker is addicted to is not what is endangering her health.[17] Nicotine, in itself, is not generally regarded as particularly harmful, and has been observed to have beneficial effects on the brain.[18] The most harmful substances, in medical terms, are the tar and carbon monoxide in cigarette smoke. But this distinction, between addictive agent and source of harm, cannot be made in a discourse which constructs dependence and physical harm as interlinked elements of the one overarching disorder. The NA philosophy, supported by Walker, argues that the evil effects of smoking and the tyranny of addiction cannot be separated, because the disease of addiction is itself the source of physical and psychological harm.

The current popularity of nicotine replacement devices as aids to smoking cessation brings the double identity of the drug to the fore. Good nicotine in the form of gum, patches, and nasal spray are succeeding as treatments for attachment to bad nicotine. Ironically, nicotine as cure may, at least in the short term, cause more distress to the user than nicotine as poison: nausea, vomiting, dizziness, sore mouth and throat, rashes, and insomnia are possible side effects of treatment. Another danger is excessively accurate mimicry, causing the good to blur into the bad. Addiction to nicotine gum can occur after long-term use, with some users experiencing symptoms 'very similar to those associated with cigarette withdrawal'.[19]

The final irony is that while Walker insists that smokers are 'junkies', the authority and appeal of her story depend on the fact that she is a respectable, law-abiding, middle-class citizen. Identifying with her struggles is easy because they represent the mundane but heroic efforts of a woman to do her best by her husband and children, her work, her friends, and her community. Walker does not deserve the indignities of addiction because she is otherwise respectable and competent.

Despite Walker's best efforts, smoking fits awkwardly into the twelve-step disease model of addiction. Given the tensions and paradoxes already discussed, it is perhaps not surprising that the pleasures rather than the costs of cigarettes emerge most clearly in her text. She confesses that smoking 'gives me a peace that I've found no place else', and that 'Nicotine does everything asked of it. It works'. Later, she adds that the drug becomes a god to smokers because, 'It never fails. It is always there'. These tributes are powerful and resonant in their conciseness. No wonder smoking cessation guides talk about quitting as mourning the loss of a loved one, and warn neophyte ex-smokers to expect vivid smoking dreams.[20]

It is not only narratives such as Walker's which evoke smoking's virtues as supremely reliable and inimitably versatile. Much mainstream anti-smoking material contains clinical, but no less enticing, portrayals of the unique qualities of nicotine and the efficiency of the cigarette as a drug delivery device. We are told that the drug is both calming and stimulating, that the nicotine from a cigarette can reach the brain in seven seconds, which is faster than if it were injected. Dedicated smokers can deliver up to four hundred hits of nicotine to their brains a day, and far from becoming intoxicated, their mental efficiency is increased. The pleasures of nicotine are subtle, the alterations in consciousness slight, compared to the euphoria and dramatic changes produced by some other drugs. But as one author points out, the subtlety is part of the attraction. Nicotine enables a kind of emotional fine-tuning, it allows its users to 'stay medium' rather than get high.[21]

What is more, smokers learn to maintain a constant level of nicotine in their blood. They are sensitive to tiny variations in dose, and if given milder cigarettes will inhale more deeply to achieve their preferred concentration. Anti-smoking texts portray this as an entirely unfortunate reaction, reducing the potential benefits of low-tar brands. For them, the finely tuned and specialised corporeality of the smoker is a corruption of the body's natural state of organic and self-contained integrity. But the inhaling and exhaling of the smoker's body, its connection with the atmosphere through the medium of smoke, also brings to mind the radically different understanding of embodiment constructed by French philosophers Deleuze and Guattari. In *A Thousand Plateaus* they theorise bodies as inorganic and untotalisable assemblages, formed through the making of provisional linkages between heterogeneous objects. No ontological or hierarchical distinctions are made between animate and inanimate bodies, biological, social or textual bodies. As already noted in Chapter 1, Deleuze and Guattari define bodies by their specific capacities or 'affects': by what they can do, the sensations they can experience and the range of their potential interactions with other bodies.[22] From this view, the smoker's connection with the cigarette and her responses to nicotine appear as increases in the range of the body's powers, that is, the body's capacity to affect and be affected. In addition to the delicate manipulation of drug levels are the sensory and aesthetic stimulations of smoke in the airways ('pulmonary eroticism'), object in the mouth, and movement of the hand. The actions and reactions of smoking can be read as a testimony to the adaptability and sensitivity of a body which can actively produce and experience pleasure through all sorts of connections, flows, and intensities, including regulated flows of toxins.

Of course, the recognition that cigarettes are not only useful, but contain a 'darkly beautiful, inevitably painful pleasure' has been convincingly expressed elsewhere, most comprehensively, in the work of Richard Klein. But locating the pleasures of smoking in unequivocally anti-smoking texts has a sly appeal of its own. As Klein notes, it is not surprising that anti-smoking warnings can incite the practice they hope to discourage. Even the resolute and no-nonsense anti-smoking text *SmokeScreen: A Guide to the Personal Risks and Global Effects of the Cigarette Habit*, demonstrates a tension on this point. It is illustrated with American and European cigarette advertisements dating from the turn of the century to the 1940s. Their elegant graphics and beautiful colours make them the most visually attractive elements of the book, a striking contrast with the numerous bar and line graphs and tables demonstrating the dangers of smoking.[23]

Smoking and Future Risk

In the broad field of contemporary anti-smoking literature, Walker's autobiographical narrative and Hoffman's twelve-step guide are unusual in their emphasis on psychic and spiritual damage. As smoking does not have the obviously life-disrupting and socially harmful consequences of other addictions, most texts give a dominant role to physical health in their production of tobacco use as a major social issue. But as noted earlier, for most smokers the seriously deleterious medical consequences of their habit lie in the future, while its rewards are experienced in the present. Hence anti-smoking material highlights links between the remembered past, present behaviour, and the anticipated future, constructing a unidirectional and linear notion of time. Through its deployment of the notion of risk, anti-smoking discourse tries to negate the gratifications of the present in favour of the dangers of the future.

In the plane of two-dimensional time, a 'smooth flowing continuum in which everything in the universe proceeds at an equal rate',[24] the smoker is produced as at best a time waster, at worst a perverse and self-destructive time destroyer. The idea that addiction is a form of disordered temporality appears in many different locations. One of the official diagnostic criteria for substance dependence is spending much time using the substance, trying to obtain it or recovering from its use. Another is abandoning or reducing other important actitivities because of substance use, which is also a matter of time allocation. Smoking is strangely located in relation to these criteria. In the DSM-IV chain-smoking is given as an example of a great deal of time being devoted to substance use. But chain-smoking is usually combined with other activities, rather than using up time on its own, even in the age of smoke-free public and work places. As another diagnostic guide admits, 'Most people can use it [nicotine] without interfering in any material way with their other, non-substance-related pursuits'.[25]

But there are more existential understandings of addicted time. For example, sociologist Norman Denzin, drawing on Heideggerian categories, calls alcoholism a disease of time. The alcoholic is living with an altered and inauthentic temporal consciousness, out of sync with and alienated from 'normal time'. He is fearful of the future and the past, but trapped within them, unable to live in the now of the present. In contrast, normal time grounds us in the present and is not threatening or anxiety-producing, but is part of our on-going presence in the world, allowing us to work towards achievable goals. In Walker's text, being an addict means failing to live up to the challenge of passing time. She sees herself as stuck in a 'perpetual teenagedom', slave to an impulsive decision made thirty years ago by a naive and lonely college student. Relying on a drug to solve her problems has meant missing her chance to learn how to be an adult. Her addiction holds her present hostage to her past and is destroying her future.[26]

Mainstream public health literature is less metaphorical in its use of temporal explanations. It depends explicitly on the truth of the connection between smoking and future ill health, aiming to make the probable and the possible real enough to motivate behaviour change. While accepting that nicotine addiction is a central aspect of smoking, this literature downplays its power, placing faith in the ability of education and awareness to provide the resolve needed to quit. In this approach, accurate information about risk is the key weapon against smoking and nicotine addiction. It is exemplified in *SmokeScreen: A Guide to the Personal Risks and Global Effects of the Cigarette Habit*. Much of the highly detailed (and rather tortuous) information provided in this Australian book is presented in the form of statistical links between smoking, disease, and premature death. In the preface, author Barry Ford sets out its field of inquiry:

> To really understand the dangers of smoking, people need information that will provide explicit answers to questions like: What are the chances that it *will* happen to me? What are the odds of a smoker developing lung cancer, some other form of cancer, emphysema, heart disease, or one of the other diseases that can be caused by smoking? What is the overall probability of one's death being caused by smoking, and for those who are killed by smoking, how many years prematurely do they die, on average?

After reviewing the research, the text suggests that people who die as a result of their smoking are likely to do so fifteen to twenty years before their time. Overall, US smokers suffer a life-loss of about eight years. More precisely, according to one study cited, men aged around thirty lost 4.6 years of life expectancy if they smoked up to ten cigarettes a day; 5.5 years for ten to twenty cigarettes; 6.2 years for twenty to forty; and 8.3 for more than forty. In terms of specific diseases, *SmokeScreen* estimates that, on average, long-term smokers face a one in six chance of dying of lung cancer, a one in eight chance of dying of heart disease, and a one in nineteen chance of dying from emphysema.[27]

'Real understanding' then depends on accepting isolated and precise probabilities as accurate reflections of reality, and on seeing one's future as an individually held commodity that one either judiciously protects or recklessly gambles away. One reason put forward to explain why smokers do not want to quit, despite knowing the dangers, is that they labour under particular 'cognitive defects' or forms of irrationality. One of these is 'time discounting', the tendency to attach too little importance to the future relative to the present.[28]

But the relationship between the present and the future promoted in health literature represents a particular view of the world, not a transparent window on the real. While not denying the reality of the dangers, the argument is not as straightforward as anti-smoking texts suggest. Mary Douglas has observed that the contemporary concept of risk has departed from an earlier neutral meaning in which high risk described a probability of great gain or great loss. Stripped of its connections with positive outcomes, and with the element of chance de-emphasised, '*risk* now means danger; *high risk* means a lot of danger'.[29] In health promotion texts like *SmokeScreen*, the valorisation of specific risk calculations into 'the truth' brings the future smoothly into existence in the present, imbuing it with a solidity which masks the uncertainty and inaccessibility which are its necessary attributes. The very unpredictability of the future is translated into a series of solely negative outcomes. In fact, in the world of *SmokeScreen*, the practice of smoking is reduced to its potentially most undesirable outcomes; namely, various premature, painful, and protracted forms of death. The enhancements of existence that can come with smoking are dismissed as illusory and excluded from the calculations of risk. How could they be included? The benefits of such things as solitary peace, self-sufficiency, style, concentration, camaraderie and rebellion cannot be quantified. Moreover, in the discourse of 'health risk' there are no willing gamblers, lucky or unlucky; there are only pitiable or foolish victims. It is assumed that making choices about risk can and should be done 'objectively', but this ignores the diversity of values and commitments people draw on, and refer to, when assessing risks in daily life.

Also obscured in public health anti-smoking discourse is the extent to which our individual futures are not separate channels which we can steer independently in any direction. They are more like threads in a woven fabric, the pattern of which is determined by social forces and the relations of power in which we are all embedded. Our decisions alone do not control our futures, and our decisions themselves are not made in an abstract space of pure choice. The irony is that it is only the future's supposed openness which makes it possible for people's actions to influence it, but they must assume the yet-to-be can be known in order to choose their actions rationally.

Reference to risk inevitably has political dimensions; the concept brings with it questions of responsibility and blame. Douglas notes that the contemporary language of risk works as 'a common forensic vocabulary with which to hold persons accountable'.[30] For smoking, the attribution of blame is complex. The logic of addiction does not cancel out the belief in individual responsibility for health which is central to health promotion discourse. As an addict, the smoker is not to blame for her current dependence on cigarettes; the role of tobacco companies as predatory risk-mongers is also acknowledged. But on the other hand, for texts like *SmokeScreen* to make sense, individuals must be presumed to have control over their 'lifestyle' choices, and hence, their health.

Again this tension is resolved through contrasting the unalterable necessity that is the present with the possibilities of the future. The implication is that the forces of culture and addiction which currently imprison and deceive the smoker will somehow weaken their grip or disappear in times to come, allowing her to free herself from dependency. Anti-smoking texts can thereby maintain an optimistic tone despite their grim message. Armed with the truth, smokers can ensure that their future is different from their present; they are reassured that giving up is 'highly effective' in reducing the risks and that the body has an 'astounding repair capacity'. Bittoun states that after four smoke-free months there are no remnants of the four thousand chemicals in smoke left in the body;[31] after ten to fifteen years the risk of premature death is said to return close to that of people who have never smoked.[32]

However, the smoking body's potential for recovery is only half the story. The notion of future risk simultaneously produces the smoker's body as always already diseased and unhealthy. According to the information provided in *SmokeScreen*, the addiction will prove fatal for one long-term smoker out of two. There is no way of knowing who will be struck down and who will be spared. Therefore all smokers must presume they will be among the former. In addition, the statistical construction of smokers as people who die eight years younger than non-smokers produces all smokers as already suffering a loss of life. As Nelkin and Lindee have observed in another context, 'possible future states, calculated by statistical methods, are often defined as equivalent to current status'. The smoker who takes comfort in her present health and fitness is therefore viewed as living in ignorance of the true identity of her body which lies in its future deterioration.[33]

Social theorist Helga Nowotny's work is useful for thinking about the production and deployment of future risk in these texts on smoking. She argues that in contemporary western life the future has disappeared, replaced by what she calls the 'extended present'.[34] We believe we can, and should, determine the future in our activities in the present through technological innovation, planning, and solving of impending problems. This allows us to imagine a better future, but also means problems reach into the present which could formerly be deferred into the future. And as the future is worked out in the present, the limitations of the utopian dream become apparent. Thus there is a tension between the desire for the yet to be conceived to remain inconceivable, and the desire to control and know the repercussions in advance.

Nowotny's focus is on technology, but her ideas can fruitfully be applied to the way the boundaries between the past, present, and future are made porous in anti-smoking and health promotion texts. The culturally endorsed habit of thinking in terms of health risks means our present behaviour is seen as determining the quantity and quality of our individual futures. This knowledge both opens up possibilities and closes them down. We know we can look forward to a longer and happier future by giving up smoking, and by exercising and eating well, but every day as we fail to do these things, fulfilment of the promise becomes less likely. In making the choices we make today, we have to consider our responsibility to our future selves, just as we can berate our past selves for choices which have had negative outcomes. Seemingly small and trivial acts, such as the impulsive trying out of cigarettes as a teenager, are refigured into 'deadly choices', to quote the title of a popular book.[35] The distinction between the disordered temporality of addiction and the natural, unthreatening passage of normal time is hard to maintain. It is not only the addicted who are unable to live in the present. They may be controlled by their pasts, but joining the ranks of the healthy brings control by, and obsession with, the simultaneous knowability and unknowability of the future.

In both the discourses of addiction and of future risk there are strains and gaps through which alternative understandings of smoking can be glimpsed. If the attractions of cigarettes are taken seriously and thought of in relation to temporality, it becomes possible to construct a different relationship between smoking and time, one from which the smoker emerges as an active and skilful producer of time and pleasure. This not only refigures smoking, it also brings out positive attributes of addiction itself. In relation to the broader themes of this thesis, the exercise of refiguring smoking shows how the production of addiction as a disorder located in the individual excludes certain experiences of self-enhancement and certain types of pleasure.

Temporality and Addiction

The pleasure of smoking is connected to temporal effects, the small ritual marking the passage of time as well as taking up time. Indeed, cigarettes can be argued to make time. Klein states that:

> The moment of taking a cigarette allows one to open a parenthesis
> in the time of ordinary experience, a space and a time of heightened
> attention that give rise to a feeling of transcendence . . .[36]

This image is translated into a matter of everyday survival by
the young working-class mothers studied by sociologist Hilary
Graham. Cigarettes enabled them to bring structure and order to
otherwise chaotic working days. In addition, the assertively self-
directed activity of smoking represented making and taking space
and time for themselves. In lives dominated by the demands of
others, the availability of such a resource made the difference
between coping and losing control. The women interviewed in
another recent study mentioned similar distancing functions fulfilled
by smoking. For example the danger represented by the lighter, the
burning cigarette and the smoke provided reasons for insisting that
young children keep their distance when mother is having a cigarette. The distance provided can even be literally protective—one
woman had found that her abusive husband would not hit her if she
had a cigarette in her hand. A consideration of temporality thus adds
to understandings of sexual difference and smoking, by suggesting
that women are not only victims of smoking but use it actively as
a resource.[37]

The vulnerability of women to the lure of cigarettes and the difficulty with which they quit have been discussed and lamented by
many. In feminist accounts like Bobbie Jacobson's, women's dependence on cigarettes reflects their subordinate status. They smoke to
deal with the frustration of always having to be 'nice', with the stress
of their multiple roles, and because they have few other opportunities to exert control. Another often cited factor in women's
smoking is fear of weight gain, described as coming 'close to para-
noia' in some. Interpreting this as a symptom of patriarchal oppression, Jacobson states that, 'Being thin is one of the few sources of
self-esteem society allows us'. In contrast to the dependent and
oppressed female smoker central to these interpretations, there is
the popular representation of a new breed of hard-drinking, heavy-
smoking career women who adopt 'masculine' habits in their quest
for power and success.[38]

Whatever their veracity, these explanations construct women
as motivated by lack, while leaving the male smoker unmarked and

unproblematised. Women are said to use cigarettes as substitutes for power, self-esteem, self-confidence, freedom or love. Men, by comparison, are smoking purists, they smoke for smoking's sake. But if smokers are viewed as manipulators of time and space, it is possible to imagine typically male needs filled by the practice. In the Wayne Wang film *Smoke* (1994), smoking is an enabler of male intimacy. Protected by a haze of smoke, the male characters share secrets and stories, console each other, give advice, and cement friendships. Perhaps the location of smoking somewhere between activity and idleness brings about a space that is open enough to allow self-exposure and emotional connection, without being so gapingly and threateningly empty to inhibit the cautious unfurling of masculine forms of responsivity.

The important, if obvious, point is that the nature of the time and space created by cigarettes is not universal, but depends on the context and the identity of the smoker. In contrast to the male characters of *Smoke*, Ellen Walker, the self-described nicotine addict, calls cigarette smoke a 'tangible wall' which she uses to distance herself from others, both physically and emotionally.[39]

By bringing together the themes of addiction and time, it is possible to argue that the temporal qualities of smoking are as central to its addictiveness as the pharmacology of nicotine. Like the reader of novels, the lone smoker can remove herself, at least partially, from common social time, shielded behind a curtain of smoke as she indulges in a solitary pleasure. Nowotny observes that in the West, making more time is the supreme principle of human activities.[40] Time is understood to be in short supply, and the wish for 'more time' is common and heartfelt. Usually the longing is not merely for more time, but for a different kind of time. People want 'time for themselves' beyond the socially organised and solidified mappings of work and leisure.

Smoking can be seen as an efficient method of acting on the 'longing for an [autonomous] moment'.[41] One remains in touch, but a contemplative distance is placed between the doer and the deed, mediated by the actions of smoking. Smoking is not considered doing anything, but neither is it doing nothing. A smoker quoted by Walker states that having a cigarette generates a sense of accomplishment, 'even if I'm doing nothing else—I feel as though I'm getting something done . . .'.[42]

The temporal otherness of the cigarette depends in part on circularity and repetition. The sameness of each act suggests a recursive and reversible time, a soothing contrast to the steady marching on of linear time towards death. Klein observes that:

> Every single cigarette numerically implies all the other cigarettes, exactly alike, that the smoker consumes in series; each cigarette immediately calls forth its inevitable successor and rejoins the preceding one in a chain of smoking . . .[43]

In the context of this chapter the chain is more like a wheel. Each cigarette makes a link with past and future cigarettes, but not necessarily its immediately preceding and succeeding neighbours. The connection is between repeated moments which recall and foreshadow each other: the morning coffee cigarette, the waiting for the train cigarette, the cigarette after sex, the last cigarette of the day. On the wheel of smoking, the sense of accomplishment engendered by smoking results from the incitement of desire as well as its fulfilment. This makes addiction not the terrible cost of smoking, but an intrinsic part of its pleasure, ensuring as it does the predictable return of desire. Anti-smoking texts promote the tendency of each cigarette to be a disappointment as a reason for quitting. But their ability to deliver an unsatisfied promise of fulfilment has also been celebrated as part of cigarettes' perfection. What ultimately emerges is the addictiveness of desire itself; in Barthes' words, 'it is my desire I desire, and the loved being is no more than its tool'. After all, it is addiction which guarantees a potentially endless repetition of pleasure.[44]

Smoking, by creating another time outside of ordinary duration, a time that is neither busy nor idle, is like other technologies which are valued for their temporal alterity: listening to music, swimming, meditation and S/M rituals, to name a few. Rather than simply destroying time in the future, smoking also creates a different time in the present, where the need for it is felt most forcefully. The addictiveness of cigarettes, an aesthetic as much as chemical property, is part of this power, and this power is an element in their addictiveness.

The smoker who quits is trading one form of extra time for another. The inclusive ideal of health celebrated in the discourse of health promotion obscures this exchange by collapsing together avoidance of future disease with the adoption of self-enhancing and fulfilling practices. The use of 'health' to encompass almost all that is worthwhile and valuable ignores the fact that the desire for a long and disease-free life can, and often does, conflict with practices which make us feel like we are doing more than merely existing. Another difficulty, downplayed by health promotion discourse, is the possibility of conflict between different health-related goals. The healthy lifestyle it promotes is presented as an interconnected set of practices which logically fit together into a harmonious whole: not smoking, exercising, eating well, and maintaining a desirable weight. But many smokers who give up gain weight, and one of the factors in the increasing prevalence of overweight in the United States is the decline in smoking.[45] Therefore, one trend which is welcomed as the source of significant health benefits is linked to another trend which is regarded as a major threat to public health. By obscuring the tension between exhortations to stop smoking and encouragement to stay slim, health discourse suggests that individuals who fail to realise both goals are the problem, rather than questioning the feasibility or desirability of its utopian dream of health.

Walker's self-portrait presents her inability to quit despite the risks as testimony to the strength of her addiction. But it could also be read as a product of the tension between living in the present and protecting and improving one's future. Striking the balance is perhaps a question of taste, rather than truth. Such questions of how to live well are faced by us all, not only by those obviously subject to the struggles of addiction.

5

Disorders of Eating and the Healthy Diet: How to Eat Well

How we enjoy eating! Yet we seldom remind ourselves that almost everything we swallow is foreign to the human body.
—Adrien Albert, *Xenobiosis: Foods, Drugs and Poisons in the Human Body*

Sugar is a time, a category of the world.
—Roland Barthes, 'Toward a Psychosociology of Contemporary Food Consumption'

How does the concept of addiction work when applied to a substance which is necessary for survival? Food addiction seems contrary to logic, in that we are all 'food dependent' and experience hunger as a powerful, recurring desire, outside of rational control. We need to eat regularly, but unlike breathing it is not a reflex action. Food must be produced and prepared, with considerable expenditure of time and effort. As well as meeting the need for physical nourishment, food and eating habits operate as important signifiers of social meaning and generators of social relations. Twenty-five years ago Roland Barthes commented on the remarkable polysemy of food as sign, a sign which signals other activities such as work, sports, leisure and celebration, and communicates identity.[1] This richness of meaning has, if anything, intensified with the increase in health and food consciousness, and the vast array of food items now available to the Western consumer. The (assumed) connection between eating habits and body size and shape adds further levels of meaning to food consumption. In the contemporary West, slenderness is read not only as physically attractive and healthy, but as a sign of moral rectitude; evidence of self-control, self-reliance, and industriousness. The fat body, in turn, connotes greed, laziness and lack of care for the self.[2] Given these realities, preoccupation with food and eating at both a cultural and individual level is to be expected. Such a morally loaded and inescapable aspect of life is bound to attract strong investments and attachments.

This is the context in which the idea of addiction to food has gained credibility. The disorders of anorexia nervosa and bulimia, as well as the less dramatic but widespread unhappiness of the compulsive overeater and perpetual dieter, have been constituted as addictive disorders by both popular and medical discourse. Anorexic and bulimic patients were found to display 'addictive personality characteristics' in a study which argued that 'An addiction model involving a self-perpetuating downwardly spiraling cycle of compulsive exercising and weight loss' seemed ideally suited to describing the psychobiological progress of eating disorders. One explicitly gendered psychoanalytic model of substance abuse describes alcohol abuse and bulimia as brother and sister disorders because both forms of abuse are attempts to compensate for 'ego deficiencies'. Anorexia is also understood as an addictive disorder by some because it is marked by an overwhelming obsession with an oral behaviour, albeit a negative one of food refusal. Another theory claims that self-starvation is actually driven by a dependence on internally produced opioids.[3] Whatever the clinical verdict about food addiction, the personal experiences of those troubled by disordered eating lend support to the idea that food can become a forbidden, yet magically alluring drug-like substance.[4] What is meant by the terms food abuse or food addiction varies widely, ranging from the case of a young girl who dies of self-induced starvation to the woman who worries about being five kilograms overweight and is distressed by her inability to resist chocolate. Food addiction can be a matter of an attachment to particular foods or substances such as sugar or carbohydrates, of eating for the wrong reasons, of eating too much, or not enough.

Much has been written on the cultural and social conditions which make food and eating predominantly female obsessions. I will not rehearse these arguments; they are covered in detail in the feminist texts discussed. However, by focusing on the production of addicted bodies in eating disorder discourses, the issue of sexual difference and its discursive reproduction is inevitably brought into the frame.

While hunger is often used as a metaphor for addictive desire in general, the actual construction of eating disorders as addictions results in interesting reformulations of the concept of addiction. Since everybody has to eat and because hunger is not regarded as under the control of the will, a recurring, irrational desire for the substance cannot define food addiction. Distinguishing between use and abuse, the normal and the addicted, requires the categorisation of styles of eating and reasons for eating. Disordered bodies, desires and eating styles of food abusers are constructed against the idea of normal hunger and normal eating. Therefore the notion of healthy, natural eating is as constructed and as culturally encoded as the food rituals of the anorexic and bulimic. Despite, or perhaps because of, the range of prescriptive discourses on food and eating, the distinction between the pathological, disordered and addicted and the normal is difficult to maintain. In part this is because food itself has a double identity: it is the good substance that sustains us and promises health, but it also the foreign substance, the poison that attacks us from within. The dilemma of food for humans has been perceptively described as 'the omnivore's paradox' by psychologist Paul Rozin. We need variety in our diet, but the unknown may be poisonous. Therefore we are driven by both 'neophobia', fear of new foods, on one hand, and 'neophilia' on the other, curiosity towards them. According to Claude Fischler, modern food practices, which involve the vast majority of people being mere consumers rather than producers of food, tend to increase the anxiety of this paradox. This suggests a cultural psychopathology around food as the background for the development of various individual disorders of consumption.[5]

Anorexia: The Good Addicts

Anorexia nervosa is one of the most talked about disorders of contemporary society, generating documentaries, magazine articles, autobiographies, self-help guides for sufferers and parents and fictional accounts, as well as thousands of clinical and research publications. The anorexic is a compelling figure, often evoking a response of horror tinged with admiration. On one hand her self-starvation is bizarre and inexplicable to those close to her, yet it is also an emblematic, intelligible form of bodily discipline. She appears to be enacting a terrible and extreme parody of feminine virtue, physically frail but morally powerful, demonstrating a triumph of will over the flesh. She has sealed her body off from the outside world and is demonstrating its self-sufficiency, but also the great price of that self-sufficiency. The meanings available in the anorexic's emaciation and refusal to eat give her a strange prestige, even though she is simultaneously regarded as deluded and obsessed.

A girl who exists on two hundred calories a day is surely the opposite of the addict controlled by a wayward appetite, unable to stop consuming ever-increasing amounts of a harmful substance. Rather than taking in the unnatural, the anorexic is rejecting the natural. Her addiction is to control, her obsession with *avoiding* a substance; and, not surprisingly, she is constituted in quite different terms from compulsive eaters, alcoholics, or drug addicts. Some earlier descriptions of the disease, by emphasising the perfectionism, determination to succeed, and energy of the sufferer constructed her as a prom-queen ideal of young womanhood. In 1975, an article in *Seventeen* magazine described the young anorexic as 'bright, energetic and articulate. Good in school, good in sports, [she] . . . rises to competition and achieves. She is slender, attractive, usually fun to be around. But she worries . . . about grades, about her friends, about her looks'.[6]

In western cultures the symptoms of starvation are easily interpreted in positive moral terms, as 'symptoms of excessive virtue'. Hyperactivity is interpreted as energy, sleeplessness leading to early rising is seen as a sign of diligence, while the desire for solitude is regarded as self-sufficiency. Psychiatrist Hilde Bruch demonstrates admiration for the struggle for self-respect that she believes the disease represents, especially in comparison with her contempt for the bulimic. Lamenting the passing of 'classic anorexia' and the rise of bulimia she says:

> They [bulimics] make an exhibitionistic display of their lack of control or discipline, in contrast to the adherence to discipline of the true anorexics . . .
>
> Though relatively uninvolved, they expect to share in the prestige of anorexia nervosa . . .[7]

Although viewing her in quite different terms, some feminist writers have reinforced the prestige or at least the fascination of the anorexic. The vast majority of sufferers are female (although eating disorders may be under-reported and under-recognised in males) and the disorder obviously cannot be understood without taking gender into account. Some feminist commentators have interpreted anorexia as a form of political struggle, an embodied cry against female oppression, furthering its elevation from the ranks of other compulsive and addictive disorders. This position draws on feminist literary critics' interpretation of the nineteenth-century diseases of hysteria, neurasthenia and anorexia as rebellion against the restrictions of Victorian bourgeois femininity. Similarly, the emaciated body of the contemporary anorexic is read as a statement about the impossibility of being 'a good girl' without destroying herself.[8] The anorexic body is also inscribed as a kind of corporeal enactment of western philosophy; feminist philosopher Susan Bordo highlights the similarities between the anorexic's experience of food, hunger and her body and the western philosophic tradition of dualism, from Plato to Descartes. Other feminist writers are wary of the understanding of anorexia nervosa as a form of politics, pointing out the dangers of venerating the victims of such a debilitating disorder.[9]

The view of the anorexic's behaviour as philosophically, politically, and morally intelligible reveals the links between addiction, freedom of will, and self-control. The anorexic contradicts the assumed dichotomy between self-control and addiction, thus stretching and destabilising the concept of addiction. The anorexic, along with the work addict and the exercise addict, is a paradoxical figure, addicted to the exercise of will, addicted to non-addiction. The possibility raised by these addictions is that the voluntarism/

addiction dichotomy operates in a circular fashion. If control and exercise of the will are taken to extremes they can be interpreted as lack of these very qualities. It appears that there is a normative level of self-control which is viewed as healthy and acceptable (which varies according to context). Deviations in either direction end up meaning the same thing: a disturbed inner self. Thus we must work hard, but not too hard, and control our appetites and exercise our bodies, but only within cultural norms. If such behaviours become something the individual is compelled to do rather than freely chooses to do, they lose their positive meaning.

One particular medical understanding of anorexia as addiction to endorphins brings it much closer to other forms of substance abuse and defuses the paradox of addiction to control. The basis of this theory is that starvation causes euphoria through the release of endorphins, the opiate-like chemicals produced by the brain. Just like a heroin addict, the anorexic becomes tolerant to increasing doses of a drug, and experiences withdrawal symptoms if the source of the drug is cut off (through enforced eating).[10] In common with the compulsive exerciser and gambler, then, the anorexic is produced as a type of auto-addict; the chemical she is addicted to is produced by her own body. The idea of addiction to a drug produced within the addict's own body challenges the dichotomy of body/foreign substance which informs much of addiction discourse. It suggests that most of us, in one way or another, enjoy the effects of drugs on a regular basis. Moreover, the user becomes the manufacturer and dealer of their own fix.

The intellectual shutdown caused by food restriction is also a vital element of the anorexic process in this model. The sufferer's categories of thought are reduced and her thinking becomes polarised, leading to the characteristic black-and-white thinking of the anorexic. She experiences this positively as an escape from confusion and indecision, while it simultaneously reinforces the anorexic behaviour. The anorexic's rigid beliefs about 'good' versus 'bad' food are particularly fitted to interpretation in these terms. She allows herself to eat a very limited range of 'good' foods—fruit, salad, diet soda, crackers. All the rest are fattening and polluting and must be avoided at all costs.[11]

The stress on the physiological source of the anorexic's most firmly held convictions constructs her as not just deluded, but bordering on the insane. Psychiatrist Hans Huebner, researcher and supporter of the endorphin addiction theory, states that 'She has been, in the true meaning of the word, "brainwashed" by endorphins'.[12] From this perspective, the dualism of her thinking is not an expression of Platonic and Christian views of the relationship between the body and the soul, but a symptom of malnutrition. She is as controlled by a chemical as any drug addict. In fact, because her body is a closed system of drug production and consumption, her state of alienation from reality is more complete than that of the addict, who at least is consciously aware of his substance use.

In these approaches, the anorexic is physiologically, psychologically, and cognitively a site of disorder and lack of fit between inside and outside. While she appears to be 'addicted to control' she in fact feels out of control, and *is* out of control. Her chaotic inner state is masked by her maintenance of rigid control over food, but it emerges in the sign of her extreme thinness. The chemical addiction model allows a refusal to take in a substance to be 'really' about dependence on another substance. The anorexic's seeming control and discipline, source of her self-respect, and the respect she receives from others, is revealed to be a manifestation of chaos and dependence. The cultural and political dimensions of a disorder in which the contemporary feminine ideal of slenderness is taken to an extreme are obscured. As Bordo has pointed out, the supposedly flawed and distorted beliefs attributed to women with eating disorders, such as, 'I am special if I am thin' and, 'If I have one cookie, I'll eat them all', are actually fairly accurate representations of prevalent social attitudes and the realities of dieting.[13] The endorphin addiction approach instead produces them as symptoms of physiological dysfunction, basically the type of thinking that all starving people exhibit. Even so, the conduct and appearance of the anorexic remains a challenge to the idea that addiction has a straightforward and fixed meaning.

Bulimia as an Addictive Disorder

Bulimia, identified by cycles of binge eating followed by self-induced vomiting and purging, fits into an addiction model much more obviously than anorexia. The way bulimics report their overwhelming urges to binge eat certainly mirror descriptions of cravings for drugs, as the following passage demonstrates:

> It would start to build in the late morning. By noon I'd know I had to binge. I would go out, almost driven like a machine to the super-market down the block and buy a gallon, or maybe even two gallons of maple-walnut ice cream and a couple of packages of fudge brownie mix . . . On the way home, the urge to binge would get stronger and stronger. I could hardly drive my car because I couldn't think about anything except food.[14]

Because of the similarities between bulimia and drug abuse, some researchers regard the two phenomena as related addictions. Bulimics relate a 'high' while bingeing, followed by a feeling of calm and relaxation that descends after vomiting.[15] Taking a different approach, Lorraine Gamman and Merja Makinen view bulimia as a form of fetishism, noting that bingeing and vomiting follow the oscillating fetishistic pattern of gratifying desire then disavowing it. To them bulimia cannot be an addiction because in addiction there is a clear chemical explanation for the fixation: 'Alcoholics drink not for the experience of drinking *per se*, but for the chemical effects of being drunk. Bulimics eat for the experience of bingeing (since the food is almost immediately purged)'. While their understanding of the bulimia as an active use of food for pleasure is compelling, the distinction between chemical and non-chemical effects and motivations is certainly not as clear as they suggest. Neither is it possible to simply confine addiction to the realm of the chemical.[16]

Like drug addictions, frequent binge eating involves deception and feelings of great shame, and can lead to serious financial problems. A significant number of bulimics steal to maintain their supply. But the rapid ingestion and regurgitation of food is unlike drinking and some forms of drug taking in that it is never a socially acceptable practice. Neither has bulimia any of the prestige of anorexia; it signifies greed rather than denial, corporeality rather than ethereality. Women with bulimia tend to be regarded with hostility not only by the general public, but by therapists and medical professionals. Disgust, anger and contempt are the usual feelings to emerge, plus outrage at the waste of food.[17] At least compulsive eaters wear the visible signs of their weakness on their bodies and thus pay the price for their greed. By regurgitating the food they eat, bulimics seem to get away with having their cake and eating it too.

Bulimia is associated with other anti-social and impulsive behaviours, such as alcohol and drug abuse, shoplifting, sexual promiscuity, and self-harm and suicide attempts. The overall picture in the medical discourse is of a woman who cannot control any of her bodily appetites or impulses, her disordered relationship with food reflecting a generalised chaos in her life. Not only does the bulimic damage herself, she also fails to fulfil her social and domestic duties to others. Weiss, Katzman and Wolchik state that:

> The bulimic is constantly thinking about food and planning her next binge. This preoccupation with food results in deliberate or inadvertent neglect of other areas. Because she binges in secret, she plans her day around the time when she can be alone so she can binge, thus neglecting friends and family. Her social and family relationships as well as her functioning at work or school suffer.[18]

Here the construction of the bulimic's social impairment underlines the sexed nature of the disorder. Apart from the actual bingeing and purging, it is as if the desire for uninterrupted time alone is itself pathological. Normative femininity includes sociability and caring for others. Women who are obsessed with a solitary activity which they find more rewarding than family life are much more disturbing than men who neglect family and friends for the sake of a solitary pursuit, whatever those pursuits might be. In addition, a male body which eats voraciously then voluntarily ejects the food will accrue quite different meanings. The male body is not seen as already fluid, formless and uncontrollable, and powerful expressions of male desire are not viewed as inherently threatening to the social order. Elizabeth Grosz's claim that in the west women's corporeality has been inscribed as a form of seepage suggests that the bulimic body could well represent one of the phallic masculine's most vivid nightmare/fantasies of female desire and the engulfing, liquid and polluting female body.[19]

Texts on bulimia inevitably mention the serious health consequences of the disorder. However, alongside frightening lists of dramatic outcomes such as cardiac failure and oesophagal rupture, it's also noted that the majority of sufferers escape serious physical damage, suffering mainly from bad teeth and sore mouths.[20] The relative rarity of serious medical complications adds to the idea that bulimics are 'getting away' with something, while the noble anorexic stoically endures her physical suffering and risks permanent physical damage. Perhaps the descriptions of irreversible physical deterioration arising from bulimia are expected to act as deterrents or inducements to stop. They can also be read as the physical damage such an unnatural practice *should* cause, whether it actually causes it or not.

Many writers, especially those writing from a feminist or 're-covering' perspective, criticise the dominant negative view of women with bulimia. They offer alternative, positive constructions which are almost the exact opposite of the medical view. Feminist therapists Dana and Lawrence state that most bulimic women

> are highly competent and successful at what they do. They tend to be copers; women who always mange to hold things together and get things done . . . women who become bulimic are really women whom most people would admire . . . as well as being an impressively accomplished group, they tend to be responsive, caring and very good listeners.[21]

Because they read bulimic binges as symbolic of conflicts about creativity, goodness, and desire, Dana and Lawrence can neutralise the abject mess of bingeing and vomiting into a picture of a loving and competent woman. According to their theory, women with bulimia are expressing a fear of their messy, needy side. More specifically, bulimia fills the same space in these women's lives as their potential creativity. Dana and Lawrence note with pride that many of the bulimic women they work with have outstanding artistic and literary talent, and that development of these gifts is part of the recovery process.[22] While it may well be the case that women with bulimia are accomplished and talented, this analysis reveals a premature desire to make order out of disorder, to move from bodily appetites to art and literature, not unlike the fear of chaos attributed to the bulimic. Like the bulimic woman, it cleans away the vomit to present a sanitised image to the world.

In their own description of their binges, bulimic women stress the 'out of control' nature of the eating and emphasise that it is not only the amount of food consumed which breaks normal rules. They describe eating with their hands standing up at the fridge; even eating food that is not normally considered edible: frozen food, raw meat and fish, pet food and half-cooked cakes. They violate the rules which order the progress of a meal, mixing sweet and savoury foods. Once they have consumed favoured foods, such as cakes, ice cream and bread, they will turn to whatever is available: dry cereal, stale bread, scraps from the rubbish bin. Cherry Boone O'Neill relates stealing leftovers from the family dog's bowl.[23] Another woman, 'beautiful' and 'frail-looking', is described as eating her own vomit, and then regurgitating it again.[24] These activities arouse stronger 'gut reactions' of disgust than any other form of excessive consumption. Although food would seem to be a much more benign and morally neutral substance than alcohol or heroin, the bulimic's abuse of food threatens deeply held cultural rules of consumption in a way that alcoholism and drug addiction do not. Eating food scraps from the floor and eating one's own vomit are animalistic behaviours; being human means not eating in this manner. Because eating is such a central part of our social interaction, the bulimic's apparent disregard for the rules of eating and her distortion of practices usually taken for granted raises the spectre of civilisation itself under attack.

The bulimic's intimate relationship with her own body wastes is as shocking as her abuse of food. In her ritual of consumption and ejection she brings together the functions of eating and elimination and transgresses the internal/external bodily boundary. She puts her fingers down her throat. She checks her vomit until she is sure she has emptied her stomach completely, sometimes using food like liquorice, beetroot or orange juice at the beginning of a binge as 'markers'. To escape detection she hides the vomit in plastic bags or in the garden. Only slightly less disturbing is the practice of 'tasting', reportedly employed by a significant number of bulimics. This involves chewing food without swallowing, then removing it from the mouth.[25] Once food has been chewed, consumed and taken into the body, its recognisable and appealing form as food is broken down into a mass of abject matter. If this is immediately ejected, the bodily functions underneath our culinary pleasures are exposed. As

Grosz argues, bodily fluids and wastes arouse a particularly power-ful repulsion:

> The personal disgust and the various social taboos associated with *waste* also attest to a psycho-social horror at what transgresses borders and boundaries. Bodily fluids, wastes, refuse—faeces, spit, blood, sperm, etc.—are examples of corporeal byproducts provoking horror at the subject's mortality. The subject is unable to accept that its body is a material organism, one that feeds off other organisms and, in its turn, sustains them. The subject recoils from its material-ity, being unable to accept its bodily origins, and hence also its im-manent death.[26]

The bulimic attracts fascinated revulsion because she plays with and manipulates the boundaries between clean and unclean, order and disorder and the inside and outside of her body. Many report a cleaning up process which is as much a part of their binge–purge cycle as the eating and vomiting. By cleaning up the kitchen, the bathroom and themselves, and destroying all evidence of the binge, the woman restores order where before she created disorder. This raises the important point that the characterisation of the binge as evidence of loss of control obscures the highly ritualised nature of the binges. While bulimic women often say they eat anything and everything while having a binge, they also recount the rigid and ritualised nature of these episodes. Many consume the same foods in a fixed order.

Binges are also often elaborately planned, with food purchased in advance, to be eaten in private, perhaps after work or while other family members or housemates are absent. They have a definite beginning and an end, after which 'normal' life resumes. And measures are always taken to ensure secrecy. Women with bulimia are both out of control of their consumption of food, and in control of their interactions with it. Linking this with other addictions, it is always the case that the 'loss of control' of the drug taker and alcoholic is not an absolute absence of control; some rules and limits are always observed. Although addiction is in part defined by loss of control, to be recognisable and intelligible as an addiction a behaviour has to fit within certain parameters.

Looking more closely at the role of vomiting in the bulimic ritual suggests another aspect of the bulimic body. While the huge amount of food bulimics consume during a binge suggests that food is their addictive substance, some writers regard vomiting as an addictive practice which drives the cycle.[27] Rather than vomiting to get rid of the food she couldn't resist, she eats in order to vomit. That vomiting can become a rewarding and sought after experience disrupts the idea of bodily functions as fixed and natural processes. For most people vomiting is actively unpleasant: a painful, malodorous, embarrassing and involuntary act associated with sickness or repulsion. The bulimic's transformation of vomiting into a source of pleasure furthers her status as disturbed, almost inhuman. Suggestions that the pleasures of binge eating and vomiting are sexual further enhance the perversity of the bulimic body. Lindsey Hall, who binged four or five times a day for more than five years, comments that she 'sometimes had sexual feelings from the emerging, private excitement, complete involvement, fullness, stroking, and sudden release'.[28]

Yet the determination of the bulimic to rid herself of the food at the end of the binge, and her ability to obtain a pleasurable and relaxing release from the act, speaks of an unusual level of bodily control. Through practice and training she becomes more adept at this difficult task, modifying her relationship with the contents of her stomach, and eventually learning to vomit spontaneously.[29] Another contradiction on the control/lack of control axis is that while the bulimic appears as deeply disturbed and animal-like while in the midst of a binge, she is described in some texts as maintaining a public life of healthy social and professional functioning. This is commonly described as part of the problem by sufferers and therapists alike: the woman feels she is trapped in a double existence and experiences her public persona as a sham. On the other hand, it is possible that the surface appearance of healthy functioning is in fact healthy functioning. This possibility is supported by research comparing compulsive exercisers and a group of women with bulimia. The researchers found that their original hypothesis—that the apparent health and success of the 'obligatory runners' they studied masked a hidden pathology—was incorrect. The runners, who ran every day whatever the weather and despite injuries, clocking up hundreds of miles per week, were healthy and well-functioning, intelligent, high-achieving, hardworking and independent. There were similarities between this group and what the researchers described as a new type of eating-disordered woman. These women were bulimic but well-adjusted and emotionally healthy, and functioning very well in social, educational and vocational spheres. It seems that both groups developed addictive disorders not because they were sick, but because they were healthy. They had applied their healthy attitudes, their initiative, resourcefulness, self-reliance, ability to keep going in the face of adversity and high self-expectations to an activity which they ended up depending on for its ability to organise, energise, stabilise and soothe.[30]

Thus in eating disorder discourse, both a good bulimic subject and a bad bulimic subject are produced. Good bulimics are able to practice a 'recreational or pragmatic bulimia' which does not escalate to an all-encompassing obsession and is no more deleterious to the health and well-being than 'normal' dieting.[31] The good bulimic can be viewed as responding rationally to a cultural condition which celebrates indulgence but demands slenderness. After all, as Schlundt and Johnson admit, 'Self-induced vomiting is a very effective way to eliminate calories, and functions quite nicely as a weight control strategy'.[32] But such a rational assessment of bulimic practices disavows their violation of cultural boundaries and their invocation of a form of female corporeality deeply threatening to social order.

Compulsive Eating

Compulsive eating is regarded as the cause of many health problems, but is not recognised widely as a disease in itself. It lacks the sensational aspects of anorexia and bulimia: the symptoms are less dramatic, the health risks not so immediately severe, obvious, or unusual. Compulsive eaters do the same thing with food as 'normal' people, their deviation is quantitative rather than qualitative. Overeating to the point of discomfort, followed by feelings of regret and guilt, is a common enough experience. At certain times it is viewed as abnormal not to overeat, Christmas being the most obvious example. 'Binge-eating syndrome' has been included as a disorder in the most recent edition of the American Psychiatric Association's compendium of diseases, but much of what is included under the general term compulsive eating would not meet its relatively strict criteria.[33]

Judging from textual evidence, it seems that compulsive over-eaters are not as interesting to medical experts as sufferers from other more exotic forms of disturbed eating. In medically oriented texts, the sections on compulsive eating usually follow the sections on anorexia and bulimia and are usually shorter. Many of the more traditional medical texts slip between compulsive eating and obesity as if they are the same thing, or include a section on obesity rather than compulsive eating. Abraham and Llewellyn-Jones's *Eating Disorders: The Facts* is a good example. The tenor and content of their section on obesity is quite different from their discussions of anorexia and bulimia. Rather than discussing the reasons for and meanings of the 'disorder' and the psychology of its sufferers, they provide a weight-reducing menu, discuss bypass operations and jaw wiring, and take a firm but jovial and patronising tone reminiscent of popular diet books. This is how they introduce their diet plan:

> The suggested menu, which is low in energy and in carbohydrate and rich in fibre, has many advantages. It is nutritious; it is relatively easy to understand and to follow; it doesn't make you feel a freak; it avoids gimmicks; you can stay on it a long time, and, most important of all, it works! These criteria form the basis of a sensible diet for a sensible person.[34]

The authors then urge obese (and presumably not sensible) readers to work on their motivation because otherwise it will be 'easy to cheat—just a little!' In this section of their text food is not taken seriously as an addictive substance, and the overeater is constructed as someone not very bright who just needs to learn how to control herself, be sensible, and avoid 'no-no' foods. She lacks the feminine appeal of the anorexic, and she is excluded from the masculine romantic anti-hero model of drug use. Instead, she is represented as the comic figure of the greedy fat woman.

Given that the link between food consumption and weight is not at all straightforward, the categorisation of obesity as an eating disorder is in itself rather strange. Some research suggests that as a group, the obese eat the same or less than the lean. As Orford has noted, the confusion between obesity and excess eating is instructive, however, because it ties in with a strong theme of addiction discourse —the search for psychological phenomena to explain troublesome physical or social events.[35] Obesity, with its associated health risks and powerful social stigma, is perhaps easier to construct as a serious pathology than excessive eating itself. However, compulsive eating and obesity are discursively if not causally connected, because in the absence of unhappiness about their weight, people who eat much more than is considered normal would probably not consider themselves compulsive eaters or food addicts. Those who remain thin despite eating much more than others are more likely to be considered lucky than viewed as suffering from an eating disorder. And because they would not experience the intense conflict between appetite and desire to lose weight which characterises the overweight overeater, they escape the feeling of being out of control which defines compulsion. Put simply, it is only people who are trying to restrain their eating who experience it as compulsive.

Given these links it is not surprising that feminist and self-help therapeutic discourses on compulsive eating are also concerned with weight loss. While both discourses insist that the key to recovery is to shift the focus from weight to healthy non-addicted eating, they nevertheless assume that their readers are overweight, and that healthy eating will ultimately bring about weight loss. In contrast to traditional medical texts on eating disorders, feminist therapeutic discourse pays serious attention to compulsive eating, and popular self-help discourses on food addiction focus on this problem, rather than anorexia and bulimia. Orbach's *Fat is a Feminist Issue* was the groundbreaking work which related compulsive eating to women's feelings of deprivation and lack of control over their lives, while also constructing it as an addiction to food which required therapy. Orbach argues that for compulsive eaters fat represents both a protection against the world, and a rebellion against dominant ideas of femininity. But she also believes that the compulsive eater's dependence on food is unproductive and damaging; a need for emotional nourishment can never be met by eating. Her approach sets up an ideal of eating according to genuine, physiological 'stomach' hunger.

The key to breaking an addicted relationship to food is for compulsive eaters to give up the idea of forbidden foods, and instead eat exactly what their body tells them it wants:

> We do not believe in good or bad foods. *We believe that our bodies can tell us what to eat, how to have a nutritionally balanced food intake and how to lose weight.* The body is a self-regulatory system if allowed to operate.[36]

The notion that there is a right reason to eat (genuine hunger) and many wrong reasons (from boredom, anger or loneliness, as a reward, out of habit) has become a central pillar of both feminist and self-help therapy models. In this approach, the problem demonstrated by the compulsive eater is one of interpretation rather than quantity control; she eats when it is not food she needs. Lawrence and Dana take this view, describing a compulsive eater as:

> someone, usually a woman, who eats more than she needs or wants to, not in response to signs from her stomach indicating hunger but for quite different reasons. For the compulsive eater, physical and emotional cues become confused. She senses a need within herself, but then interprets it as a physical rather than emotional sensation.[37]

In this discourse, bodily desire is the true expression of need, with the mind as the corrupting and alien force. The problem is that compulsive eaters, often because of years of dieting that have destroyed their natural recognition of hunger and satiety, do not listen to or trust their bodies. The natural, balanced and straightforward relationship between the body and food has been distorted by the harmful cultural practice of dieting and the attachment of powerful meanings to different foods. The key to recovery is the demystification of food, especially those 'forbidden foods' like chocolate which attain almost magical status. The idea of normal, healthy eating based on responding to the natural signals of the body is a reassuring and attractive image. It seems to offer a simple way of eating well and choosing amongst the huge range of food options competing for our attention. The author of a text based on interviews with women recovering from anorexia nervosa provides this utopian image of one of her subjects:

Helena is listening to her body—paying attention to the hunger cues, instead of ignoring them, and eating in response to these signals. When she does this, maintaining her weight is easy. It's a simple concept. All it takes is eating exactly what she needs, exactly what she's craving, and stopping when she has had enough.[38]

This text also urges women to forget about being thin and instead focus on being healthy, as if this will ameliorate anxiety about food. But being thin and being healthy are intimately connected in contemporary western culture. Moreover, the pursuit of the healthy diet and the decision to eat 'exactly what the body needs' has its own complications and difficulties. In an age inundated with information about the dangers and risks of different foods and substances, identifying a healthy diet is just as likely to result in a list of taboo foods as worrying about one's weight. What is excluded in this optimistic model of natural, healthy eating is the possibility that some people's bodies will tell them to eat enough to maintain a weight that is categorised as obese and unhealthy and which violates cultural norms. Orbach states that by listening to their bodies overweight women will gradually but permanently lose weight. Texts on overcoming bulimia admit that many women who resume normal eating gain weight. But this always turns out to be a matter of a few kilos or less, leaving them at a weight which may not be thin, but is aesthetically and medically acceptable.[39] Thus the championing of the natural never threatens or contradicts the cultural norms of eating and weight. It is assumed that all bodies will respond to natural eating by stabilising at a healthy weight. While advocates of natural eating are vocal in their criticism of the cultural obsession with the slender body, the fat body is still negatively valued in their discourse. It is unnatural, as well as unattractive.

Writers who support the idea of natural eating as the solution to food addiction are critical of Overeaters Anonymous (OA) because its twelve-step program promotes a strict regime of abstention from certain foods. In addition, OA locates the disorder firmly within the individual, minimising the role of social forces. OA is unconcerned with the gendered politics of food, instead constructing the compulsive eater on the physiological disease model of the alcoholic. Kay Sheppard's text *Food Addiction: The Body Knows* is a detailed guide to the twelve-step approach to compulsive eating. She argues that overeaters are the victims of a disease caused by imbalances in brain chemistry, and that food addicts suffer from all the classic symptoms of addiction: obsession, compulsion, denial, tolerance and withdrawal symptoms. By constructing a category of potentially addictive foods which trigger binges in the susceptible, she appropriates the idea of recovery via abstinence from Alcoholics Anonymous. Just like drugs, certain foods—flour, all forms of chocolate and sugar—have chemical qualities which make them addictive. The addict must avoid these for life. One mouthful of a food containing flour can trigger a binge. Sheppard gives the example of a woman who relapsed after eating some gravy:

> At the time she ate it, she thought, 'just that little bit of flour won't bother me.' The fantasy was, 'My body won't notice that I just ate an addictive substance.' Such rationalizations will not change the course of addiction because THE BODY KNOWS otherwise.[40]

Sheppard's repetition of the slogan 'the body knows' emphasises the physiological nature of the addiction. Refined carbohydrates will always trigger a binge; it makes no difference if the individual likes the particular food or not. The discourse produces the truth of food as residing in its constituent components, its micro-properties. Overeaters must learn to see foods as diverse as gravy, pasta, and bran as addictive because they all contain flour or wheat. However, there is a tension in this model between the insistence that food addiction is fundamentally about micro-substances such as amino acids and carbohydrates and the fact that food addicts only crave and consume these substances in particular, culturally specific forms. For example, in *Anatomy of a Food Addiction*, recovering food addict and therapist Anne Katherine places tryptophan and insulin and their role in neurotransmitter production and release at the centre of the addictive process. Basically food addicts crave carbohydrates because they cause increases in insulin and allow more tryptophan to enter the brain. However the 'are you a food addict?' questionnaires in her text ask about highly specific situations involving boxes of candy, holiday foods, popcorn at the movies, leftovers in the fridge and so on. For example, one of the questions in the 'Are you a refined carbohydrate addict?' quiz asks 'At a spaghetti dinner, do you look at the garlic-bread basket and identify a piece you really want? As they pass the basket, do you watch in suspense to see if anybody takes it before the basket gets to you? If somebody takes it, do you feel disappointed? If your husband takes it, do you feel angry?'.[41] It is a long way from this question, which seems to involve the desire for a very particular piece of food, feelings of competitiveness with others and resentment of a spouse, to the physiological processes of insulin production.

It is easy to see why this approach antagonises those who champion the demystification of food as the solution to eating disorders. The idea of abstinence insists that certain foods must be forbidden because of their power to control behaviour. Food is unashamedly and explicitly divided into healthy, clean and good, and addictive, polluting and bad. A recovering addict states in Sheppard's text:

> When I got binge food out of my body, I stopped thinking about it. When I'm clean, I don't think about food. I certainly thought about it a lot when I was using. Being clean relieves me of the obsession.[42]

The OA program challenges the idea of hunger as natural and the body as self-regulatory. Instead the relationship between food and the body is constituted as inherently problematic. If a food addict responds to her cravings and eats exactly what she wants, she will end up fat, sick, depressed, her life controlled by a chemical compulsion. Freedom from addiction can only come from strict external control: no sugar or flour, no eating between meals, meticulous recording of everything eaten, and regular reporting to a food sponsor. Critics who argue that the strict OA program promotes an obsession with food are on one level undoubtedly correct. Rather than a freedom from obsession, OA offers a different kind of obsessive relationship with food. However, it is also possible to see the program as a revealing response to issues ignored by the supporters of 'natural eating'. OA admits that for some people the only way to achieve a stable and culturally acceptable weight and a 'normal' relationship with food is to give up the possibility of choice and submit to a rigorous disciplinary regime. It unintentionally reveals the violence necessary to maintain concepts of normal weight and natural eating. Other technologies also speak to the same problematic: that for some the attainment of a body that meets standards of health and normality requires the relinquishment of normal eating. 'Stomach stapling' operations and very low calorie diets based on liquid fasts are advised for the 'morbidly obese'. These solutions to problems of food regulation signal the limit point of the natural body and its ability to regulate food.

Medical texts often demonstrate a contradictory stance on normal eating which reveal the constructedness of normality. On one hand, they argue that normal eating is how the body relates to food naturally, without interference from externally imposed rules. But they also feel it necessary to give quite detailed guidelines on what normal, healthy eating is. For example, Abraham and Llewellyn-Jones list eighteen criteria for normal eating. These include: eating something at least three times a day; eating more than you feel you need on some occasions; eating less than you feel you need on some occasions; eating more of the foods that you enjoy the taste of when you choose to; eating in a flexible way so that it does not interfere with your work, study, or social life; eating both 'good' and 'bad' foods; eating when out socially, in a similar manner to the other people in the group; and eating fast food on occasion.[43] Interestingly though, a woman following the diet plan they recommend for compulsive eaters would violate most of these criteria. It seems that if one is overweight, eating normally is not for you.

To summarise, in different discourses eating disorders are produced as quite different forms of disturbance, with a range of aetiologies from the forces of patriarchy to a malfunction in brain chemistry. However, a strong theme in eating disorder discourse is that food becomes addictive for the eating disordered because of their mystification of it as a forbidden, magical pleasure, rigidly divided into categories of the good and the bad. This is the case even in OA discourse which produces its own rigid categories of good and bad. It still argues that recovery comes with a demystification of food, of eating to live instead of living to eat. By identifying compulsive eaters as driven by a physiological anomaly, OA allows the ideal of natural eating in response to bodily signals to remain intact for those without this flaw.

Nutrition: Eating for Life

What is not a poison? All things are poisons, and nothing is without toxicity. Only the dose permits anything not to be poisonous. For example, every food and every drink is a poison if consumed in more than the usual amount: which proves the point. I admit that a poison is a poison; but that is no reason for condemning it outright.

—Paracelsus, *Sieben Defensiones*

Anorexics, bulimics, and compulsive eaters are exhorted not to demonise food or to imbue it with magical powers and qualities. To return to health they need to realise that food is not the answer to coping with life, and to separate eating from the creation of a self-identity. But turning to contemporary nutrition and health promotion guides on healthy eating, one finds a discourse which constitutes the right diet as the key to health, well-being, and longevity and a failure to care for the self in this way as a route to disease and decay. In many government public health texts, food is classified as either or good or bad, acting as a medicine or a poison. The categories of good and bad are unstable, however, making the ideal of fully informed, rational eating for health impossible to attain.

Attempting to change the eating habits of the population through devices such as national guidelines for a healthy diet and provision of nutritional information on packaged food is now a central aspect of government public health programs. The nutritional projects of Western democracies combine the emphasis on choice and self-regulation that characterises neo-liberal governmentality. As a number of critics have pointed out (and as I suggest below) nutritional advice can be considered a disciplinary discourse.[44] However, it is important to recognise that the goal is a freely-choosing subject who makes the correct choices, not a rigid follower of a strict regime. The existence of resistance to nutritional advice is also apparent, especially in the face of food scares, contradictory advice from different experts and debates about irradiated and genetically engineered food, which undermine faith in the government and food industries.[45]

A typical government nutrition text is the (Australian) National Food Authority's *Food for Health* which begins with the standard food pyramid and divides good food into five groups. It tells readers,

'Each day, check your diet against the Five Food Group plan. Have you selected foods from each of the Five Groups and in the servings recommended?' 'Extra' foods such as confectionery, soft drinks, biscuits, cakes are to be added to the diet only after foods from the five food groups have been incorporated. The guidelines recommend that we eat four serves of vegetables and fruit daily, including one serve of the dark green or orange vegetables and one serving of citrus. We are also told to check our diet every day, to know where to look for fat, to spread butter and margarine very thinly, to read the ingredients of packaged foods and to not eat too much sugar. In these guidelines mundane foods are presented as collections of micro-properties which need to be analysed and deciphered before being eaten. That is, they promote the kind of anxious attitude to food which is the object of concern and management in eating disorder discourse. Moreover, food is decontextualised from the social realm and becomes something unfamiliar, a realm of life requiring expert advice. To enable ordinary consumers to make the right choices, *Food for Health* provides food composition information for 650 foods, giving levels of fourteen different nutrients, plus how they measure up to recommended daily intakes. From these tables one can learn that ten green stuffed olives have 146 kilojoules, 0.3 g protein, 3.5 g fat, 0.7 g carbohydrate, 3.1 g fibre, no cholesterol, 830 ug sodium, 39 ug calcium, 19 ug retinol, 110 ug beta-carotene, 0.1 ug niacin and no vitamin C, riboflavin, thiamine, zinc or iron. As one leafs through pages and pages of this kind of information, one gets the feeling of entering a disembodied, unfamiliar, and obsession-driven world.[46]

A similar approach is taken in the US publication *Eat for Life: The Food and Nutrition Board's Guide to Reducing Your Risk of Chronic Disease*. It begins by telling its readers that when they sit down to a dinner of roast chicken, rice and green beans what their body sees is 'a huge collection of matter to process, providing both energy and nutrients'. Continuing the production of food as matter, the text provides nine guidelines for healthy eating, including limiting the amount of fat, saturated fatty acids, and cholesterol, eliminating added salt, eating more complex carbohydrates, eating a moderate amount of protein and cutting down on added sugars. It also urges consumers to plan meals carefully to reduce risk of chronic diseases such as heart disease and cancer: 'Sitting down with your family, a pile of cookbooks, and a list of favorite recipes in front of you and planning meals for the week can be an enjoyable part of ensuring that your eating pattern is a healthful one'.[47]

Despite the domestic cosiness of this image, what is being encouraged is an approach to food which privileges the micro (nutrients) and the macro (diet), over the quotidian reality of dishes and meals which are the way food is generally consumed. Elements of chance, spontaneity, and unscientific preferences and desires are to be avoided, with the rational decision-making process dominating the intake of nutrients into the body.

Again, a problem with this model is that the distinction between good and bad food is not straightforward. For example, standard advice for many years was to switch from butter to margarine because polyunsaturated fats were considered better for the heart than saturated fats. But now the 'trans fatty acids' created by processing oils into margarine are described as 'highly detrimental to the health', to quote one healthy living guide, making 'Natural fresh farm butter . . . far healthier than margarine'.[48] Equally as disquieting as the revelation of hidden dangers in 'good' foods is the 'bad' emerging as beneficial. This has happened recently in the case of alcohol: warnings of liver and brain damage now coexist with the advice that moderate alcohol consumption decreases the risk of heart disease and strokes. This seems to have caused some anxiety among the health conscious and abstemious in the United States, with one alcohol and drug abuse prevention publication suggesting grape juice as a possible compromise.[49]

Some diet and food authors produce the activity of eating in general as a very risky proposition by constructing common foods, including those recommended by texts like *Food for Health*, as toxic. In *Diet for a Poisoned Planet: How to Choose Safe Foods for You and Your Family*, David Steinman argues that genuinely healthy eating is only possible by knowing exactly which foods have high levels of chemical and pesticide contamination and which are relatively uncontaminated. This cannot be ascertained by reading labels:

> The bottom line is that industrial pollution and pesticides that come in drinking water and with breakfast, lunch, and dinner can accelerate cancer, increase chances of secondary disease, decrease mental clarity, and shave years from your life.[50]

Alarmingly for the diet-conscious, healthy foods such as cottage cheese, whole wheat bread, apples and raisins are hazardous in terms of their pesticide levels. In Steinman's text the gap between the appearance of wholesomeness and the reality of toxicity is painstakingly described. But the question of how to eat well is still unresolved. We learn, for example, that canned fruit and vegetables have less toxic residues than fresh. But they may have more lead and often have added salt or sugar. The broad point is that anxiety about food and food choice is clear at a cultural, not just an individual level. As Fischler has argued, the shift of food processing from the kitchen to the factory has undermined confidence in the purity of food. The industrial processes which transform raw ingredients into the edible no longer guarantee the symbolic purity of food, even though they may meet objective standards of purity and non-contamination. The increasing use of genetically modified products and ingredients has produced another level of public concern about the purity and indeed, identity, of food.[51]

Finally, nutrition discourse has a double identity in relation to eating disorders. On one hand it is part of the cure. Treatment programs for anorexics and bulimics often include education in nutrition and the role of carbohydrates, fats and proteins in the maintenance of health. One medical text argues that 'While information alone may not be sufficient to overcome these fears, knowledge about energy and the body's energy needs is essential if the patient is ever to become comfortable with food'. Specifically, it advocates the use of a mechanical metaphor to explain the importance of nutrition, likening the body to a car which requires gasoline to function.[52] However, this analogy could well be compatible with the anorexic's view of her body as an efficient machine which runs best on very little, high quality fuel. After all, modern fuel-efficient cars are valued over big, gas-guzzling ones. And machines can easily be clogged up with excess oil. Nutrition discourse can work with eating disorders as well as working against them. It is often observed that anorexics and bulimics have a much better knowledge of nutrition than the general public and devour articles on diet and health. And while their interpretations of nutrition guidelines may diverge from the meanings intended by the authors, they are definitely based on elements present in the texts.[53]

In health promotion and nutrition discourse, eating is not just a response to physiological need and nutritional requirements. Eating is also about a commitment to a particular vision of the self and of the good life; the term 'diet' itself connotes individual improvement and achievement through rational acts of choice. As Robert Crawford has argued, health has become a goal that one strives for through intentional action and incorporation of particular disciplines into one's life.[54] It is not just that people follow nutritional guidelines in order to become or remain healthy, but that healthy living means eating according to nutritional knowledge, exercising, and adopting other health-promoting measures. Health becomes an ethical issue; those who have the proper, thoughtful relationship to themselves and their bodies achieve it, those who do not have only themselves to blame.

The connection between diet and the construction of oneself as an individual is illustrated in Steinman's text. He promises that following his 'low-toxin high-energy diet' will enable you to separate yourself from the ignorant and self-poisoning masses, 'You'll have the extra assurance of knowing that you're not accumulating more twentieth century poisons with every bite you take . . . It's a liberating feeling'.[55] Low-toxin eating is the key to a new kind of harmonious and vibrant existence, characterised by physical energy and mental alertness. The right food will save you, the wrong food will slowly poison you.

Seeking to change one's life through diet and the desire to 'let your body do the talking' are valued practices of contemporary self-formation. It is not only anorexics or bulimics who seek to create themselves through their relationships with food. An anorexic woman quoted by Way says, 'food is my mainstay and that's the little high that I'm on. I'm still on it and it still possesses my life. I have fun with it. It's my little thing. It's my toy; it's my game; it's *mine*—don't take it away!'.[56] How different is this from the careful label-reading, weighing and calculating nutritionally aware consumer? It is not that it is necessarily a bad thing to fetishise food and use it to make statements about the sort of person one is, but rather that it is not only the pathological who manipulate food in this way.

Our relationship and understanding of food can never be as simple and straightforward as the idea of natural healthy eating suggests. Orbach's ideal of pure 'stomach hunger' cannot be isolated from all the cultural and social meanings and functions of food and eating. The needs of the body can only ever be understood through different discourses of food and eating, including that of 'listening to your body'. The exasperated cry of the nutritionally over-informed, 'everything gives you cancer', is more than a wry joke; it is a recognition of the dilemma of consumption in an environment riddled with conflicting discourses of health and an abundance of chemicals and substances, good, bad and indifferent. The anorexic who has reduced her diet to lettuce, apples and non-fat yoghurt can be seen as no more than an extremely cautious consumer who is taking no chances in a toxic world.

6

Sex and Love Addiction: The Ethics and Erotics of Intimacy

At issue is not a movement bent on pushing rude sex back into some obscure and inaccessible region, but on the contrary, a process that spreads it over the surface of things and bodies, arouses it, draws it out and bids it speak, implants it in reality and enjoins it to tell the truth: an entire glittering sexual array, reflected in a myriad of discourses, the obstination of powers, and the interplay of knowledge and pleasure.
—Michel Foucault, *The History of Sexuality, Volume One*

Love is a very funny place to go for safety.
—Michael Ventura, in James Hillman and Michael Ventura, *We've had a Hundred Years of Psychotherapy—And the World's Getting Worse*

The idea that sexual desire can act like a powerful drug, transforming a rational individual into the slave of an irrational obsession, is hardly an unfamiliar one in modern western culture. The conventions of romance accept, indeed celebrate, intoxication, compulsion, and reckless indifference to the rest of the world as markers of true passion. Love stories tell us that all lovers worthy of the name are addicts. They demonstrate many of the diagnostic criteria for substance dependence: persistent desire for the loved object despite harmful consequences; impaired judgement; loss of interest in other things; and even distressing withdrawal symptoms on separation. Consider the couple whose thirty-year clandestine affair is chronicled in Benoîte Groult's novel *Salt on our Skin*. The narrator of the story is a sophisticated Parisian intellectual. Her lover is a Breton fisherman, uneducated and inarticulate but incredibly virile and possessor of a natural, earthy dignity (as well as a very large penis, which is the subject of many rhapsodic passages). Their sexual obsession begins while she is a young student, on a family holiday at his village. Describing the emotions she felt while waiting for their first private meeting, George (named after George Sand) celebrates the intensity of her youthful passion. The fact that they are practically strangers and have almost nothing in common only increases her desire:

> From the moment I got there I was caught up in the exquisite state of passionate anticipation, aware that this was the highest experience life can offer. That evening I would have sacrificed ten years of my life—well, five anyway—to ensure that nothing would now come between us and the drama we were about to play, though neither of us yet knew our lines. What are a few years of age when you're twenty? I was preparing for a night with no tomorrow—outside convention, outside caution, outside even hope.[1]

The adult George relates her extravagant teenage emotions with some irony, but we know her feelings were genuine and appropriate; the first night with her lover *was* the start of the most significant experience in her life. The love between George and Gavin survives until his death, despite their marriages to other people, children, geographical separation, and differences of values and interests which could hardly be more extreme. The willingness of the lovers to deceive their families, disrupt their lives, and take great risks to meet once a year are presented in the novel as a triumph of passion over the dull conventions of daily life.

In common with these romantic narratives, sex addiction discourse is concerned with the experience of overwhelming and insistent erotic desire. But in sex addiction texts, those at the mercy of uncontrollable desires are victims of a virulent disease. Patrick Carnes, psychologist and foremost authority on sex addiction, states:

Contrary to love, the obsessional illness transforms sex into the primary relationship or need, for which all else may be sacrificed, including family, friends, values, health, safety, and work. As life unravels, the sex addict despairs, helplessly trapped in cycles of degradation, shame, and danger.[2]

To replace the roller coaster ride of passion and desire, sex addiction discourse offers the safety and contentment of healthy intimacy. The problem is that while the pleasures of lust and romance may well be shallow and shortlived, in love as in shoes the sensible is rarely the most appealing. The difficulty faced by sex addiction discourse is not confined to persuading the sceptic of the addictive nature of sex or love. It also includes the task of convincing her that a healthy relationship is preferable to the highs and lows of a doomed and dysfunctional desire.

It should also be noted that the status of sex addiction is still highly contested. Unlike gambling addiction, it does not appear as a distinct disorder in the latest *Diagnostic and Statistical Manual of Mental Disorders*. However, psychiatrists specialising in sex addiction point out that 'addictive sexual behaviors are ... subsumed in various categories of the DSM-IV' including paraphilias and impulse control disorders. According to Irons and Schneider, the most common diagnostic category for patients identified as sexual addicts is 'Sexual Disorder Not Otherwise Specified' which includes the example 'Distress about a pattern of repeated sexual relationships involving a succession of lovers who are experienced by the individual only as things to be used'.[3] The issue of DSM nosology is obviously of more than theoretical importance, as it is commonly used to assess insurance payments for treatment.

Here I examine both sides of the issue; that is, the construction of some sorts of sex as pathological and addictive, and the construction of other types of sexual relationship as healthy. This model of healthy intimacy has little space for the body and its desires, except as servants of a higher goal of self-realisation. Ultimately, it is the development of a certain relationship with the self that is the concern of recovery, and healthy interaction with the other is necessary to this goal. The overt message of the discourse is that what is ultimately wrong with sex addiction is that its victims use people as objects, as means rather than ends in themselves. But the type of relationship celebrated as the key to recovery is also open to the charge of the objectification of the other.

Making a Sexual Disorder

A striking aspect of sex addiction literature is the diverse array of behaviours which are read as symptoms of the one disease. Having affairs, sex with prostitutes, fantasising about sex, wearing revealing clothes, flirting, seducing students or patients, sexually harassing employees and committing sexual crimes such as rape and child abuse are all possible signs of sex addiction. The disorders of romance and love addiction have further expanded the field of problematic conduct; the typical case is a woman obsessed with the trappings and rituals of romantic encounters and lost in fantasies of perfect and unattainable lovers. Another immediately apparent characteristic of sex addiction is the tendency of the boundaries marked out between healthy and unhealthy sexuality to conform to the precepts of traditional sexual morality. In fact, the hierarchies of sexual value constructed by sex addiction discourse bear a remarkably close resemblance to the general system of sexual stratification described by Gayle Rubin in her classic article 'Thinking Sex: Notes for a Radical Theory of the Politics of Sexuality'. Varieties of sexual expression which deviate from norms of 'loving intimacy' within a long-term, heterosexual and preferably marital relationship are constructed as pathological and risky. The use of pornography and sex toys, the enjoyment of sexual role-playing and casual sex are viewed as signs of addiction and inner disorder. While homosexuality is nominally accepted as a valid form of sexual expression for a small minority, gay sex is only classified as healthy when indulged in by a monogamous couple. If gay sex comes into conflict with the stability of a heterosexual couple it is always the gay sex which is the problem.[4] In the threatening world constructed by sex addiction texts, sexual experimentation and exploration outside monogamous coupledom is perilous, even lethal, and a search for sexual excitement and freedom can only lead to heartbreak, shame, and sickness. The case studies and examples which punctuate sex addiction texts act both as illustrative devices and as cautionary tales of sexual peril, moral decline and terrible punishments. The vignettes of sexual addiction presented by Carnes include a young couple who are both dying of AIDS because the husband failed to get treatment for his sex addiction soon enough. His body is 'being destroyed by the advanced stages of cancer' but he struggles to look after their two young children because his wife is in hospital with pneumonia.[5]

Following Foucault, the notion that sexuality is a major vector of power, through which pathological subjectivities are produced and techniques of normalisation mobilized, is a familiar one. Sex addiction is a vivid example of the constitution of a new form of sexual disorder, one which demands that the individual scrutinise and work on himself in order to achieve happiness, health and personal autonomy. The social context in which sex addiction emerged as a concept helps explain these invocations of danger and chaos. Sociologist Janice Irvine's Foucauldian account of the 'invention' of sex addiction argues that its success as a discourse is due to its expression of, and resonance with, specific cultural concerns and anxieties dominant in the United States in the 1980s. Irvine identifies the AIDS epidemic and the restrictive morality of both conservative and feminist challenges to sexual liberalism as two of the major historical and cultural forces which shaped the new addictive disorder. AIDS and social purity campaigns fostered anxieties about lust as well as supporting a view of sex as a dangerous force with a universal, unchanging essence.[6]

However, as Foucault's account of the operations of sexuality and power would suggest, the ethical dimensions of sex addiction discourse are not limited to an anti-sex prudery backed up by a prohibitive moral code. In the introductory volume of *The History of Sexuality*, he argues that since the eighteenth century sexuality has been the subject of a discursive explosion: '[a] multiplication of discourses concerning sex in the field of the exercise of power itself: an institutional incitement to speak about it, and to do so more and more; a determination on the part of the agencies of power to hear it spoken about, and to cause *it* to speak through explicit articulation and endlessly accumulated detail'.[7]

In its concern with autonomy and choice, sex addiction discourse can be read as part of a regime of liberal governance in

which individuals are governed through their freedom and aspir-
ations, rather than in spite of them. Like other addiction discourses
which have proliferated in recent years, sex addiction demonstrates
the operation of freedom as a regulative ideal. Through various
techniques individuals are encouraged to liberate themselves from
troubling feelings, desires and behaviours which are constituted as
alien to the true self.

In the case of sex addiction, freedom demands a marshalling
of sexual desire to conform not so much to a prescriptive moral
code, but to a vision of a harmonious self in which the erotic is in
perfect balance and agreement with other aspects of being. Sex
addiction is as much about confession and redemption as it is about
restraint. Rather than repressing sexual expression, the discourse of
sex addiction encourages individuals to develop a habit of obsessive
attentiveness to their sexual desires. This includes the interpretation
of apparently innocent thoughts and habits as signs of sexual
pathology:

> To halt the addictive cycle, sex addicts need to begin to look at the
> little things in their lives, the details that might at first glance seem
> inconsequential, but have actually served as triggers or permission
> givers.[8]

Sex addiction discourse also fosters a huge volume of sex talk,
between sex addicts in twelve-step meetings, between addicts and
their partners, between addicts and their therapists. Talking about
what you are going through, says psychiatrist Eric Griffin-Shelley, is
the treatment of choice for sex addicts struggling with withdrawal
and recovery. Reading about sex (known as bibliotherapy), learning
about sex, and writing about sex in daily journals are also prescribed, although only therapeutic and confessional genres of sex-
writing are approved for this purpose.[9] In fact, sex addiction
experts are eager to distance their project from traditional sexual
moralism. They are critical of 'repressive', prudish and punitive
views about sex, using the language and technologies of clinical psychology and psychiatry to constitute sex addiction as a scientific
category rather than moral judgement. Carnes has developed a
highly influential model of sex addiction based on studies of self-
identified addicts which illustrates the taxonomic and nosological

construction of the disease. The model identifies eleven broad types of sex addiction: fantasy sex, seductive role sex, anonymous sex, paying for sex, trading sex, voyeuristic sex, exhibitionist sex, intrusive sex, pain exchange, object sex, and sex with children. 'Presenting behaviours' are also classified into three levels of addiction, ranging from the socially acceptable to the illegal and highly taboo, and there are developmental phases which describe the progress of the addiction from initiation to the terminal 'chronic phrase'. Carnes has also developed standardised screening tests for sexual addiction, the SAST for heterosexual men, the G-SAST for gay men and the W-SAST for women. The development of these specialised versions of the test from the original SAST, which was found to be useful only for assessing heterosexual men, demonstrates the reproduction of sexual and gender norms in this field. For example, the question which asks the subject whether he regularly buys sexually explicit magazines is expanded to include romance novels in the women's test. The women's test also includes a question about participating in sado-masochism which is absent from the men's tests (which suggests that this behaviour is pathological for women but not men). There are also several questions for gay men only, asking about anonymous sex, problems maintaining intimate relationships once the 'sexual newness' has worn off, sexual encounters that could lead to arrest for public indecency, public restroom cruising and engagement in risky sexual behaviour despite HIV-positive status.[10]

In all these tests, affirmative answers to thirteen of the twenty-five questions strongly suggests addiction.[11] However, many of the questions seem to almost guarantee affirmative replies from any member of a culture which constitutes sexuality as a central yet problematic aspect of the individual. Questions include: Do you often find yourself preoccupied with sexual thoughts? Has anyone been hurt emotionally because of your sexual behaviour? Has sex been a way for you to escape your problems? Do you ever think that your sexual desire is stronger than you are? The tests have the effect of solidifying sex addiction, imbuing it with the facticity of a disorder that can be detected through the application of a diagnostic test.

Carnes deploys the familiar trope of the hidden yet widespread and virulent disorder, arguing that sexual addiction is easily misdiagnosed or missed altogether because the variety of behaviours involved is confusing to the untrained eye.[12] The potency of the notion of the hidden disorder is also evident in an article entitled, 'How to Recognize the Signs of Sexual Addiction', written to educate physicians 'to spot addicts and coaddicts among [their] patients'. The author presents sex addiction as a frequently unrecognised pathology, affecting three to six per cent of the American population.[13] She advises doctors that sex addiction can only be uncovered by 'asking the right questions':

> When patients present with multiple somatic complaints, depression, dependency on tranquillisers, or compulsive behaviors, asking about the family situation may be extremely productive. Obtaining a thorough sexual history and asking about addiction problems in the patient's family of origin are helpful. A few minutes of empathetic conversation can lead to clues that suggest addiction or coaddiction.[14]

Here clinicians are being encouraged to read a confluence of general symptoms and complaints in a certain way, and are thereby being trained to see the presence of sex addiction in individuals. This is not just a matter of recognising an already-existing pathology, but of producing a recognisable disease entity through epistemological labour. Family and personal histories are to be elicited and causally linked with current somatic and psychological distress. In this article and most other sex addiction texts, the disease is solidified through an aetiological narrative. Its genesis is traced back to families of origin that were dysfunctional, either too chaotic and unstructured or too rigid and authoritarian, headed by parents who were either too sexually repressed or too sexually open. The narrative connecting childhood pain, low self-esteem and adult pathology is familiar and satisfyingly coherent, and through it sex addiction becomes a disease which makes sense.

Love is a Drug

A strategy used by both popular and specialist texts is to draw on the credibility of disease models of alcoholism and drug addiction, constructing sex addiction as a direct analogy of these better known dependencies. Irvine points out that the sex addiction movement was started by individuals already involved in self-help groups for drug and alcohol abuse, who began to articulate the idea that sex could be addictive and as potentially dangerous as other mood-altering pursuits. These recovering alcoholics and addicts posited the existence of a disease which compelled its sufferers to repeatedly engage in self-destructive sexual activities, and set up twelve-step groups to help the afflicted attain 'sexual sobriety'.[15] Hence it is not surprising that sex addiction discourse emphasises the similarities between sex and drug use as 'mood altering experiences'. The professionals who began writing on the new sexual disorder further developed the analogy by pointing out the ability of sexual activity to produce endorphins and other opiate-like chemicals in the brain. The theory is that even activities not involving physical contact, such as flirting, planning seductions and getting ready for a date can produce a trance-like euphoria through the release of endorphins. This is the 'high' which becomes the sex addict's 'fix'.[16] Thus, the notion of endorphin addiction enables sex addiction to be constituted as a literal as well as metaphoric chemical dependence, in a similar way to eating disorders.

Griffin-Shelley extends the idea of sexual compulsivity as a kind of drug addiction in his descriptions of the increased tolerance, compulsion, cravings and withdrawal symptoms experienced by sex addicts. In the context of drug and alcohol use these concepts, especially those of tolerance and withdrawal are used as markers of physiological dependence, signs of the brain adapting to the presence of a chemical. Applying them to sex addiction represents a strong claim for its existence as a biological disorder, but description of their operation demonstrates a move back to a metaphorical level of meaning. To illustrate tolerance, Griffin-Shelley gives the example of a man whose addiction to pornography started with advertisements for underwear and progressed to hard core porn. This movement from soft to hard, in search of ever-increasing stimulation, echoes the inexorable progress from soft drugs to hard drugs which exists in popular images of drug addiction, but it relies on cultural rather than chemical measurements of increasing potency.[17]

However, a central criterion for chemical dependency is continued use despite serious harmful consequences, and here the irrepressible differences between heavy drinking and drug use and excessive sexual desire make for some strange conclusions about sexual safety and danger. Unlike drugs, which are easily constructed as unnatural and inherently damaging to the human body, sex is regarded as a natural urge and fundamental human need. Sexual activity itself cannot be constituted as a threat to health in a contemporary psychological discourse. Yet the physically damaging and life-threatening potential of sex is a vital part of the claim for the status of sex addiction as a serious illness. The need to demonstrate the physical dangers of addictive sex leads to bizarre examples of addicts masturbating so frequently that they cause what is vaguely described as physical harm, others collapsing with exhaustion from over-strenuous activity, or suffering from back pain caused by sex in 'an unusual place or position', female addicts suffering vaginal infections and unwanted pregnancies, not to mention erotic self-asphyxiators dying from suffocation.[18]

The trump card is, however, the spectre of sexually transmitted diseases, especially HIV/AIDS. Introducing his text, Griffin-Shelley attributes the recent emergence of the truth about compulsive sexuality to the AIDS epidemic: 'Until recently, most people had trouble considering love and sex addictions as potentially fatal problems. Now, especially with the presence of human immunodeficiency virus (HIV), people are beginning to respect the potential lethality of unsafe sexual activity'.[19] His statement swiftly elides the distinction between unsafe sex in terms of HIV transmission and 'unsafe', addictive sex as classified by sex addiction discourse. This confusion also appears in another text, *Sex, Lies and Forgiveness: Couples Speaking Out on Healing from Sex Addiction*. The focus is very much on the marital relationship, the deleterious effect of outside sexual activity on its functioning, and the process of rebuilding trust within it. In nearly all the couples who 'speak out' it is the husband who is addicted. The danger of AIDS recurs as a theme, always connected with the threat posed by addictive extramarital sex to the health of the marriage. The authors state that:

> In the AIDS era, many spouses asked their [addicted] partner for information about sexual activities that would put them at risk, especially if the activities had been with gay men or prostitutes. Since the HIV virus is transmitted via body fluids, unsafe sexual practices

are those in which any body fluids are exchanged. Anal intercourse is particularly dangerous because the lining of the rectum is easily torn and semen or blood containing the virus can be absorbed.[20]

This passage manages to invoke an-all-too-common notion of deviant bodies as sources of pollution, through a series of apparently innocuous statements. The exact nature of the connections between the various symbols of disease mentioned: gay men, prostitutes, bodily fluids, anal intercourse and HIV infection are not made clear; instead there is a general sense of uncontrollable contamination which emanates from outside the marriage in the bodies of prostitutes and homosexuals and invades the previously pure and safe marital space, via the (addicted) body of the husband. This is as much an image of moral as viral contamination. In all the references to the risk of AIDS courted by married men who have homosexual affairs or frequent prostitutes, there is no mention of the danger of the husband infecting his homosexual lovers or the prostitutes he hires. The transmission only ever occurs in one direction, from the outside in.

The use of condoms and other safe sex practices are not mentioned as ways of making sexual activity less risky. In the example from Carnes, cited earlier, the tragedy of the young couple dying of AIDS is attributed to the husband's failure to get treatment for his addiction, not to his failure to practice safe sex. The reluctance to mention safe sex is partly attributable to the fear that it would be tantamount to telling addicts it is 'safe' to enjoy their disease as long as they are careful. Recommending AIDS prevention safe sex practices would also contradict sex addiction discourse's own model of safe and unsafe sex. As far as the disease of sex addiction goes, a condom has no effect on safety or risk.

The treatment of sex addiction as analogous to alcoholism leads to simplistic dichotomous models of safety and danger, responsibility and irresponsibility. What gets lost are the complex and important ethical questions of consent, mutuality, power and the relationship of representations and fantasies to the real. The significance of distinctions between consensual and coercive acts, practices that are safe and unsafe in terms of HIV transmission, and experiences that are solitary or involve interaction with another person are minimised in favour of the classification of the act as either addicted or healthy. Rather than paying attention to the specific meanings of different sexual encounters and experiences, the discourse focuses on producing sex in conformity with an already existing model of disease. It is possible to argue that sex addiction discourse is not very interested in actual sexual practices and experiences, except as surface indicators of deeper realities and truths. The capacities of a body in interaction with other bodies and with itself are reduced to indicators of a bigger truth, the opposition between health and addiction. This is how it is possible for sexual fantasising, prostitution, and rape to be regarded as sharing the same fundamental meaning. A consequence of this lack of interest in actual sexual acts is an absence of the explicit and detailed personal accounts of addictive behaviour which are common in texts on alcoholism and drug addiction. Sex addiction texts do contain first-person stories of sex addiction, but they only allude to sexual activity in general terms and do not describe the individual's physical feelings and sensations while getting her fix. For example, one of the women Kasl interviewed at length for her book talks about her life before joining Sex Addicts Anonymous:

> Nothing worked anymore . . . I was always sneaking around, lying to everybody, and feeling paranoid that one of the four guys I was seeing would bump into another one and there would be a big scene. On top of that, I had broken one of my sacred rules. My sister and I have a pact that we'll never mess with each other's boyfriends, but I had flirted with her boyfriend and we started making out.[21]

This inoffensive and euphemistic account is very different from Alcoholics Anonymous stories which vividly relate the sordid and fundamentally carnal pleasures and agonies of drinking with a kind of relish. The expurgated nature of sex addiction stories is explained in part by the need to avoid the possibility that sufferers could be avidly devouring texts on sex addiction for prurient purposes. Griffin-Shelley actually warns sex addicts not to use 'honesty' as an excuse for relating graphic and lurid stories of sexual exploits at self-help meetings or therapy sessions. Such story-telling could easily become a source of addictive pleasure and a way of trying to turn the listener(s) on. But the preference for the vague and general over the explicit is part of a broader effacement of actual sexual acts in daily life, and is related to the reduction of sexual behaviour to a cipher, a symbol of an inner disorder. Every point made about sex quickly boils down to a point about the nature of the inner self.

Bad Sex and the Absence of the Other

Judgements of quality are more important than quantity in defining sex addiction. While some sex addicts are described as spending nearly every waking minute either thinking about sex or having sex, it is the nature of their sexual interactions which is the root of their problems. In his first book on the topic, Carnes defined 'absence of relationship' and 'search for heightened excitement' as the 'twin pillars' of sex addiction. The objectification and exploitation of others is also a key element of addictive sex. Sex addicts 'do not see people as real human beings. Rather, they perceive others as objects. To them another person is an object that may provide the sexual or romantic high that is sought'.[22]

The concept of sexual objectification is taken (without acknowledgment) from the theories of sexuality and power developed by radical feminists such as Andrea Dworkin. For Dworkin, the sexual objectification of women is a manifestation of the power of men, a power which is exercised and reinforced through the institution of heterosexuality. The representation of women as sexual objects to be possessed, taken and used is intrinsic to patriarchal social relations and the functioning of a social order based on the subordination of women. But in sex addiction discourse the notion of sexual objectification is emptied of its political and institutional elements. The viewing of humans as sexual objects is a sign of individual pathology. For Griffin-Shelley it is consensual sado-masochism which is the apotheosis of objectifying and demeaning sex, because in these encounters 'There is little or no tenderness or love; rather, the sexual passion is enhanced by fear and pain'.[23]

Anne McClintock's thoughtful reading of S/M scenarios suggests that it is not only the presence of fear and pain and the violent imagery which disturbs sex addiction experts. McClintock argues that S/M is a theatre of conversion and transformation, reversing the social meanings it borrows from regimes of power. In its exaggerated use of costume, script and scene it reveals that social order itself is unnatural, scripted and invented. Sex addiction discourse has a heavy investment in the conceptual opposition of nature and performance which S/M undermines. It operates on the premise that healthy sexuality is natural and therefore safe, and that the sexuality of artifice and performance, of heightened pleasure, is uncontrollable and dangerous, while S/M reveals the performance and theatricality at the heart of all sexual encounters. At the same time as it disrupts assumptions about the naturalness of sex, S/M refigures what sex addiction discourse regards as pathology into a highly controlled subcultural form. Condemning S/M as the ultimate in objectifying sex and ignoring its theatricality shores up the idea of sexuality and sexual desire as natural. The significance and fragility of the idea of natural sex also explains why sexual accessories and toys are so often demonised in sex addiction texts. Sex toys represent the world of commodities, commerce and consumption which corrupts the innocence of nature; therefore they are attributed with great power, as if the intrusion of these often comic inanimate objects can, on its own, alter the fundamental meaning of an encounter between two people. In feminist therapist Charlotte Davis Kasl's view, even books on sexual techniques are suspect, 'Because warm and caring sex evolves from a warm and caring relationship and does not have to be artificially created'.[24] The perfectionist view of sexual relations being promoted is that of pure and unmediated communion between two souls, unsullied by any intrusion from the outside world. But the line drawn between the artificial and the natural reflects cultural and aesthetic norms. Pretty lingerie, candlelight and massage oils are acceptable natural enhancements to sexuality while a leather mask and a whip are the signs of an exploitative search for 'heightened pleasure'. Moreover, the assertion that good sex evolves naturally between couples is undermined by the prescriptive and pedagogical approach of sex addiction discourse itself, which suggests that this natural evolution requires significant cultural input.

Beyond the rituals of S/M, the sex addict's use of 'unsuspecting persons' as sexual objects is frequently raised to underline the damage caused to innocent victims. The metaphor of a hunter and its prey is used to drive home the predatory nature of the addict's stalking and seduction of a partner. Since the revelation that all they want is a quick sexual fix is unlikely to lead to success, sex addicts become polished deceivers, not caring who they hurt in their quest for satisfaction. Alongside this model of the addict as sexual predator is a very different vision of the addict as passive and fearful, addicted not to the exploitation of others, but to solitary masturbation. Given that exploitation of their partners is one of the major forms of unethical conduct that sex addicts are accused of, it is interesting to note the ambiguous place of masturbation in sex addiction discourse. One might expect that masturbation would be preferable to embroiling innocent partners in the games of sex addiction. However, solo sex (and the fantasising that accompanies it) is produced as an equally problematic and potentially dangerous form of sexual expression. Pornography, fantasy and masturbation are constituted as the unholy trio which introduce individuals into the illusory thrills of addictive sex; they appear harmless but are 'the opening that allows the addictive process to gain control'.[25] In the early stages of recovery, sex addicts are required to abstain from all forms of sex, including masturbation and one of the stricter recovery groups believes that addicts must abstain from 'any form of sex with one's self' for life.[26]

The disapproval attracted by masturbation is explained by the significance of motivation. Sex addiction discourse classifies some reasons for having sex as good, others are bad. Good reasons are always to do with the creation and maintenance of an intimate relationship with a life partner. The bad reasons are more diverse: for physical pleasure, to boost self-esteem, to escape feelings of loneliness, to avoid problems, to secure someone's love. Using sex to avoid negative feelings is seen as a particularly dangerous strategy, since it becomes all too tempting to retreat to a fantasy world whenever the challenges and tasks of life become too difficult.[27] This is where masturbation comes in, as the refuge of those unwilling or unable to do the hard work of developing real relationships.

The suspiciousness with which masturbation is viewed could be easily read as further evidence that sex addiction discourse is prudish and anti-sex. But mainstream understandings of masturbation are themselves ambiguous. On one hand masturbation is accepted as a healthy, almost compulsory, part of normal sexuality, but it is simultaneously devalued against the norm of mature sexual coupling. Despite the fact that, as Sedgwick observes, the link between masturbation and degeneracy no longer has respectable currency, masturbation still arouses ridicule and suspicion, if not fear. In 1994 Dr Jocelyn Elders was dismissed as United States Surgeon General after she stated that children should be reassured that masturbation is normal. Critics Paula Bennett and Vernon Rosario argue that Elders' dismissal proves that the 'profound fears' inspired by masturbation as a sexual activity and as 'an occasion for erotic imagining' can still be enlisted to justify the political control of sexuality.[28]

Sedgwick remarks that when masturbation is practised solo it escapes 'the creation of any interpersonal trace' and it is this quality which makes it an alluring and dangerous activity for sex addicts.[29] Just like the S/M devotee and the predatory seducer, the compulsive masturbator avoids personal interaction and concentrates on self-gratification. In a way his sexual objectification of others is even more extreme than that of the more obviously exploitative addicts. He has done away with the other altogether; for him people are simply actors in his fantasies, their actions and responses under his complete control. The importance of the contrast between solitary pleasures and the rewards of relationship is further revealed by looking at the ideal of healthy sexuality promoted in sex addiction discourse.

Good Sex and the Absence of the Other

Sex addiction discourse adheres to the belief that sexuality is central to identity and self-fulfilment, and that sexual relationships are a vital part of life. Thus 'sexual sobriety' cannot be based on total life-long abstinence, which is itself an unhealthy state. For these addicts, recovery does not mean renouncing their sexuality but developing healthy sexuality, which is based on intimacy. Judging from the histories recounted in sex addiction texts, healthy sexuality means being married to a respectable person not too different from oneself, having sex only with them, and enjoying it, but not to the detriment of other shared activities. The ideal of intimacy which underlies it is based on verbal exchange between rational individuals. Intimacy is produced through honest communication, self-disclosure, and the exchange of information, feelings, and secrets. Its ultimate realisation is a state of 'knowing and being known by another'.[30] The healthy relationship is a joint enterprise between equal individuals. Both partners are aware of their 'equal investment and responsibility for the success of the venture'.[31]

Simply put then, sex can only be meaningful after the partners have agreed on the nature and organisation of their mutual project. Absent is any notion of erotic desire or corporeal connection. The possibility of a kind of bodily intimacy independent of 'knowing and being known' is excluded. I am not alluding to a romantic view of love as an inexplicable force beyond language; rather suggesting that encounters viewed as worthless by sex addiction discourse could provide a different, possibly fleeting, but real sense of belonging and recognition based on mutual erotic desire. In this hierarchical model of sex, sexual pleasure is not valuable in itself, but only when it can be rendered useful and productive, working in the service of 'higher' goals. As I go on to argue, the ultimate goal of sexual relations is not so much the relationship with the other, but the self-realisation and self-knowledge fostered by this relationship.

The celebration of intimacy as the measure of the worth of sexual relationships also disavows the heterogeneity of people's values and interests. As Robert Solomon has argued, intimacy is not for everyone. For some, it violates the sense of individuality, independence and solitude crucial to their identity. For others, it is a distraction from public life or more expansive community and friendship ties.[32] Preferring different forms of engagement with the world does not necessarily imply a pathological fear of intimacy.

If we turn to the role of the other in the project of healthy intimacy, the instability at the core of the sex addiction model of sexuality is revealed. Sex addiction texts state that intimacy requires sex addicts to develop the capacity to see the other as an equal, separate but connected, instead of as an object to be used for their own purposes. How to relate to the other while recognising their alterity is a profound ethical challenge,[33] but for sex addiction experts it is a simple matter. True intimacy with the other is not easily achieved, but is potentially attainable by all who follow the guidelines. It is talking which can facilitate an authentic relationship, one where partners reveal their true selves, simultaneously giving up their false, projected images of the other. But there is a curious lack of such others in the texts I have been discussing. While the case histories recount what sex, love and romance addicts have done to, with, and for other people, we never have a sense that these other people are also active participants in the dramas described. For example, Schaef's case of the woman with 'sexual anorexia' contains no information about her husband or her marriage, apart from the fact that the relationship appeared normal from the outside. Could this not be a case of relationship breakdown involving two people, rather than an addiction involving only one? In the same text, romance addicts are described as expressing their pathology by planning elaborate dinners and showering their lovers with extravagant gifts. One wonders if these attentions are welcome or unwelcome, pleasurable or distressing for the recipients. In the terms of the discourse, however, the reaction and feelings of the other are not relevant; what matters are the motivations of the diseased self. The elision of the other as a responsive, autonomous agent in sex addiction discourses results in remarkable ethical vacuums in these texts, despite their concern with sexual conduct. Two of the case studies presented in a guide for professionals by Earle & Earle provide a striking example. The first case is of David, a sex offender who molested his stepdaughter regularly for eight years, starting when she was ten years old. The second is of Maria who had a long series of extra-marital affairs, and also spends much time fantasising about men. These two cases are presented as homologous examples of the same fundamental process of addiction. This is only possible because the experiences of the other people involved have been effaced. Even though the authors make strong statements about the 'severe damage' sex offenders cause to their victims, analysing such dissimilar conduct under the same rubric undermines ethical differentiation. David's use of his stepdaughter and Maria's use of her lovers are produced as analogous, as are David's betrayal of his daughter's trust and Maria's betrayal of her husband.[34]

The absence of the other, except in the most shadowy form, extends into the models of intimacy provided by sex addiction texts. According to Schaef, the requirements of a healthy relationship include: to share feelings; to be honest with oneself about who the other is; to have and respect boundaries; and to know that dependency in any form kills relationships, and to honour the integrity of the self and the other.[35] In this static vision of a subject who knows and is known, there is no sense of the misrecognitions and conflicts inherent in any confrontation with a specific and unpredictable other. The intrusion of an independent entity with a history and desires of their own, and possibly divergent understandings of what their boundaries are, what constitutes their integrity and what dependency is (or indeed whether it is such a bad thing), would disrupt the harmony of such communion. This ideal of intimacy is predicated on a self who is already fully formed before the other arrives on the scene and it is the state of this stable, bounded, autonomous inner self that is the final measure of the health of the relationship.

Despite all the statements about respect for the other, there is no space for a concrete other in these formulations of relationship. The 'concrete other' is a term used by feminist political theorist Seyla Benhabib to describe a conception of human relations which requires us to view every person as 'a unique individual, with a certain life history, disposition and endowment, as well as needs and limitations'. In contrast, the concept of the 'generalized other' enjoins us to view others as rational beings endowed with the same rights as ourselves. The generalised other is the dominant liberal conception of the abstract individual, in which relations between individuals are based on formal equality. As Benhabib explains, in this version of ethical relations, what constitutes the moral dignity of the other is not what differentiates us from each other, but rather what we have in common. In adopting the standpoint of the concrete other we instead abstract from what constitutes our commonality and focus on individuality. 'We seek to comprehend the needs of the other, his or her motivations, what she searches for, and what s/he desires'.[36] Benhabib develops these conceptions in discussion of moral psychology and theory, but her work is useful in describing the ethical standpoint of sex addiction discourse. It adopts and promotes relations based on the concept of the 'generalized other', it assumes that the other is fundamentally the same as the self. The fluidity and undecidability of desire for the other is classified as a symptom of disease; in its place the relationship of self with an identical self is promoted as the model of healthy interaction. The truism that to truly love anyone else one must first love oneself is widely repeated in sex addiction texts, but their central claim is more that truly loving someone is the same as truly loving oneself. The ideal ethical connection thus turns out to be a sort of solipsism in which difference is either absorbed or excluded.

There is a strange proximity between the ideal of intimacy promoted in these texts and the very forms of relationship they condemn as exploitative. In the former, the other is not produced as a sexual object, but as a therapeutic device, a way of improving oneself and knowing oneself better.

Conclusion

Sex addiction discourse demonstrates the use of the trope of addiction to translate codes of morality into avowedly scientific and objective diagnostic categories which classify people as healthy or sick. By producing certain forms of sex as potentially addictive, sex addiction experts reflect and reproduce cultural anxieties about the destructive power of erotic desire. But the insistent and intense nature of erotic desire is also exalted in the western tradition of romance. As the alternative to the destructive pleasures of addictive sex, sex addiction discourse posits an ideal of healthy intimacy between two committed and secure individuals. This ideal has the appeal of safety, but disavows the significance of bodily connection. Moreover, it produces the other as a mirror of the self and a means to the higher goal of self-actualisation, rather than as a unique, concrete and embodied subject.

7

The Recovery Habit

The only unfailing and permanent source of improvement is liberty.

—J. S. Mill, *On Liberty*

We know ourselves, we govern ourselves, and we make ourselves only at a cost, which we often pay without recognizing, or without realizing that it is not necessary to do so. One task for 'critical thought' is thus to expose these costs, to analyze what we did not realize we had to say and to do to ourselves in order to be who we are.

—John Rajchman, *Truth and Eros*

The previous chapters have delineated a range of addicted subjects produced by popular addiction literature. The recovering addict was present in these texts too, as the always desirable and always possible future of the addicted subject. The relationship between the addict and the recovering addict is one of distance and proximity or, to put it another way, difference and identity. On one hand the recovering addict's state of physical, emotional and spiritual health is the mirror opposite of the addict's pathological and unenlightened being, but the recovering addict is also the promise of what the addict could become. In popular therapeutic discourse the possible addictive disorders are many and diverse, but the models of healthy personhood they promote are very much alike in their basic structure and constitutive elements.

It is assumed in self-help discourse that addiction is conceptually prior to recovery, that is, that addiction exists 'out there' as a problem and that the processes of recovery are a response to this prior entity. On this logic it makes sense that the good of recovery can be predicted from the bad of addiction, and that the two exist as mirror images of each other. If addiction is characterised by dishonesty, self-hatred and despair, recovery must be built around honesty, self-esteem and hope. My starting point is to reverse the direction of this logic so that the normative standards of health and happiness that define recovery can be studied not as the logical, necessary and natural counterparts to the forces of addiction but as specific and autonomous formations. The healthy and productive life of recovery is a particular mode of existence that comes about not from natural processes of healing or growth, but from a concerted and multifaceted project of self-production.

Nikolas Rose's work on the psychological disciplines and their invention of the contemporary self enables this aspect of recovery discourse and practice to be understood within a broader category of regimes of freedom. Rose argues that during the second half of this century, the 'psy disciplines', in particular psychology, produced a regulative ideal of the self, characterised by a 'profound inwardness' and a concomitant personal autonomy. In schools, hospitals, clinics, workplaces, within the family and in the popular media, human beings were subjected to therapeutic authority and enjoined to live as autonomous and responsible individuals. The crucial point about the regimes of the self established by therapeutic authority is that they are regimes of freedom. They 'translate the enigmatic desires and dissatisfactions of the individual into precise ways of inspecting oneself, accounting for oneself, and working upon oneself in order to realize one's potential, gain happiness and exercise one's authority'. Therapeutic authorities work in the service of liberty and personal choice, which ironically makes them more profoundly subjectifying than other more obviously oppressive forms of authority. Therapeutic authorities seem to emerge from inside ourselves, from our desires for happiness and our striving for fulfil-ment.[1] The understanding of freedom as a regulative norm provides a useful insight into recovery discourse, which urges troubled individuals to attain autonomy and find happiness through open-ended projects of self-examination and self-improvement.

· The concepts of habit and ethical self-formation are also drawn on in this chapter to highlight some of the tensions in recovery discourse, in particular the unstable relationship between inner transformation and everyday conduct. In his later works, Foucault turned to questions of ethics, by which he meant the relations of the self to itself. His reconstruction of the sexual ethics of ancient Greece in *The Use of Pleasure: The History of Sexuality Volume Two* demonstrates that the ethical problem of how to turn oneself into the right kind of person can be formulated and understood in a way foreign to the modern obsession with desire and the duty to expose it. For the ancient Greeks, according to Foucault, sexual morality was a question of the correct use of pleasure, rather than inner purity or the control of desire. Instead of adherence to a universal code which defined permitted and prohibited practices, what was required was the correct attitude to the self. Terming Greek practices of self-formation as 'arts of existence', Foucault describes an ethics concerned with aesthetic values and stylistic criteria.[2] The goal of such ethical regimes was the making of oneself as a work of art befitting an appropriate oeuvre.

Foucault's studies of the constitution of the self in Greek, Roman and early Christian ethical regimes make clear that subjectivity is not a transcendent feature of human beings. Rather it is variably constituted through prescribed, historically and culturally specific 'technologies of the self'. These technologies:

> permit individuals to effect by their own means or with the help of others a certain number of operations on their own bodies and souls, thoughts, conduct, and way of being, so as to transform themselves in order to attain a certain state of happiness, purity, wisdom, perfection, or immortality.[3]

The programs designed to take the individual from addiction to health which are found in recovery guides can be understood as technologies of the self. They are made up of detailed techniques, from how to attend a cocktail party as a recovering alcoholic, to how to become aware of one's inner voice.

A distinction again needs to be made here between the practices of Alcoholics Anonymous and other twelve-step programs as they are carried out by individuals in meetings around the world, and the practices promoted in the self-help texts which have emerged from the contemporary North American recovery movement. It is the latter with which I am here concerned. AA still has a conventionally (Protestant) Christian and masculinist flavour which survives from its origins in the 1930s as a fellowship group for middle-class white men. It arose out of the spread and intensification of industrialism and consumerism, responding to the particular stresses faced by male workers as their traditional roles and authority were challenged. The recovery movement and the literature it has produced are very much phenomena of the late twentieth century, incorporating not only AA's twelve steps but concepts and language from feminism, psychoanalysis, new age spiritualism and bio-sciences such as genetics and neurochemistry. Its growth was fuelled in large part by the frustrations and unhappiness of a generation of women who expected liberation, equality and rewarding personal and professional lives but found themselves stuck in destructive relationships and ungratifying jobs.[4] I return to consequences of this difference later in the chapter, but here it is enough to note that the homeliness of the AA approach, and its eschewal of leaders, experts and spokespeople in favour of anonymous not-for-profit fellowship, contrasts with the psychological discourse of the recovery movement and its production of celebrity authors and therapists. In AA the twelve steps are unquestionable and unalterable, but their interpretation and implementation is not set out in an explicit or detailed program.

The Recovering Addict

The identity of 'recovering addict' is marked by difference from the addict, but also by its difference from the non-addict. The addict in recovery may be distinguished by his sobriety and self-awareness; but this does not make him a 'normal' non-addicted subject. As a subject engaged in a perpetual process of recovering from the fracturing effects of addiction, the recovering self cannot achieve the unselfconscious normality of the non-addicted. 'Recovering addict' operates as a 'master' identity, one that defines individuals and explains all their actions, but it is also protean. In one manifestation it is constructed as a higher form of being with special epistemic status, calling to mind an Ayn Rand hero or a Maslovian self-actualiser. In another, a type of standpoint theory operates, suggesting that recovering addicts have special insight into the human condition, gained from battling a disease that demands rigorous honesty and an unflinching commitment to facing reality, without any of the comforting rationalisations, illusions and defences the non-addicted can resort to. Linda Leonard, recovering addict, author and Jungian therapist, states in a magazine article on addiction and creativity:

> The entire experience of addiction forced me to face directly the human condition, to acknowledge my mortality, and in the face of this to make a vow to life—a vow to create a new way of being.[5]

The recovering addict is on a journey or pilgrimage, the tribulations of addiction leading to the attainment of a higher level of functioning and awareness. The narrative of descent into addiction, the hitting of 'bottom' and the ascent of recovery constructs a life with direction, a satisfying and meaningful trajectory of progress and development. In this discourse, addicts in recovery are produced as courageous actors in a grand drama, compared to the unremarkable, static and mundane lives of the masses. Gratitude for their disease is a common sentiment among recovering addicts. According to Cocores, 'Without the disease, they feel, they probably would have done what most people do: just go on the same way, doing the same things, reacting and responding in the same fashion, not learning or changing'. Recovery is also constructed as a type of rebirth which offers addicts a second chance, cleansed of past sins. According to Patrick Carnes, sex addicts in recovery can go through a second adolescence and emerge with a new sense of innocence. Many accounts, like the words of the young female recovering alcoholic quoted below, describe a heightened sensibility and a childlike capacity for finding joy in the things others take for granted:

Feeling good while waking up was an incredible feeling! I hadn't felt that way in five years . . . In addition to the physical improvements were some wondrous feats: On my nineteenth day of sobriety, I was able to go grocery shopping with the rest of the world; on my twenty-seventh day, I vacuumed my apartment. It got better and better.[6]

Not surprisingly, recovering addicts are warned about the lack of understanding with which others will greet their experiences, and are told to expect responses ranging from lack of interest to the defensive hostility of those who are in denial about their own addictions. The community of recovering addicts is the only place where unfailing support and encouragement can be found. Thus, while 'recovering addict' is a highly individualised identity, it gives the individual membership in an instant community with a clear boundary separating insiders from outsiders.

On one hand recovery appears as a utopian state of redemption and salvation. A well-known passage from AA literature (known as 'the promises') portrays recovery as nothing short of paradise on earth, where 'We are going to know a new freedom and a new happiness . . . We will comprehend the word serenity and we will know peace . . .'.[7] But in its less exalted form, the recovering addict identity is a precarious and uncomfortable state marked by constant self-surveillance, and the ever-present threat of relapse. One effect of the formulation of recovery as enlightenment is to suggest that the apparently normal and functioning self which existed before the onset of active addiction was in fact unhealthy and constricted, or at least vulnerable in its lack of authentic self-knowledge and purpose. Recovery then demands a retroactive alienation from this earlier experience of normality as part of the process of moving away from addictive conduct and thinking. Addicts must work on themselves in relation to their past as well as their future, questioning the normal as well as challenging addiction.

The other side of the joy and sense of meaning found in recovery is self-monitoring and discipline. A twelve-step handbook warns that sustaining recovery requires 'constant vigilance' and that 'complacency and forgetfulness' are its worst enemies. The recovering addict must remain ever vigilant and ever aware of her difference. She must practice a painstaking form of memory work to protect against a return to addiction because:

[Relapse] begins when alcoholics and addicts feel 'safe' enough to stop going to meetings. It begins when they stop remembering the harm they did to others and to themselves as a consequence of their addiction: when they start to forget what it was like to lose their jobs and their friends, to ruin their relationships and their health, and to feel hopelessness and self-hatred.[8]

Such (literally) sobering warnings remind recovering addicts that the price of their recovery is actively maintaining the memory of their past pain, and recognising that for them there is no safety.

Images and metaphors found in recovery discourse compare recovery to a natural process of growth: a butterfly emerging from a chrysalis, the opening of a flower. Yet, the pathology of the addict raises questions about her capacity to recover through simple evolution. Indeed, the content of self-help texts presents a picture of recovery as a mode of existence that is achieved only through a rigorously concerted and multifaceted project of self-production. Attaining health and happiness is not a matter of allowing a process of maturation simply to unfold, but demands a lifelong commitment to the practices of recovery, comprising both techniques of everyday conduct and a transformation of the inner self. The hierarchical relationship between the two dimensions of recovery tends to privilege the 'true self', the inner core of being, as the site of genuine and deep recovery. Mastering sober deportment represents an important but ultimately superficial activity, the precursor to the personal growth which leads to the more advanced stage of enlightenment.

Indeed, most of the steps of the twelve steps concern attitudes, beliefs and processes of self-examination. The final stage of recovery involves 'a spiritual awakening' which cannot be forced or hurried, but emerges only after patient and dedicated 'working' of the steps. Recovery literature insists that this spiritual awakening is a progressive and open-ended process which lasts for a lifetime, a growing awareness of a power greater than the self, a sense of letting go and moving from darkness into light.[9]

But on the other hand, the connections between 'lifestyle' changes and internal shifts are stressed, and it is acknowledged that, in the words of an AA slogan, 'right acting leads to right thinking'. Change can occur from the outside in; 'what we practice we become' is another AA slogan. Still, there is suspicion of those who are too compliant; the easy adoption of recovery 'talk' and conduct can obscure a resistance to 'genuine' acceptance and inner change.[10]

This dichotomy of interiority/exteriority is central to the notion of autonomy promoted in recovery discourse. According to this view, a healthy person (whether 'normal' or recovering) has a strong and clear boundary around their self, which separates it from what is not-self. This allows them to differentiate their inner voice from the claims of external authorities, enabling the moral self-determination which in this framework is the essence of freedom. But paying attention to the techniques and practices of recovery reveals the difficulty of maintaining the distinction between outer and inner change. Enacting the exercises recommended in the texts operates as a training program which both requires and produces an inner self that is always present, coherent and intelligible, and available to be 'worked on'. Focusing on these practices refigures recovery as a matter of habit and self-conduct.

Abstinence and Beyond

The necessary condition of recovery is abstinence from the addictive substance or behaviour. The form this takes obviously depends on the addiction. When the substance is a drug, abstinence requires no ingestion of the drug. But what this means in practice varies. Alcoholics must avoid all alcohol and are warned about cough medicines, dealcoholised wines which still contain traces of alcohol, and even desserts flavoured with rum or brandy. Drug addicts must eschew mood-altering drugs including tranquillisers, sleeping pills, narcotic painkillers and non-local dental anaesthesia unless absolutely necessary. Nicotine, as a widely used and non-intoxicating legal drug, has a special status; sobriety in Alcoholics Anonymous or Narcotics Anonymous does not preclude smoking. Common advice is not to attempt to give up smoking while in 'early recovery' from alcohol and other drug addictions, because life is going to be difficult enough without adding another source of stress. But once this stage is over, giving up cigarettes is insisted on as part of the healthy new lifestyle, along with regular exercise, learning to eat healthily and getting enough sleep. In the case of addiction to food, which cannot be given up, or activities regarded as necessary for a good life such as sex, work or relationships, abstinence is a more complex matter. It takes the form of prescribing certain behaviours, prohibiting others, and limiting others to 'moderate' or 'non-addicted' forms. Not eating sugar in any form and weighing all food portions are practices of abstinence for food addicts. For sex addicts, abstinence might require not wearing make-up or provocative clothing, or avoiding public restrooms if they had previously been the site of sexual encounters. For work addicts, taking lunch breaks, working a set number of hours a day and going on a vacation once a year are suggested abstinence rules.[11]

Even for alcoholics and drug addicts, abstinence in addiction/ recovery discourse is much more than saying no. Prohibition is combined with incitement to new forms of behaviour. For example, the question of drinking for alcoholics in recovery is about what they should drink and how, rather than just what they shouldn't drink. Jack Mumey, in his guide *The New Joy of Being Sober,* advises that at parties the recovering alcoholic should drink soft drink straight from the can or coffee from a cup. This ensures against his glass being refilled with an alcoholic drink and, just as importantly, makes it clear to himself and others that he is not the same as the other party-goers enjoying gin and tonics or beer. He also recommends never having punch, even if it is supposedly non-alcoholic, and refusing soft drinks that have come out of mixer nozzles which may have been used to dispense alcohol. Although the rationale for these actions is that they safeguard against inadvertent alcohol consumption, they also reinforce a certain identity, marked by a meticulous 'care of the self' in relation to consumption.[12]

The negotiations necessary to maintaining sobriety, like those above, involve speaking as a recovering addict and occupying this identity openly in public. Speech acts produce the identity as well as present it to the world. The most formal occasion of self-production is the addict's announcement of identity and narration of their life story at a twelve-step meeting. This moment is central to the formation of a new identity. In one account by a compulsive eater, saying the words, 'I am Eliot' and 'I am a compulsive eater', brings about a tectonic shift in sense of self. 'The instant' he speaks them he is 'immediately overcome with emotion' and begins weeping, 'Speaking those words . . . meant everything to me. I was speaking a deep truth, a truth that lay at the very heart of my life and my pain'. Eliot's new identity is reinforced by the requirement that he call his Overeaters Anonymous sponsor every night and report exactly what he is going to eat for breakfast, lunch and dinner the following day. This is called 'committing food'. Less public and more mundane speech acts continue the production of the identity. Part of recovery is telling friends, family, colleagues and acquaintances. While the nature of the 'telling' depends on the particular relationship, it always involves acknowledging to oneself that one is speaking from the position of recovering addict. Even interactions with waiters and bartenders are important. Once Eliot has begun his recovery with Overeaters Anonymous, he no longer orders from restaurant menus, but asks for a special meal, 'six ounces of broiled swordfish, a baked potato, green salad with oil and vinegar on the side' or 'broiled breast of chicken, four ounces of pasta, a salad'. Again, he orders this way to stick to his food plan, but the act of speaking is just as important in itself. In his story 'coming out' as a food addict and embarking on recovery gives him the right to say things he has never been able to say before, such as 'I am hungry and I need to eat now'. In the case of sex addiction, new ways of speaking are conceived as duties rather than rights. One of the elements of recovery is 'telling the truth', meaning practising particular types of confession and self-disclosure with a therapist or spouse as audience. The demands of abstinence include an incitement to verbalise the self, using a psychological and therapeutic vocabulary.[13]

Too much focus on the prohibitive can be as damaging for recovering addicts as too little attention to the maintenance of abstinence. For food, sex and work addicts, overdoing abstinence can lead to the equally addictive processes of anorexia, sexual avoidance and work phobia. Former drug addicts and alcoholics stuck on 'saying no' will end up in a state known in AA literature as 'white knuckle sobriety'. This is a state of dislocation and torment in which the body is drug-free, but addictive urges and addicted thought patterns continue. Cocores reassures his readers that although 'white knuckle sobriety' is 'like gritting your teeth and just barely hanging on', it is not nearly as bad as being an alcohol or drug abuser. But in some respects it does seem a worse, or at least equally unhappy state, stuck in a limbo of anger and depression, without a chemical scapegoat. Seymour and Smith in *Drugfree* paint an even grimmer picture:

> White knuckle sobriety is more than just uncomfortable. It can be dangerous and debilitating. It can become a source of constant negative stress, eroding the immune system and theoretically could make the knuckler especially vulnerable to dangerous, even terminal illness.[14]

Here 'white knucklers' are just as out of control as addicts, and in some ways their situation is worse, because they can easily convince themselves and others that they are in control of their disease. The concept of 'white knuckle sobriety' is a clear demonstration that in self-help recovery discourse, abstinence is the beginning of the project, not its fulfilment. Genuine and deep recovery, the sort that brings with it the enlightenment and peak experiences mentioned earlier, requires 'a psychological overhaul', systematic work on and with the desires and emotions. Since the addictive behaviour is the surface manifestation of a deeper disturbance, stopping the behaviour without working on the underlying pathology is pointless. Genuine and long-lasting change will only occur when recovery is approached as a project of work on the self, work that is wide-ranging and difficult. A new mode of existence must be embraced, comprising both a new way of life and a transformation of the self. The goal is not just to resist the addictive desires but to transform them. Cocores offers the enticing example of those recovering addicts who are living 'full and satisfying lives without *wanting drink or drugs*, without for one moment wishing they could go back to it, without for one moment feeling sorry for themselves because they're "not like other people" when it comes to chemicals'. He holds out the promise of a moment of mastery when 'You no longer have to think about staying sober, you just are'.[15]

This is an image of a perfect, unified and transcendent self; but as the examples of the food addict at the restaurant and the alcoholic at the cocktail party have illustrated, recovery also involves a rhetorical and performative practice. One becomes a recovering addict by doing and saying the things that recovering addicts do and say. How are the mundane acts of everyday life and the transformative experience of spiritual awakening connected?

Both are the result of work on the self which establishes habits of action and thought. Paradoxically, these habits are the basis of the freedom experienced by the recovering addict.

In the following examination of the techniques of recovery I make a distinction between the work of early recovery, which involves a practical problem-solving approach to life without drugs or alcohol, and the continuing and broader project of gaining self-knowledge through self-examination and introspection. I begin with a discussion of Mumey's *The New Joy of Being Sober* and *Restore Your Life* by Anne Geller, a medical doctor and recovering alcoholic. Both are detailed guides to the work of early recovery, and promote recovery as a new way of life in which physical, psychological and spiritual health become the guiding principles.

Styles of Conduct: Millions of Moments of Everyday Living

> To become a truly sober person—someone leading a normal, healthy, productive life without using mood-altering chemicals—you need a <u>living plan</u>, that is, a simple, organized way to conduct your life. Sobriety may begin, often dramatically, with throwing away your bottle, pills, powder, or needles. But it by no means ends there. It is an ongoing proposition, one that encompasses millions of moments of everyday living.
> —A. Geller, *Restore Your Life: A Living Plan for Sober People*

In their detailed and painstaking attention to the everyday, Mumey's and Geller's guides to managing life in early recovery de-naturalise the mundane activities of daily life. They are reminiscent of etiquette guides as they set out of rules for social life, techniques of daily deportment and correct conduct toward oneself and others. They also have an air of the ethnographic, as if the newly recovering addict is being introduced to a foreign culture, the culture of sobriety, and needs instructions on how to fit in.

The areas covered by the guides include work, relationships, sex, leisure, exercise and diet. Their 'practical' and 'common sense' stance has the effect of constituting all aspects of life as fundamentally alike. They all require active management and the application of problem solving strategies and tools. Diligence and effort are as appropriate to family life, sexual relations and hobbies as they are to career success and health maintenance. For example, to rebuild the family into 'a strong, healthy unit' Geller prescribes regular family meetings with 'frank, open discussions', written contracts between family members and plans of action to solve problems.[16] In fact, her healthy living program relies heavily on a model of sound business practice; routines and time management, risk assessment, prudent decision-making, honesty and communication are the keys to success. Living is a serious and challenging task which can only be successfully executed with the help of personal schedules and devotion to list-making.

Progress is built on a base of emotional stability and a healthy body, which are in turn the result of following a code of moderation. This involves planning daily and weekly routines that are not too taxing, but do not leave too much empty time, learning how to reduce stress and defuse negative moods, and obtaining regular exercise, adequate sleep and good nutrition. Even pleasure becomes a servant to the goal of recovery, another task to be ticked off the list. Geller admonishes the recovering addict to remember to reward herself when she has had a hard day or achieved a goal; 'sober life has to have its celebratory moments'. But how is the recovering addict to celebrate without turning to 'the familiar rewards of a drink, a snort, a joint?'. The answer is to make a list of (non-drug-related) pleasures and the occasions on which you might enjoy them, then work your way systematically through them.[17] Pleasure, which for the addict used to be a destructive and chaotic force, is tamed and brought into the fold of rationality. Emphasising the individual's ability to take control of his or her life, Geller's program is a blueprint for producing an active, autonomous and responsible self. This is an individual who is linked 'into a social field not primarily through constraint or injunction, but through regulated acts of choice'.[18]

Geller's authority as a recovering alcoholic is combined with her status as a medical doctor who specialises in treating addiction. She speaks as both understanding fellow sufferer and objective professional, and presents her book as a text that, like a Bible, should always be kept close at hand and read in small doses, in response to whatever aspect of life is particularly troubling at that time. *The New Joy of Being Sober* by Jack Mumey is, as the title suggests, more casual in style and is written in a relentlessly upbeat tone, covering topics such as 'the singles game without booze' and 'handling the cocktail party'. Mumey emphasises collecting a set of tools and strategies rather than building an overall living plan, and he encourages friendliness and openness as part of recovery. He believes that recovering addicts should not be shy about disclosing their disease, whether to family, friends, employers, workmates or even to their bank and insurance company. In the world created by this text, no irreparable damage or significant loss ever occurs from such disclosure. If an application form for a job asks if you have ever been treated for alcoholism, Mumey advises the recovering alcoholic to reply honestly, and attach a letter explaining the details:

> Ask for a personal, additional interview to elaborate on this point. You'll get your chance to be open and honest with this company right from the start. You may be surprised at the number of administrators who will disclose to you their own battles with the bottle; they will take the same risk with you as part of their program of recovery.[19]

Similarly, bankers, lawyers and insurance agents will be understanding and sympathetic as long as you make the effort to explain your disease and your commitment to recovery. Unlike Geller, Mumey promotes adventurousness and risk-taking as elements of recovery. He urges his readers to 'cast a long line out into the world' and share their recovery with everyone they meet; 'You may lose a few rolls of the dice, but the odds are that you will come up a winner more often than you ever thought possible'. If Geller's text constructs the living of a happy, healthy life as analogous to running a solid business in a prudent and conscientious manner, Mumey's vision is of a more entrepreneurial and expansionist enterprise. After all, Mumey is the owner and president of a drug and alcohol treatment centre, a successful businessman in a rapidly expanding and highly profitable field. No wonder he envisages health as an energetic embracing of challenges, whether the enterprise is finding a religious life or finding a better job. According to Rose, the ideal of the enterprising self, a self characterised by energy, initiative, ambition, calculation, boldness and vigour now imbues the political, institutional and ethical cultures of the modern West.[20] In Mumey's text the successfully recovering addict is an enthusiastic convert to enterprise culture.

What is most striking about *The New Joy of Being Sober* is its very detailed advice about specific situations. A chapter on flying without drinking takes the reader through a step-by-step plan covering every stage of the flight from waiting in the airport to leaving the aircraft. Some of the techniques are closely connected to drinking, others are aimed more at general reduction of anxiety and enhancement of 'the flying experience'. They include choosing reading material which you have already begun (rather than a new book which will be harder to concentrate on), not leaving your seat unless necessary, greeting the flight attendants cordially, preparing yourself for the appearance of 'the formidable monster' (the drinks trolley), and paying close attention to how few people on the flight actually drink alcohol.[21] This plan, along with many others among Mumey's strategies, is about altering conduct rather than attitudes. The point of the plan is not to unearth the reasons why one hates flying, but to behave in a calm and self-controlled manner. Similarly, Geller's approach is also about conduct, and the establishment of new habits. It is through repetition of the small acts of sobriety that a new mode of existence is instilled, not through contemplation or self-examination. Geller explicitly advises against too much intro-spection during early recovery, recommending activity and distraction rather than analysis to overcome negative moods.

Despite their self-identification as down-to-earth and prag-matic, these two texts do promote a utopian view of recovery, in that its many benefits come without the loss of anything genuinely valuable. Telling a boyfriend that you will no longer be able to drink with him may cost you the relationship, but this proves that it was of little value anyway. It may take a bit of effort to get used dating and meeting new people without alcohol, but ultimately it will be a lot more fun. Having to leave your job because it involves too much contact with alcohol and drug use turns out to be a blessing in disguise when it allows you the chance to find more rewarding work.

Mumey and Geller are also committed to a totalised and co-herent model of the self. I have discussed their guides to living as treatises on good habits to highlight the extent to which recovery is a matter of conduct, but their rhetoric invokes the healthy subject as an identity based on a lifestyle and ethical code which one must adopt as a whole. For example, *The New Joy of Being Sober* connects recovery with a particular type of sexuality:

> The need to care about someone before sex, during sex, and after sex is essential if, in recovery, you are going to make progress toward a lasting sobriety . . . Sobriety, and the joy of it, means that you have a sincere concern for meeting the needs of your partner as well as your own. Sexual encounters become a matter of what you can do for each other instead of what you can do for yourself.[22]

The alcoholic who wishes to stop drinking but is keen to continue his pursuit of casual sexual encounters is in trouble. Valverde states that one of the virtues of habit as a technique of self-government is that habits are contingently, not necessarily, linked to each other; while people who exercise regularly are likely to eat healthily, this link is not necessary.[23] In recovery discourse, however, habits are merely stepping stones to the attainment of a new identity; thus they are inevitably tied together as components of a healthy lifestyle, which is in turn the base for the transformation of the inner self. Self-examination and self-reflection are valorised by Geller and Mumey as the source of greater understanding and continuing personal growth. They are not useful in early recovery, but once the addict has successfully mastered the daily conduct of sobriety the work on the inner self, in particular the gaining of self-knowledge, should begin.

The Whole Person and The Healthy Self

At the beginning of this chapter, I highlighted the utopian element in recovery discourse. This is not a vision of a perfect society where individuals flourish because of enlightened forms of social organisation, but an individual project of self-formation, in which happiness is found in the clear recognition of the difference between the self and other, and in an absence of lack within the self. It is a humanist ideal of individual self-sufficiency and completeness, combining a romantic belief in self-expression with the ideals of enterprise culture. The self in its highest form contains a rich but harmonious inner world of imagination and emotion, and this enables it to act effectively and productively in the world. Healthy personhood means finding fulfilment in these inner resources and then projecting the self outwards into the world. In contrast, the addict's mode of being is seen as driven by the need to incorporate outside objects into an empty inner space in order to feel whole.

The wholeness of the healthy and flourishing person is expressed as 'well-roundedness'. The self is thought of as a container for a set of 'potentials'. If these are developed the result is a 'fully functioning person', active in a range of different activities and relationships, someone who goes to the gym and also studies part time, who enjoys friendships and has a rewarding family life but also devotes time to meditation and prayer, who takes their career seriously but knows how to have fun. Again, addiction is the antithesis of the balanced and well-rounded life: the addict has neglected the range of her personal potentials in favour of a total obsession with one activity. The fully functioning person constituted in recovery discourse is a model of balance more than one of moderation. The ideal is the pursuit of self-development in a range of areas, as opposed to a narrow and restricted focus. What is excluded is the possibility of conflict between the demands of different aspects of life, or recognition that 'having it all' may be impossible and/or undesirable. Any limits on the chance to 'grow' are experienced as negative and oppressive.

The fantasy of balance is succinctly summarised in psychologist and therapist Sharon Wegscheider-Cruze's 'whole-person model' of health. Her understanding of the healthy, functioning person is represented as a circle cut into six equal pie-shaped pieces each symbolising a different aspect of being: the physical, emotional, mental, spiritual, social and volitional. The segments are equally important:

> When any one is incomplete or damaged, the entire circle loses its integrity . . . If we imagine for a moment that the circle is a wheel, it becomes clear what a strong effect deformity in one segment can have on the functioning of the whole.[24]

Wegscheider-Cruze's circular model of personhood includes a clearly defined boundary between the inner self and the outer world.

Recovery discourse produces the boundary 'where you end and I begin' as one of the crucial indicators of healthy personhood.[25] According to recovery discourse, addicts often lack a strong emotional boundary which enables the self to relate to others while retaining a sense of separateness. Although it is commonly stated that overly rigid boundaries are as harmful as excessively weak or amorphous ones, it is the need to establish and maintain stronger boundaries which is emphasised. The analogies used to describe the emotional and relational boundary between two selves stress the protective functions of such boundaries. The boundary around the self is compared to the skin around the body which keeps out invading organisms, or a nation's territorial border which is armed against foreign invasion. Another description compares a self with weak boundaries with a cell that has been invaded by cancer. The boundary of the self must keep what belongs outside out, so that what is inside, the raw material of the recovery process, can be worked on. Attempts to exercise power outside the boundary, to change other people and control the outside world, are diagnosed as signs of codependent or grandiose thinking, part of the addictive disease. The famous serenity prayer of Alcoholics Anonymous can be read as an expression of the importance placed on boundary recognition, of knowing the difference between self and other:

> God grant me the serenity to accept the things I cannot change,
> The courage to change the things I can,
> And the wisdom to know the difference.[26]

The prayer constructs the distinction between the changeable and the unchangeable as open and flexible; each individual 'I' must be the judge of their sphere of influence. Concealed is the fact that recovery discourse has already written the answer to the question of what the individual can and cannot change. Health means knowing that one can change oneself but not others, and certainly not the world.

Detachment and boundedness are also necessary prerequisites to the experience of genuine freedom. If balance is the organising principle, then freedom, understood in both negative and positive terms, is the content of the ideal self. First, there is freedom from the compulsions of addiction, from the power the addictive substance has over the self. In the discourse of recovery, relinquishment becomes an exercise of liberty: 'giving up cigarettes' is re-formed as 'breaking free from nicotine'. This negative freedom makes space for the possibility of freely choosing what one *really* wants, establishing the moral authority of the self and learning to follow one's own voice rather than listening to the dictates of external rules and authorities. Abstinence is therefore crucial, not because self-denial is inherently virtuous but because, for addicts, it is a necessary part of honouring the real needs of the self; the alien desire for the addictive substance or process must be removed so that access to genuine desires can be gained. The danger is that many external rules and authorities will have been interiorised. An action believed to be freely chosen, for example spending Christmas with one's parents, is actually a response to cultural beliefs and norms about families, love and the behaviour of good children, especially daughters. Psychotherapist Shirley Smith in her recovery guide *Set Yourself Free* describes the following of external rules and role expectations as imprisonment by labels and their accompanying 'shoulds' and 'oughts'.[27] This is a theme especially prevalent in codependency literature, since codependents are defined as people who are so busy living for and caring for others that they are unable to recognise their own needs and desires.

The placing of cultural norms under suspicion in the name of freedom and arguing against addiction in the name of the same freedom is a somewhat awkward position to maintain. The discourse of recovery in fact conforms to cultural norms and dominant beliefs about substance use, sexuality and relationships. References to peer group pressure and the desire to be popular are used to overcome this paradox. Using heroin or being sexually promiscuous can then be categorised as the consequences of paying too much attention to other people's expectations of how one should behave. Another paradox is that in recovery, freedom means creating and living by self-authored rules, but it is self-help discourse which defines what such rules and freedom look like. As Gary Greenberg has argued, recovery literature conceals its own position as authoritative 'other' to its audience of readers. Codependency literature in particular insists that sole authorship of one's life is the key to health, enjoining readers to liberate themselves from entanglements with other people. Yet these texts themselves act as 'co-authors' of their readers' narratives of self, summoning the reader into an already written narrative.[28] Setting aside the fact that the admonition to create and live by one's own rules is itself a cultural imperative, the individual rules that are possible and recognisable are highly circumscribed by the limits imposed by the discourse. Rules such as 'I will no longer recognise private property rights' or 'I will devote my life to wasting time' would surely be classified as expressions of pathology rather than the authentic self, even if they were self-chosen.

An individual's rules must be personally chosen, but also compatible with a liberal understanding of human nature and human flourishing. As befits a process of self-production, the attainment of freedom depends on an active and energetic engagement with the world. A strong sense of inner self reduces the need to find security in rigid routines and belief systems. Instead openness to change, spontaneity and curiosity are the hallmarks of the healthy person's relationship with the world. Creativity is valued in itself as a form of self-expression rather than in the value of what is created. *Off the Hook: How to Break Free of Addiction and Enjoy a New Way of Life* recommends activities for 'everyday creativity' including cooking, gardening, singing, playing a musical instrument, playing with children, dancing, writing letters or stories and painting.[29] A life of playful self-expression appears to fit in with an ethic of 'living for the moment', but here spontaneity and creativity are valued because they serve the goals of productivity and progress, with the healthy well-rounded self as the final product.

It is authenticity which is the ultimate condition of possibility for freeedom, and the result of freedom. Authenticity is located in the inner core of the self, the 'true' and unchanging part of the self that has been buried by the denial, deceptions and illusions of addiction but can be excavated in recovery. It is this 'inner kernel' which allows the discourse to talk of recovery as both rediscovery of an already existing authentic self and the making of a new healthy self. The inner core is rediscovered, which allows the whole self to be remade in its image. An authentic life is marked by transparency and consistency between the inner and the outer selves. In a healthy person, appearance and reality coincide; nothing is hidden, from oneself or others. Genuine desires and emotions emerge uncorrupted and undistorted from the inner self; one knows what one wants and what one feels.

If the addict is presented as the consummate actor, saying things he does not mean and pretending feelings he does not feel, the recovering addict must come out from behind the mask. In recovery, maturity is the ability to live in accordance with a singular personal truth that does not alter according to context. Meeting different role expectations may be necessary, but it is a necessary evil rather than a skill to be promoted, as illustrated by a codependency text's description of the consequences of dedicating your life to being 'good':

> The roles of adulthood become stereotypes; grown men just strive harder to be good husbands, good fathers, good breadwinners, while grown women strive harder to be good wives, good moms, good nurturers. But these are just roles to play, a script or a set of rules. These people may be virtuous and laudable in their roles, but their personal development is still incomplete. Fulfilling a role creates the part of a self that follows external rules, but it doesn't develop a grown-up, wholesome inner self.[30]

In recovery discourse, a world made up of people committed to expressing their authentic selves is viewed as desirable because it is assumed that authentic selves are both inherently good and fundamentally identical. Individuals each living according to their own self-created rules will nevertheless recognise the same overarching truths, and most conflict will be able to be resolved through communication and compromise. As I argued in Chapter 6, there is little or no place for the alterity of a concrete other in such conceptualisations of health.

It is not that the goals of freedom, all-round development and creativity as expressed in the identity of the recovering addict are necessarily bad. They represent, however, only one form of selfhood, produced as an ideal of health so that deviation from it becomes a disease or disorder that requires remedy. The cultural and historical specificity of the model, and the costs of forming ourselves in its image, are obscured. Alternative modes of being are either devalued or remain unthinkable. Why is the 'well rounded' individual any more admirable or any better 'functioning' than the passionately obsessed? Recovery discourse not only pathologises the addicted and the compulsive, but rejects the existence of benign eccentricity: the lives of the bodybuilder, the misanthropic loner, the tireless social butterfly, the dandy, are all reduced to expressions of distortion and lack.

The emphasis on wholeness, while seemingly uncontentious, also acts to pathologise experiences which may be experienced as positive or valuable in their ambiguity. Feelings of dislocation, of fragmentation and unreality, can be sought after as life-enhancing or transformative as well as being evidence of disease and disorder. The sense that one has dissolved into the other has been celebrated as rapture. And, as Greenberg has stated, the ideal of the individual as the sole author of the story of their life ignores the significance and the role of those narratives which 'claim us ... without our choosing'.[31] It is not so much that we are 'contaminated' by such entanglements with others, but that they make us what we are. In spite of its celebration of 'individuality', homogenisation is one of the effects of recovery discourse. Underneath their differences, the masks they have adopted to hide their pain, everyone is good and everyone is good in the same way. What is more, their fundamental needs and true desires can be confidently predicted on the basis of this goodness, and again they are more or less the same. Everyone 'really' wants love and self-esteem. No one really wants drugs or anonymous sex or any other unimproving experiences.

Self-Knowledge, Truth and Conduct

The freedom and authenticity of the recovering self depends on a particular form of self-knowledge and self-awareness. To create a life that is healthy, happy and meaningful, the recovering addict must unearth and identify the truth of himself. This is done by turning inwards and isolating the essence: his enduring traits, deeply held beliefs and values and deeply buried feelings. Interestingly, it is emotional capacity rather than rationality which is central to human identity in this discourse. Neither is knowing the self about listing achievements, actions, relationships or interests, except if they reveal underlying truths. These surface qualities are in fact often seen as obstacles to self-knowledge, the power and authority of the successful lawyer and respected father conceals the lack of self-esteem and insecurity at the man's core. Hence the project of knowing oneself, carried out in contemplation and solitude, contrasts with the activity and routines of staying sober in early recovery. Smith states that once you stop outer distractions, 'the feelings you have suppressed and repressed will arise within you. Allow yourself to feel them all. Especially, allow yourself to grieve over the pain of your lost childhood. As you move through this pain, you'll begin to experience an increasing sense of inner freedom and joy'.[32]

The critical approach I have been taking suggests that the experience of the inner, as a discrete and bounded space filled with unmediated feelings, is produced by the discourse of self-examination. The techniques and written exercises offered by self-help texts as ways of helping 'you to let go of destructive thoughts, feelings and behaviour patterns, determine and express your own reality and thereby discover who you really are', represent the instilling of a habit of introspection and a practice of self-expression. Such techniques are just as programmatic as the exercise routine, eating plan and daily schedule of early recovery.

The form of self-knowledge which readers of these texts are guided toward is highly specialised. The truth which lies at the heart of recovery is the addict's identity as someone who is powerless over the substance or process in question, and whose powerlessness is the result of an incurable disease. Paradoxically, accepting powerlessness brings a source of power: a demand that cannot be refused. All the texts are adamant that someone who is in recovery must always put their recovery first, before family, friends or work. The addict must do whatever has do be done to protect his or her recovery.

Accepting this truth about the self is only the first step of self-knowledge. In the twelve steps of AA, number four, 'making a searching and fearless moral inventory of ourselves', is regarded as the foundation of the ongoing and honest self-assessment and self-acceptance necessary for recovery. While the inventory involves a review of past behaviour, the point of the exercise is to reinterpret this behaviour as the expression of broad character traits. One handbook lists twenty-eight headings such as false pride, humility, perfectionism, ability to admit mistakes, phoniness, being yourself, selfishness, sharing, resentment, forgiveness, fear and acceptance, under which the addict is to write specific examples and descriptions of incidents which illustrate these qualities.[33] Through this exercise, events and interactions are removed from their social context and converted into timeless and abstract attributes located in the self. Once the inventory has been taken, the next step is admitting to God, to oneself and to another person 'the exact nature of our wrongs' based on the inventory. Although the inventory is supposed to include good points as well as bad, the focus is on admitting wrongdoing and mistakes, and therefore gaining relief from guilt. For example, while self-deception is damaging to the self, the emphasis is on how the addict's dishonesty has damaged others. In traditional Alcoholics Anonymous literature, self-knowledge is defined largely as honesty about one's faults and misdoings. Humility and modesty are promoted as important virtues for alcoholics to practise.

In contrast with official AA literature, recovery discourse influenced by humanist psychology, feminism and new age spirituality concentrates much more on recognising feelings such as loneliness, shame, anger and guilt and identifying their genesis, usually in early childhood experiences. Here the recovering addict is much more the victim of others' bad conduct and their own lack of self-awareness than the perpetrator of dishonesty. And rather than a result of not facing one's faults, self-delusion is constructed as an ultimately dysfunctional but understandable attempt to cope with pain and loss: 'The root of addiction lies in *how* we have been hurt and whether we have been able to heal those hurts' (emphasis in original). Thus, the shame of being a lesser being in a patriarchal society leads a woman to numb herself with drugs. The knowledge she lacks about herself is that she is a worthy person who has the right to feel angry because her needs for respect and independence have not been met. The major problem faced by addicted individuals is lack of self-esteem: 'You have addictions because you feel bad about yourself, and you don't like yourself because you're addicted'.[34]

Noting the differences between the contemporary recovery movement and traditional AA discourses highlights the historical specificity of models of self-knowledge, and denaturalises them. In the contemporary model, understanding oneself as a subject defined by needs and emotions is the sign of the self-knower. According to Smith, one of the most difficult questions for people to answer is, 'what do you want?'. Therefore, recovering addicts are encouraged to work on identifying their unfulfilled needs, because it was these needs which gave rise to negative feelings about the self, which then led to 'self-medication' in the form of addictive behaviour. Self-examination is taken to be successful when the recovering addict realises that he or she is worthy of love and nurture, and learns to meet her needs and accept and express her feelings, both negative and positive. The idea that identifying and meeting their own needs is the fundamental purpose of a human being, and the key to finding freedom, is one of the surprising elements of recovery discourse. In *Off the Hook*, Sweet provides a good example of how this logic operates. She bases her recovery plan on learning to meet 'real needs', which are categorised into the emotional, physical, sexual, social, creative, intellectual and spiritual, echoing the 'whole person' ideal discussed earlier. The task of recovery is to learn to distinguish these needs from 'frozen needs', which are those left over from childhood experiences of lack. For instance, being unloved or neglected as a baby results in an insatiable need for love and an unfillable feeling of emptiness in the adult. Frozen needs, unlike real needs, can never be met and the only way to end the pattern of distress is to release the repressed feelings associated with them. Once the individual begins this process and starts looking after their real needs by eating good food, making new friends, taking up new hobbies and expressing their feelings, self-esteem blossoms and positive, joyful living without addictions becomes possible.[35]

But the problem of how to 'get in touch with' the true self and its emotions and needs after years of repression and alienation remains. Sweet puts her faith in the 'inner voice', which is an infallible authority on authentic feelings and genuine desires. Luckily, the inner voice speaks the same language as the outer person, and is unfailingly co-operative and obliging. If you close your eyes and ask yourself, 'How am I feeling, right now?' it will answer. Conversation with your inner voice should become part of your daily life, Sweet advises readers to keep asking themselves how they feel as they move through the day, interact with people and carry out different tasks.[36] Through this form of dialogue, genuine desires can be disentangled from the 'noise' of outside interference. And crucially, because what one genuinely desires is what is good for you, it is never too difficult to put this knowledge into appropriate action.

The notion of the 'inner child' is another technology enabling the truth of the self to be located and made concrete. Inner child therapies have become a staple of recovery discourse, largely through the work of prolific self-help author John Bradshaw. Briefly, the theory is that adult survivors of childhood abuse, neglect and dysfunctional families are stuck at the developmental stages of childhood when their needs were not met by their caretakers. Since inner child therapists estimate that 95 per cent of families are dysfunctional, most of us are inhabited by wounded inner children who are still acting out their unresolved traumas and vainly trying to have their needs met, via addictions and compulsive behaviour. To recover from addiction one needs to reclaim and re-parent the inner child, so that it can become a healed and creative 'wonder child'.[37]

Smith's version of inner child work constructs a whole internal family which populates an individual's interiority. Instead of representing past wounds, the inner family acts as a reservoir of wisdom and information about the self. Each member is a valuable source of information about feelings and desires, and has different qualities and talents. The inner child is spontaneous, creative and loves to play, the inner adolescent is curious and adventurous, the inner adult is mature and dependable, the inner functional parents are patient and nurturing. In addition there are the inner dysfunctional parents, who are critical and judgmental. The formulation of the inner family is another expression of the ideal of balance. It is important to develop a relationship with each of the family members because those you ignore will end up dominating your life. Each has a different contribution to make and will foster the recognition of the range of your strengths. Communication with inner family members can occur through visualisation, journal writing and drawing. Unlike the 'real' family, regular meetings with the inner family can be easily slotted into a busy daily schedule. You can dialogue with your inner family members in the shower, while driving, while working or riding on the bus. Smith adds that the answers received from the members of your inner family should not be censored or analysed. The first things that come to mind are usually the right answers for you.[38] These dialogues allow the inner self to be experienced as 'real' in a quotidian context.

What is noteworthy is the centrality of language in these processes of self-discovery. While the true inner self is valued because it is supposedly outside the social, it still operates in ways that are straightforwardly accessible and intelligible. The admonition not to censor or analyse is hardly necessary as messages from inner selves inevitably have appropriate content and recognisable form. Although the emotional and the rational are assumed to be oppositional in this discourse, the feelings expressed by the inner self operate within familiar laws of causality and logic, thus they can always be interpreted and are always meaningful. The origins of troubling symptoms can always be unearthed by tracing the chain of influence back to the 'beginning', that is, to remembered (and presumably coherent and accurate) childhood memories. The remarkable cooperativeness of the inner self, and its easy harnessing to the project of self-fulfilment can be appreciated by making a brief comparison to the psychoanalytic model of the unconscious. The unconscious as described by Freud was governed by an entirely different logic to that of the conscious system. Unknowable, except through the analysis of dreams and neurotic symptoms, the unconscious does not distinguish between reality and fantasy, does not recognise time or logic or morality.[39]

Recovering addicts are constantly reassured that feelings are neither good nor bad, even though 'society' views emotions such as envy, aggression and hate as unacceptable. Part of recovery is learning that feelings should not be feared, and allowing oneself to express anger, show grief and accept feelings of jealousy, envy and desire for revenge.[40] But the price of validating feelings in this way is that the emotional realm is evacuated of its alterity. We are told not be frightened of feelings but to value them, because, as they are constituted in recovery discourse, they are not frightening or alienating. Instead they are tools in the project of self-improvement. The potential transgressiveness of imaginative and interior life is defused by the cosy image of the inner family.

While visualisation, drawing and free writing in journals are suggested as ways to access the emotions, the texts also contain directed written exercises to be completed by readers, exercises which are reminiscent of those found at the end of each chapter in school text books. Readers have to fill in answers to lists of questions on topics like facing your emotions (Are there any emotions you fear facing? If so write them down. Why do you fear them?); do quizzes to find out how well you know your emotions (Are you frightened about people knowing the real you?); check themselves against lists of common defences used to avoid feelings (I use humour, I chew gum, I intellectualise); and complete charts on how different members of their family expressed feelings. Since it is through writing (and writing which follows strict conventions of grammar and syntax) that so much of the detailed work on the self is carried out, it is not surprising that Sweet uses the term 'emotional literacy' to describe the process of coming to understand our feelings.[41]

It is ironic that writing, and the type of written expression taught at school as part of the formation as good citizens, is the key to accessing the inner world of feelings. Some texts, particularly those which utilise the theory of the inner child, advocate writing with the non-dominant hand when expressing the thoughts and feelings of the inner self.[42] But the mediation of language itself is not problematised. Examples of letters written by inner children are in childish script using simple sentences and grammar, but the thoughts expressed are those of an adult, using adult conceptions of the child-like. A letter from a wounded inner toddler reproduced in a self-help text reads: 'Dear Big Richard, Please come and get me, I've been in a closet for forty years, I'm terrified, I need you. Little Richard'.[43]

Rather than ways of revealing the inner self to the outer, these written and verbal exercises can be seen as training in a regularised discipline of self-perception and self-expression, and a powerful production of interior forces as familiar, benign and ordered. They ensure that the inner voices and authentic feelings accessed are not unruly or chaotic and do not challenge social and cultural regimes of the normal. Just as exercise routines and a nutritious diet produce the healthy body, the healthy person emerges from routines and regimes of self-interrogation, self-description and self-interpretation focused on a set of highly invested and culturally specific feelings.

Matters of Habit

Despite the privileging of inner transformation in recovery discourse, the practices of recovery are matters of habit. The subjectivity of the recovering addict is assembled from the outside in, through repeated actions ranging from daily exercise to the identification of authentic desires. Through these techniques of the self, an inner self is produced that can be continually judged and worked on, in the name of freedom and health. As others have suggested, the concept of habit can provide a useful challenge to such totalised and interiorised models of the self, as well as disrupting some of the oppositional binaries which produce the addict subjectivity. The purpose of viewing practices of recovery from the perspective of habit is not to reveal an alternative truth of recovery; it is rather a strategic move.

Mariana Valverde points out that the realm of the habitual has lacked prestige as an object of philosophical and psychological inquiry at least since the nineteenth century.[44] In contemporary life 'habit' is used in everyday reflection about self-conduct and the conduct of our friends and family. Guides to child rearing, pet training and health improvement through diet and exercise address themselves to habit formation and reformation. However, popular psychology often regards habits merely as means to higher ends, perhaps because the concept implies a certain triviality and/or superficiality, compared with the medicalised language of addiction and the moral discourse of principles and values. Stephen Covey's best-selling management guide *The Seven Habits of Highly Effective People* is a notable example. Despite its title, the text's central message is the need to base one's life on 'correct' universal and unchanging principles, and it insists that true change can only work from the inside out.

Analyses of the habitual are also largely absent from recovery discourse, and acknowledgement of the power of habit to effect change is muted compared with the celebration of ideals of freedom and authenticity. The place of habit in the unusual four-stage continuum of patterns, habits, compulsions and addictions outlined by feminist self-help author Charlotte Davis Kasl clarifies the minor role the concept plays in addiction discourse, but also points to the concept's utility in disrupting its certainties. Kasl's continuum describes different levels of habitual behaviour: from patterns to addiction, the behaviour becomes increasingly difficult to give up, and the amount of discomfort experienced if the impulse is resisted grows. Habits are dealt with in one brief paragraph. They can be overcome, Kasl states, with a bit of effort. The slight discomfort which ensues quickly disappears. Many who have tried to change seemingly insignificant and minor bad habits would no doubt challenge Kasl's assessment of the strength of their grip. But her placement of habit somewhere between freely chosen actions and addiction is significant. As both Eve Sedgwick and Valverde have noted, in contrast to addiction, habit offers a version of repeated actions that does not rely on or reproduce absolutes of compulsion and free will. Habits are not unchangeable attributes of the individual; with effort they can be reformed and controlled. But neither are they made up of freely or deliberately chosen actions. Unlike addictions, habits are not, by virtue of being habits, either good or bad; rather there are good and bad habits. In Valverde's image, habits are 'grooves that line body and soul' which confound the binary of free choice versus determination. Creating a good habit requires much conscious effort, but once the groove has been produced the acts which make up a habitual pattern are not consciously willed.[45]

Because the habitual occupies the space between freedom and compulsion, it offers a way of contesting the constitution of recovery as the one true path to health, happiness and freedom. On one hand, viewing recovery as habit suggests that the recovering addict is not free according to the standards of recovery discourse. She is acting from habit, following routines established by repetitive thoughts and actions set out by an external authority. On the other hand, recovery is a practice of freedom, in that its techniques are applied by individuals to themselves, with the goal of enhancing their capacity for free choice. But such practices are not outside power by virtue of being uncompelled; they are examples of the kind of seductive mechanisms which govern us through our choices. Rather than a standard of health, the ideal of the freely choosing self is a specific norm, against which we are urged to measure ourselves and against which we will inevitably find ourselves wanting. The rigorous surveillance and interrogation of feelings and desires I have described as techniques of recovery ensure the continuing discovery of hidden levels of unhealthy compromise and marks of inauthenticity which must be rectified.

Regarding regimes of recovery as matters of habit and conduct is a way of resisting the incitement to search ever deeper inside ourselves for meaning, to work harder for fulfilment. For Kasl, habits are of little interest because they do not have hidden meanings and do not implicate the inner self. Unlike compulsions and addictions, which require insight into buried feelings and conflicts to be remedied, habits can be altered without any excavation or examination of the self. It is this very characteristic of habits, their location on the surface of the subject, which can disrupt the understanding of addiction as the expression of a fixed, unified and fundamentally pathological identity. As Valverde has noted, we can have an indefinite number of habits, and they need not be connected nor understood as expressions of a singular, centralised or deep identity.[46]

In recovery discourse, the addict identity operates as a master identity which comes to explain everything about the subject: not only his inability to control his alcohol or drug use, but all his past failures and disappointments, his poor relationships, his lack of self-esteem, his career difficulties and so on. The more recent identities of 'codependent' and 'adult child of an alcoholic' extend the scope of addiction even further. The addict's disease not only determines his existence, it also determines the identity of those close to him.

Thinking instead about excessive drug and alcohol use in terms of habit constitutes them as problems of conduct (with sometimes severe consequences). While this move may disturb some who see in it a disregard for the profound pain and costs of addiction, it has the benefit of seeing the addicted subject as other than defined by a lifelong and all-encompassing sickness. Thinking about problematic activities in terms of habits and conduct, while no doubt bringing its own problems and impasses, could open up the possibilities for a range of ethical self-formations not confined by binaries of health and pathology. Addiction and recovery could be thought of not as disease and cure or problem and solution, but as different ways of marking the self and the body with grooves.

8

Conclusion

WHAT IS WRONG WITH ADDICTION? A tempting response to this question is to take what seems like a step back and first attempt to determine what addiction is. After all, it surely makes sense to define the entity before evaluating its qualities and consequences. Of course the identity of addiction is equally difficult to tie down, even though there is no shortage of confident assertions of its true nature from neurobiologists, psychologists, therapists and recovering addicts. Its characteristics, location and potential objects are all subject to apparently irresolvable contestation and uncertainty. But as I hope the foregoing chapters have shown, the questions of what addiction is and what is wrong with it are difficult, perhaps impossible to separate. The statement of identity is not prior to the attachment of value, because pathology, disorder and inauthenticity are intrinsic to the contemporary concept of addiction. The excessive or otherwise troubling conduct of the afflicted individual is read as the expression of physical, psychological and moral disorder, which are in turn linked together in the totalised and distinct identity of addict. The addicted individual is constructed as a pathological subject, one whose body, self, desires and conduct require examination, interpretation and rectification through various regimes of treatment, cure and/or self-transformation.

Rather than add to the crowded field of discourses asserting the truth of addiction and the necessity of its elimination for individual and social health, this book has focused on the production of addiction as an object of knowledge and the resulting organisation of diverse arrays of problems and harms into unified disorders of the individual. It has explored addiction as a mechanism through which the bodies, conduct and desires of individuals are both formed and regulated. In the name of longevity, productivity, balance and freedom we are enjoined to examine ourselves and others for signs of addiction, for evidence of impaired control, imperfect authenticity and compromised autonomy. Discourses of addiction not only set out criteria by which some people are defined as outside the realm of proper and viable subjectivity, they also produce the right sort of body, the right way to live, the right way to be and the right sort of relationship to have to oneself and to others. But these ideals are promoted as the universal requirements of health rather than specific ethical formations.

One of the catalysts for this project was the proliferation of addictions in recent years. I have not been able to examine the whole range of activities now classified as potentially addictive which include gambling, work, exercise, and surfing the internet, but the cases of smoking, sex addiction and compulsive eating, as well as the examination of recovery guides, have highlighted some of the ambiguities which emerge when the model of addiction expands outside the realm of drug use. When applied to behaviours which are regarded as necessary, positive or benign, the diagnosis of addiction becomes even more clearly connected to evaluations of motivations and feelings and to wide-ranging programs of healthy living.

The argument developed in this book suggests that the expansion of addiction discourses should be resisted or at least questioned. The development of new and wideranging addictive pathologies cannot help but strengthen the hold of medical expertise and therapeutic authority over people's conduct and desires. Addiction attribution encourages the routine application of standards of the normal and the healthy to almost all aspects of our lives. The dualisms which organise addiction discourse such as freedom/compulsion, natural/artificial, truth/falsity and self/other are reinforced and reproduced.

In part, the growth of addiction demands scrutiny because it is a notion through which specifically liberal forms of political power and government regulation operate efficiently and seductively. Addiction is part of a whole field of expert knowledges and programs which aim to form and govern individuals as healthy, happy and productive citizens. In this regime of the self, consumption as well as production becomes a site for the constitution of the autonomous, self-controlled and self-motivating individual.

However, one might wonder if a potential benefit of the widening net of addiction could be a decrease in the stigmatisation and pathologisation of those who are still taken for granted as the truly, genuinely, literally addicted—those dependent on illicit drugs and alcohol. Unfortunately, while recovering smokers, sex and love addicts and compulsive eaters claim that their disorders are analogous to alcohol and drug dependence and are as controlling and damaging as heroin addiction, this has not produced a politics or an ethics which emphasises the similarities between the normal and respectable on the one hand and the illicit on the other. The drug addict remains a firmly marginalised other, subject to profound legal, social and medical discipline. Neither does urging the recognition of sex and food as dangerous drugs for some seem to influence the demonisation of certain drugs as uniquely physically and morally dangerous for all. Similarly, in addiction science the brain has emerged as an organ which is primed to make connections with drugs, but the message that addicts are different and drugs are foreign to the human body is still reinforced.

One consequence of this book's approach of mapping the territory of addiction in both popular and medical fields is that similarities and continuities tend to be emphasised more than differences and disconnections. While I have focused on the specificities of different sites of addiction, I have also spoken of addiction and the addict as unified notions structured around concepts such as disease, disorder and loss of control. However it seems important in concluding to speak of the differences between addicts and between addictions. The daily lives of those dependent on illicit drugs are subject to medico-legal forces not encountered by smokers, drinkers and the various varieties of 'non-substance' addictions. This is not to say that diagnosing oneself as a sex or love addict, attending support meetings, embarking on therapy and a program of work on the self are outside the operation of power simply because they are voluntary and to some degree freely chosen. Indeed, the sense that the desire for recovery comes from inside the self is a large part of what makes it so compelling. Neither should the wide array of formal and informal regulations which attempt to control who drinks and smokes and where and when they can do so be overlooked. However, the social location of illicit drug users is fixed in a unique frame of criminality and moral bankruptcy. The continuing emphasis on prohibition and punishment in government drug control increases the costs of these addictions. Moreover, drug users are assumed to be addicts, and addicts are presumed to be slaves of an all-powerful substance who can only act to harm themselves and others.

As I have outlined, understandings of addiction as a disease or condition in which the individual loses their freedom of will and is controlled by an external and alien force are found in both popular and medical discourses. Such externalisation and distancing of addiction from the self can lift a burden from victims, as it can undermine the view of the addict as a bad person who is simply unwilling to change and does not care about the pain they cause. Because it posits a distinction between the disease of addiction and the self, it also seems to offer the possibility of locating and liberating a true and innocent self which has remained intact behind the alien force of addiction. Such a magical return to innocence was celebrated in the story of the 'instant heroin cure' discussed at the beginning of this book. The idea that the young woman was suffering from a brain disorder allowed her true self to be separated from the addiction, free to re-emerge unaltered as she woke from the treatment. According to the story, it was as if her three years of 'agony and degradation' never happened, or at least happened to someone else.

But the conceiving of addicted subjectivity in terms of true and false selves also has high costs. The addict is infantilised and pathologised by the presumption of powerlessness, 'propelled into a narrative of inexorable decline and fatality'.[1] Rather than a subject she becomes 'the proper object' of therapeutic interventions of various kinds. Coercive practices can be justified as endeavours to assist the true self and respect its genuine desires, while wishes expressed by the individual which do not conform to the truth of addiction can be dismissed as symptoms of the disease. For some the outcomes can be positive, but for others, especially those unwilling or unable to fit into the category of innocent victim, the medical and legal interventions mobilised by such discourses could be far from benign.

The costs of such discourses and practices of addiction are distributed unequally, not only amongst different forms of addiction, but also according to differences of class, race, sexuality and gender. For example, disease models of alcoholism and addiction seem to heighten rather than undermine misogynist discourses about pregnant women who drink and take drugs, especially if they are poor and non-white.[2] In the context of the 'war against drugs', insisting that addiction is a medical disorder does not answer the question of who will get to count as deserving victims and who will count as criminals threatening the nation's well-being and preying on its youth.

Notions of addiction can operate as fantasies of transcendence, circulating the hope that we can transcend our physical existence, escape our histories and be cleansed of our pasts, while 'remaining (or becoming more fully) ourselves'.[3] But like all dreams of transcendence, such escapes are only available to some.

Notes

Introduction: What's Wrong with Addiction?

1. Nutt, 'Addiction', p. 31; Alcoholics Anonymous, *The Big Book*, p. 18.
2. Wodak & Owens, *Drug Prohibition*.
3. See: Goodin, *No Smoking*, p. 99; May, *Addiction and Grace*, p. 3.
4. Valverde, *Diseases of the Will*, p. 17.
5. Peele, 'A Moral Vision of Addiction', p. 228.
6. Sedgwick, 'Epidemics of the Will', p. 586.
7. Room, 'Dependence and Society', pp. 135–6.
8. Definitions of health cited in Aggleton, *Health*, p. 9.
9. Peterson & Lupton, *The New Public Health*.
10. Rose, 'Medicine, History and the Present', p. 67.
11. See: Levine, 'The Discovery of Addiction' and Berridge & Edwards, *Opium and the People* for influential historical accounts of the emergence of alcoholism and addiction as medical disorders. See Alasuutari, *Desire and Craving* and Room, 'Dependence and Society' for discussions of alcoholism and addiction as sociocultural concepts and discourses connected to Western models of subjectivity and identity.
12. Redfield, 'Introduction', p. 3.
13. Forbes, *False Fixes*.
14. See Rose, 'Authority and the Genealogy of Subjectivity', pp. 299–300.
15. Foucault, *Discipline and Punish*, p. 27.
16. Foucault, 'Truth & Power', p. 73.
17. Butler, *Bodies That Matter*, p. 3.
18. Shaffer, 'The Disease Controversy', p. 66 and 'The Most Important Unresolved Issue in the Addictions'. In the 1980s Howard Shaffer argued that the addiction field was in a preparadigmatic stage of scientific development, judging the inability of the different disciplines involved in addiction studies to agree on a common paradigm as a symptom of the field's youth. However, more than ten years later, he observed that the field remained in a state of conceptual chaos.
19. See: Room, 'The Alcohologist's Addiction'; Goodyear, 'Unresolved Questions about Alcoholism'; Jurd, 'Why Alcoholism is a Disease' and 'Alcoholism as a Disease'; Miller, 'Drug and Alcohol Addiction as a Disease'; Peele, *The Meaning of Addiction*; Fingarette, *Heavy Drinking*; Stockwell & Saunders, 'Alcohol and Drug Dependence'; Maltzman, 'Is Alcoholism a Disease?'; Meyer, 'The Disease called Addiction'. A particularly interesting exchange on nominalism, realism and the disease question is found in the *Journal of Psychoactive Drugs* (Maltzman, 'Why Alcoholism is a Disease' and 'Reply to Lilienfeld'; Lilienfeld, 'Reply to Maltzman').
20. Stockwell, 'Slaying the Disease Model Dragon—Again?'.

1 The Substance of Drugs

1 Barnao, 'I Woke Up . . . Cured of Heroin', pp. 30–4.
2 Hall et al., 'Editorial'. Naltrexone has since been approved in Australia for the treatment of opiate dependence and alcohol dependence. Rapid detoxification and naltrexone maintenance are available at a number of private clinics.
3 Barnao, 'I Woke Up . . . Cured of Heroin', p. 34.
4 Kleiman, *Against Excess*, pp. 32–3.
5 See DeGrandpre & White, 'Drug Dialectics', Wodak & Owens, *Drug Prohibition*, Fox & Matthews, *Drugs Policy*. See also Reinarman and Levine, *Crack in America* for an examination of the late 1980s crack scare in the United States, a vivid example of anti-drug rhetoric connecting a supposedly virulently addictive drug with moral decay and social disintegration amongst an already stigmatised group.
6 Ward et al., *Key Issues*.
7 Leser, 'The Way Out?', p. 16.
8 Derrida, 'Plato's Pharmacy'.
9 Douglas, *Purity and Danger*.
10 Cohen, *The Chemical Brain*, p. 64.
11 Johns, 'What is Dependence', p. 5; Uelman, G. F. & Haddox, V. G., *Drug Abuse and the Law Sourcebook*, Clark Boardman Co., New York, 1988 cited in Husak, *Drugs and Rights*, p. 20.
12 United Nations, *World Drug Report*, p. 10.
13 Husak, *Drugs and Rights*, p. 26.
14 Derrida, 'The Rhetoric of Drugs', p. 2.
15 Ron Siegel argues that the distinction between medical and non-medical drugs should be dissolved, because all drugs act to help people adjust to changes in their environments. Siegel, *Intoxication*.
16 Canguilhem, *The Normal and the Pathological*.
17 These issues are sensitively explored by Peter Kramer (*Listening to Prozac*, pp. xv–xvi) who uses the term 'cosmetic psychopharmacology' to describe the use of Prozac to make people 'better than well'.
18 See: Madden, 'Effects of Drugs of Dependence'; Schuckit, *Drug and Alcohol Abuse*.
19 DeGrandpre & White, 'Drug Dialectics', p. 45. The focus text is Julien's *A Primer of Drug Action*. Interestingly, in a more recent edition of the handbook (1998), Julien does not explicitly discuss drug classification, and his chapters are organised according to a mix of scientific and social drug categories.
20 Jellinek, *The Disease Concept of Alcoholism*, pp. 40, 147; Blocker, *American Temperance Movements*, pp. 146–7. See also Cahalan, 'Implications of the Disease Concept of Alcoholism', p. 51; Page, 'The Origins of Alcohol Studies'; Room, 'The Alcohologist's Addiction'.
21 American Psychiatric Association, *Diagnostic and Statistical Manual*, 3rd edn, p. 173; Van Dyke & Byck, 'Cocaine', p. 118; Doweiko, *Concepts of Chemical Dependency*, pp. 15, 93 and citing Kirsch, p. 86; Cohen, S. 'Reinforcement and Rapid Delivery Systems: Understanding Adverse Consequences of Cocaine' in N. J. Kozel & E. H. Adams (eds), *Cocaine Use in America: Epidemiologic and Clinical Perspectives*, National Institute on Drug Abuse, Rockville, 1985 cited in Peele & Brodsky, *The Truth About Addiction and Recovery*, p. 73.
22 Hyman, 'Drug Abuse & Addiction', p. 1.
23 Peele, *The Meaning of Addiction*, p. 1.
24 See: MacAndrew & Edgerton, *Drunken Comportment*; Marlatt & Rohsenow, 'Cognitive Processes in Alcohol Use'; Zinberg, *Drug, Set and Setting*, p. x; Peele, *The Meaning of Addiction*, p. 69.

[25] Peele, *The Diseasing of America* and *The Meaning of Addiction*; Orford, *Excessive Appetites*; Room, 'Dependence and Society', p. 134.

[26] Wilson, 'Introduction', p. 11.

[27] Peele, *The Meaning of Addiction*, p. 19.

[28] Leshner, 'Addiction Is a Brain Disease, and It Matters'.

[29] Wilson, 'On the Nature of Neurology', p. 59.

[30] Singer, 'Introduction', p. ii.

[31] Duden, *Disembodying Women*, pp. 15–18.

[32] Ibid, p. 20.

[33] Grant et al., 'Activation of Memory-Circuits During Cue-Elicited Cocaine Craving'.

[34] Swan, 'NIDA Brain Imaging Research Links Cue-Induced Craving to Structures Involved in Memory'.

[35] Peter Cohen uses this example in his discussion of craving and desire, 'Desires for Cocaine', p. 212.

[36] See: Leshner, 'NIDA's Brain Imaging Studies Serve as Powerful Tools to Improve Drug Abuse Treatment'; Swan, 'NIDA Brain Imaging Research Links Cue-Induced Craving to Structures Involved in Memory'.

[37] Cohen, *The Chemical Brain*, p. 115.

[38] Seymour & Smith, *Drugfree*, p. 50.

[39] Derrida, 'The Rhetoric of Drugs', p. 6.

[40] Cohen, *The Chemical Brain*, pp. 40–1, 116; National Institute on Drug Abuse, *Mind Over Matter*, p. 11.

[41] Ronell, 'Our Narcotic Modernity', pp. 70–1, emphasis in original.

[42] Concar, 'Prisoners of Pleasure', pp. 29–30; Nesse & Berridge, 'Psychoactive Drug Use in Evolutionary Perspective', p. 63; National Institute on Drug Abuse, *Mind Over Matter*, p. 2; Derrida, 'The Rhetoric of Drugs', p. 7.

[43] Julius, D. 'NIDA's Naltrexone Research Program' in D. Julius & p. Renault (eds), *Narcotic Antagonists: Naltrexone* (NIDA Research Monograph no. 9), National Institute of Drug Abuse, Rockville, cited in Mattick & Hall, *A Treatment Outline for Approaches to Opioid Dependence*, p. 43; Tai & Blaine, 'Naltrexone'.

[44] Deleuze, 'Ethology'. My understanding of Deleuze (and Deleuze and Guattari) is indebted to the interpretations of Patton, 'Metamorpho-Logic' and Grosz, *Volatile Bodies*, pp. 166–73.

[45] Deleuze & Guattari, *A Thousand Plateaus*, pp. 158, 150.

[46] Ibid, p. 150; Grosz, *Volatile Bodies*, pp. 170–1.

[47] Deleuze, *Spinoza*, p. 22.

2 Reading the Signs of Disorder: Diagnosing Dependence

[1] See: O'Connor, 'Routine Screening and Initial Assessment', p. 43; Kinney, *Clinical Manual of Substance Abuse*, p. 7; Valverde, *Diseases of the Will*, p. 25.

[2] Miller, *Addiction Psychiatry*, pp. 19, 24.

[3] Valverde, *Diseases of the Will*, p. 28.

[4] Jellinek, 'Phases of Alcohol Addiction'; Edwards, 'Drinking in Longitudinal Perspective', p. 178.

[5] Jellinek, 'Phases of Alcohol Addiction', pp. 678–83; West & Kinney, 'An Overview of Substance Use and Abuse', pp. 29–30; Maltzman, 'Why Alcoholism is a Disease', p. 28.

[6] The ideas set out by the WHO Working Group were a reworking of the alcohol dependence syndrome proposed by Edwards and Gross in 'Alcohol Dependence'; World Health Organization (WHO), *The ICD-10 Classification of Diseases and*

Related Health Problems, p. 321; WHO, *The ICD-10 Classification of Mental and Behavioural Disorders: Diagnostic Criteria for Research*, p. 57; American Psychiatric Association, *Diagnostic and Statistical Manual of Mental Disorders*, pp. 181, 176.

[7] Room, 'Alcohol and Drug Disorders in the International Classification of Diseases', p. 309. For examples of US medical texts, see: Kinney, *Clinical Manual of Substance Abuse*; Landry, *Understanding Drugs of Abuse*.

[8] Jaffe, 'Current Concepts of Addiction', p. 11.

[9] Room, 'Alcohol and Drug Disorders in the International Classification of Diseases', p. 313.

[10] Kirk & Kutchins, *The Selling of DSM*; Goodman, 'Pragmatic Assessment and Multi-theoretical Classification', p. 296; Room, 'The Alcohologist's Addiction', p. 1053.

[11] Goodman, 'Pragmatic Assessment and Multitheoretical Classification'.

[12] Edwards, 'Alcoholism Treatment', p. 309.

[13] This point is argued by Shaw, 'A Critique of the Concept of Alcohol Dependence Syndrome'; see also Stockwell and Saunders, 'Alcohol and Drug Dependence' for a debate on the utility of the dependence syndrome concept.

[14] Moore, 'Deconstructing "Dependence"', pp. 462, 484–86.

[15] Miller, *Addiction Psychiatry*, pp. 14, 17, 20, 21.

[16] Jellinek, *The Disease Concept of Alcoholism*, p. 40; Doweiko, *Concepts of Chemical Dependency*, p. 8; Schuckit, *Drug and Alcohol Abuse*, pp. 5–6.

[17] Room, 'Alcohol and Drug Disorders in the International Classification of Diseases', p. 310; Krivanek, *Addictions*, pp. 51–4.

[18] WHO Expert Committee on Drug Dependence, *28th Report*, p. 5; American Psychiatric Association, *Diagnostic and Statistical Manual of Mental Disorders*, p. 181, emphasis added.

[19] Schuckit, *Drug and Alcohol Abuse*, p. 16; Morrison, *DSM-IV Made Easy*, pp. 102, 74.

[20] Doweiko, *Concepts of Chemical Dependency*, p. 7. See McManus's alternative guide to overcoming addiction, *They Said I Was Dead*, for a vivid account of withdrawal as a cleansing process.

[21] Leccese, *Drugs and Society*, pp. 60–1.

[22] Schmidt & Room, 'Cross-Cultural Applicability in International Classifications and Research on Alcohol Dependence', p. 454.

[23] Jaffe, 'Current Concepts of Addiction', pp. 8–9; Edwards et al., 'Nomenclature and Classification of Drug- and Alcohol-Related Problems', p. 79; Schuckit, *Drug and Alcohol Abuse*, pp. 16, 59.

[24] Landry, *Understanding Drugs of Abuse*, p. 19.

[25] Doweiko, *Concepts of Chemical Dependency*, p. 117.

[26] Landry, *Understanding Drugs of Abuse*, p. 76.

[27] Jaffe, 'Current Concepts of Addiction', pp. 2–8.

[28] Siegel, R. K. 'Cocaine Smoking Disorders: Diagnosis and Treatment', *Psychiatric Annals*, 14, pp. 728–32, cited in Doweiko, *Concepts of Chemical Dependency*, p. 86.

[29] Edwards & Gross, 'Alcohol Dependence', pp. 1059–60.

[30] Dennison, *Diagnosing Chemical Dependency*, pp. 3, 5.

[31] Westreich & Rosenthal, 'Physical Examination of Substance Abusers', p. 111.

[32] Ibid., pp. 111–12.

[33] Dennison, *Diagnosing Chemical Dependency*, p. 113.

[34] Ibid., pp. v, 16–17, 19–20, 22.

[35] Milam & Ketcham, *Under the Influence*, pp. 48–9.

[36] Gold & Miller, 'How Effective is the Disease Model?', p. 7.

37 WHO Expert Committee on Drug Dependence, *28th Report*; Edwards et al., 'Nomenclature and Classification of Drug- and Alcohol-Related Problems', p. 80.
38 Edwards et al., 'Nomenclature and Classification of Drug- and Alcohol-Related Problems', p. 79.
39 Glassman et al., 'Cigarette Craving, Smoking Withdrawal and Clonidine', p. 866.
40 Pratt, 'Addiction Treatment for Health Care Professionals', p. 17.
41 Gossop, 'Compulsion, Craving and Conflict', pp. 241–2; Kozlowski & Wilkinson, 'Use and Misuse of the Concept of Craving by Alcohol, Tobacco and Drug Researchers', p. 33.
42 WHO Expert Committees on Mental Health and on Alcohol, 'The "Craving" for Alcohol'; Kozlowski & Wilkinson, 'Use and Misuse of the Concept of Craving by Alcohol, Tobacco and Drug Researchers'.
43 Kozlowski & Wilkinson, 'Use and Misuse of the Concept of Craving by Alcohol, Tobacco and Drug Researchers', p. 33; Hughes, 'Craving as a Psychological Construct', p. 38.
44 Kozlowski & Wilkinson, 'Use and Misuse of the Concept of Craving by Alcohol, Tobacco and Drug Researchers', p. 34; Shiffman, 'Don't let us throw the baby out with the bathwater', p. 37.
45 Davies, *The Myth of Addiction*, p. 51; Wise, 'The Role of Reward Pathways in the Development of Drug Dependence', p. 45.
46 Maltzman, 'Why Alcoholism is a Disease', p. 16.
47 Edwards & Gross, 'Alcohol Dependence', p. 1058.
48 Morrison, *DSM-IV Made Easy*, p. 79; Valverde, *Diseases of the Will*, pp. 26–7.
49 Orford, *Excessive Appetites*, p. 233.
50 See Davies, *The Myth of Addiction*, for a comprehensive discussion of addiction as a 'preferred explanation'. He argues that 'addiction attribution' serves a number of psychological and social functions including explaining 'bad' behaviour' by 'good' people as a medical symptom, thereby discouraging questioning of these categories.
51 Rose, 'Medicine, History and the Present', p. 49 (emphasis in original).
52 Rose, 'Medicine, History and the Present', pp. 67–9.
53 Jaffe, 'Current Concepts of Addiction', pp. 1–2.
54 Rose, *Inventing Our Selves*, p. 17.

3 Further and Further from the Normal World: The Addicted Self

1 Schaef, *When Society Becomes an Addict*, p. 18.
2 Johns, 'What is Dependence', p. 13.
3 Alcoholics Anonymous, 'Is Alcoholism an Illness?', p. 3, emphasis in original.
4 Schultz, *Growth Psychology*, pp. 1–3; Rapping, *The Culture of Recovery*.
5 Valverde, *Diseases of the Will*, p. 120.
6 Rose, 'Governing the Enterprising Self', p. 142.
7 See: Nowinski & Baker, *The Twelve-Step Facilitation Handbook*, p. xvii; Nakken, *The Addictive Personality*, p. 4; Milhorn, *Drug and Alcohol Abuse*, pp. 32–4; Cocores, *The 800-Cocaine Book of Drug and Alcohol Recovery*, pp. 13–14.
8 Alcoholics Anonymous, *The Big Book*, p. 58.
9 Warhol & Michie, 'Twelve-Step Teleology', pp. 330, 335.
10 Alasuutari, *Desire and Craving*, p. 60.
11 Alcoholics Anonymous, *The Big Book*, pp. 24, xxiv–xxvi; Springborn, 'Step One', p. 5.

12 See: Tournier, 'The Medicalization of Alcoholism', p. 47; Shaffer, 'The Epistemology of "Addictive Disease"', p. 112.

13 See Haaken, 'From Al-Anon to ACOA' for an insightful account of Adult Children of Alcoholics, the most visible and vocal of codependent movements.

14 See: Brown, 'What Adult Children of Alcoholics Need to Know'; Schaef & Fassel, *The Addictive Organization*; Schaef, *When Society Becomes an Addict*.

15 Peluso & Peluso, *Women and Drugs*, pp. 82, 114.

16 Sartre, *Being and Nothingness*, pp. 82–3, emphasis in original.

17 Nakken, *The Addictive Personality*, p. 34.

18 Schaef, *When Society Becomes an Addict*, pp. 50–1; Jenike, M. A., 'Drug Abuse' in E. Rubenstein & D. D. Federman (eds), *Scientific American Medicine*, Scientific American Press, New York, 1989, cited in Doweiko, *Concepts of Chemical Dependency*, p. 208.

19 Doweiko, *Concepts of Chemical Dependency*, pp. 208–9.

20 Schaef, *When Society Becomes an Addict*, p. 51.

21 Taylor, *The Ethics of Authenticity*, pp. 28–9, emphasis in original.

22 Nakken, *The Addictive Personality*.

23 Sedgwick, 'Epidemics of the Will', p. 582, emphasis in original.

24 Ibid, pp. 584, 586, emphasis in original.

25 Seymour & Smith, *Drugfree*, pp. 112, 2.

26 Nakken, *The Addictive Personality*, pp. 21–2, 9, 10, 14–5.

27 See: Cocores, *The 800-Cocaine Book of Drug and Alcohol Recovery*, p. 33; May, *Addiction and Grace*, pp. 43–5.

28 Alcoholics Anonymous, *The Big Book*, pp. 90–2; Miller & Kurtz, 'Models of Alcoholism Used in Treatment'.

29 Goldberger, 'The Concept and Mechanisms of Denial'.

30 Johnson, *Everything You Need to Know About Chemical Dependence*, p. 20, emphasis in original.

31 Ibid, pp. 38–46; Hacking, 'Two Souls in One Body', p. 458.

32 Sartre, *Being and Nothingness*, p. 113, emphasis in original.

33 Johnson, *Everything You Need to Know About Chemical Dependence*, pp. 329, 340–2.

34 Ibid, p. 368. See also: Seymour & Smith, *Drugfree*, p. 64; Milhorn, *Drug and Alcohol Abuse*, pp. 121–3; Robertson, *Getting Better*, p. 129.

35 Zimberg, 'Principles of Alcoholism Psychotherapy', p. 9; Landry, *Understanding Drugs of Abuse*, p. 233.

36 Foucault, 'Orders of Discourse', p. 9.

37 Johnson, *Everything You Need to Know About Chemical Dependence*, pp. 343–8.

38 Nowinski & Baker, *The Twelve-Step Facilitation Handbook*, p. 69.

39 Robertson, *Getting Better*, p. 256.

40 Johnson, *Everything You Need to Know About Chemical Dependence*, pp. 367.

41 Robertson, *Getting Better*, p. 26. I relate the event as told by Robertson, without any presumption of the accuracy of her account. However close Robertson's version is to the events that occurred, it is still a useful demonstration of the operation of addiction discourse. A different version of the intervention is found in Betty Ford's autobiography, *Betty*.

42 Ettorre, *Women and Substance Use*, pp. 20–3. Ettorre's analysis of dependency also marks the limits of her challenge to traditional addiction discourse. While rigorously disputing the assumption that the subordinate kind of dependency is a beneficial state for women, she leaves the negative status of 'substance dependency' largely undisturbed. A deconstruction of substance dependency, along the same lines as the fem-

inist critique of female dependency, reveals the myth of substance independence. By this I mean the tendency to ignore the fact that substance dependency is, like social interdependency, a condition of existence. Humans depend on a variety of substances and practices, and the routines and rituals built around them, for survival, well-being and meaning in their lives.

[43] For sociological, ethnographic and epidemiological descriptions of recreational and controlled use of illicit drugs, see: Mugford, 'Controlled Drug Use Among Recreational Users'; Dance, 'The St Oswalds Day Celebrations'; DeGrandpre & White, 'Drug Dialectics', pp. 50–1; Fox & Matthews, *Drugs Policy*, p. 39.

[44] Kasl, *Many Roads*, pp. 116–21.

[45] Ibid, pp. 201–2; Seymour, *Drugfree*, p. ix.

[46] Alcoholics Anonymous, *The Big Book*, pp. 103, 151.

[47] Hafner, *Nice Girls Don't Drink*, pp. 10–11, 14.

[48] Denzin, *The Alcoholic Society*.

4 Smoking, Addiction and Time

[1] See: Centers for Disease Control, 'Targeting Tobacco Use'; Australian Institute of Health and Welfare, *1998 National Drug Strategy Household Survey*; Bridgwood et al., *Living In Britain*.

[2] Anti-Cancer Council of Victoria, 'Smoking', p. 11; DuCharme, 'The Cigarette Papers', p. 87.

[3] Klein, *Cigarettes are Sublime*.

[4] United States Public Health Service, *The Health Consequences of Smoking*, pp. i, 9; Gossop, 'Compulsion, Craving and Conflict', p. 237.

[5] Brigham, *Dying to Quit*, p. 101.

[6] Harris, *Deadly Choices*, p. 154; Farquhar & Spiller, *The Last Puff*, p. 28; Unreich, 'Local Hero', p. 28.

[7] Bittoun, *Stop Smoking!*, p. 5.

[8] Matthews, 'Some are Born to be Smokers say Scientists'; Bittoun, *Stop Smoking!*, p. 6.

[9] Ibid, p. 98.

[10] Jay, 'Nicotine Anonymous', p. 329.

[11] Nicotine Anonymous, 'How Nicotine Anonymous Works'. It should be noted that writers like Bittoun, who have a narrower and more 'scientific' view of addiction understand it as a state of physical and psychological dependence. They tend to be sceptical of the spiritual and emotional elements of the NA approach. See: Bittoun, *You Can Quit*, p. 34.

[12] Hoffman, *Recovery from Smoking*, pp. 45–76.

[13] Ibid, pp. 66, 90.

[14] Walker, *Smoker*, pp. 108, 13–14.

[15] Ibid, p. 51.

[16] Farrar, 'Editors Foreword', p. v.

[17] Ibid, p. vi.

[18] See: Russell, 'Nicotine Intake and Its Regulation by Smokers', pp. 44–7. Smoking has been identified as improving concentration, memory, and performance of cognitive tasks, in part because of the actions of nicotine in the brain. See: Wesnes, 'Nicotine Increases Mental Efficiency: But How?'; Warburton, 'The Appetite for Nicotine', pp. 271–2. It is also related to decreased risk of Parkinson's disease and Alzheimer's disease. See: Ford, *SmokeScreen*, p. 129; Bittoun, *Stop Smoking!*, p. 100.

[19] Christen & McDonald, 'Safety of Nicotine-Containing Gum', p. 230.

[20] Walker, *Smoker*, pp. 19, 18, 108; Bittoun, *Stop Smoking!*, pp. 73–4.

[21] Ibid, p. 12; Bittoun, *You Can Quit*, p. 20; Harris, *Deadly Choices*, p. 172; Krogh, *Smoking*.

[22] Deleuze & Guattari, *A Thousand Plateaus*, pp. 3–4, 158–62, 256–7.

[23] Klein, *Cigarettes are Sublime*, pp. 2, 1, 89, 189; Ford, *SmokeScreen*.

[24] Whorf, B. L., *Language, Thought and Reality*, MIT Press, Cambridge, 1956, p. 7, cited in Adam, 'Perceptions of Time', p. 514.

[25] American Psychiatric Association, *Diagnostic and Statistical Manual of Mental Disorders*, p. 181; Morrison, *DSM-IV Made Easy*, p. 115.

[26] Denzin, *The Alcoholic Society*, pp. 97–101; Walker, *Smoker*, p. 64.

[27] Ford, *SmokeScreen*, pp. xi (emphasis in original), 210, 132, 131, 122.

[28] Goodin, *No Smoking*, p. 22.

[29] Douglas, 'Risk as a Forensic Resource', p. 3, emphasis in original.

[30] Ibid, p. 1.

[31] Bittoun, *You Can Quit*, p. 9.

[32] Ford, *SmokeScreen*, p. 204.

[33] Ford, *SmokeScreen*, pp. 123–7; Nelkin & Lindee, *The DNA Mystique*, p. 166.

[34] Nowotny, *Time*, pp. 51–2.

[35] Harris, *Deadly Choices*.

[36] Klein, *Cigarettes are Sublime*, p. 16.

[37] Graham, 'Surviving by Smoking', pp. 116–20; Greaves, *Smoke Screen: Women's Smoking and Social Control*, pp. 46, 48.

[38] Bittoun, *Stop Smoking!*, p. 80; Jacobson, *Beating the Ladykillers*, p. 119.

[39] Walker, *Smoker*, p. 105.

[40] Nowotny, *Time*, p. 97.

[41] Nowotny, *Time*, p. 132.

[42] Klein, *Cigarettes are Sublime*, p. 35; Walker, *Smoker*, p. 48.

[43] Klein, *Cigarettes are Sublime*, p. 26.

[44] Barthes, *A Lover's Discourse*, p. 31.

[45] Flegal et al., 'The Influence of Smoking Cessation on the Prevalence of Overweight in the United States'.

5 Disorders of Eating and the Healthy Diet: How to Eat Well

[1] Barthes, 'Toward a Psychosociology of Contemporary Food Consumption'. See: Probyn, *Carnal Appetites* for an insightful analysis of eating, identity and ethics.

[2] See: Bordo, 'Reading the Slender Body'; Yuker and Allison, 'Obesity'.

[3] Davis & Claridge, 'The Eating Disorders as Addiction', p. 472; Brisman & Siegel, 'Bulimia and Alcoholism'; Gordon, *Anorexia and Bulimia*, p. 18; Huebner, *Endorphins, Eating Disorders and Other Addictive Behaviors*.

[4] See Haddock and Dill, 'The Effects of Food on Mood and Behavior', for a skeptical view of the status of food as a psychoactive substance. After reviewing the literature they conclude that the food addiction model is unlikely to be a fruitful paradigm for understanding obesity.

[5] Rozin, P., 'The Selection of Foods by Rats, Humans and Other Animals' in J. S. Rosenblatt et al. (eds), *Advances in the Study of Behavior*, vol. 6, Academic Press, London; cited in Fischler, 'Food Habits, Social Change and the Nature/Culture Dilemma', p. 945.

6 Lynch, K., 'Danger! You Can Overdo Dieting', *Seventeen*, 34, 1975, pp. 106–7; cited in Gordon, *Anorexia and Bulimia*, p. 107.

7 Duker & Slade, *Anorexia and Bulimia*, pp. 130–1; Bruch, 'Four Decades of Eating Disorders', p. 12.

8 See: Showalter, *The Female Malady*; Gilbert & Gubar, *The Madwoman in the Attic*; Lawrence & Dana, *Fighting Food*, p. 45.

9 See: Bordo, 'Anorexia Nervosa', pp. 92–5; Brumberg, *Fasting Girls*, p. 35; Ussher, *Women's Madness*, p. 92.

10 Huebner, *Endorphins, Eating Disorders and Other Addictive Behaviors*, pp. 16, 32.

11 See: Duker & Slade, *Anorexia and Bulimia*, pp. 24, 29; Reinke, 'Counseling Techniques', p. 281; Huebner, *Endorphins, Eating Disorders and Other Addictive Behaviors*, pp. 10–11.

12 Huebner, *Endorphins, Eating Disorders and Other Addictive Behaviors*, p. 35.

13 Bordo, 'Whose Body is This?', p. 59.

14 Pope & Hudson, *New Hope for Binge Eaters*, p. 12.

15 See: Mitchell, *Bulimia Nervosa*, p. 28; Brisman & Siegel, 'Bulimia and Alcoholism'.

16 Gamman & Makinen, *Female Fetishism*, p. 136.

17 Lawrence & Dana, *Fighting Food*, p. 44.

18 Weiss et al., 'Bulimia Nervosa', p. 169.

19 Grosz, *Volatile Bodies*, p. 203.

20 See: Abraham & Llewellyn-Jones, *Eating Disorders*, pp. 115, 131; Zraly & Swift, *Anorexia, Bulimia and Compulsive Overeating*, p. 33.

21 Dana & Lawrence, *Women's Secret Disorder*, p. 15.

22 Ibid, p. 110.

23 O'Neill cited in Bordo, 'Anorexia Nervosa', p. 95.

24 Dana & Lawrence, *Women's Secret Disorder*, pp. 17–8.

25 See: Abraham & Llewellyn-Jones, *Eating Disorders*, p. 115; Schlundt & Johnson, *Eating Disorders*, p. 87.

26 Grosz, *Sexual Subversions*, p. 75, emphasis in original.

27 See: Huebner, *Endorphins, Eating Disorders and Other Addictive Behaviors*, p. 125; Gordon, *Anorexia and Bulimia*, p. 27.

28 Hall & Cohn, *Eating without Fear*, pp. 15–16.

29 Schlundt & Johnson, *Eating Disorders*, p. 94.

30 Yates, *Compulsive Exercise and the Eating Disorders*, pp. 146, 40–2, 5, 152–3.

31 Cooper, 'Anorexia and Bulimia', p. 182.

32 Schlundt and Johnson, *Eating Disorders*, p. 95.

33 American Psychiatric Association, *Diagnostic and Statistical Manual of Mental Disorders*, pp. 729–31.

34 Abraham & Llewellyn-Jones, *Eating Disorders*, p. 165.

35 Wooley & Wooley, 'Overeating as Substance Abuse', p. 43; Orford, *Excessive Appetites*, p. 77.

36 Orbach, *Fat is a Feminist Issue*, p. 122, emphasis in original.

37 Lawrence & Dana, *Fighting Food*, p. 30.

38 Way, *Anorexia Nervosa and Recovery*, p. 119.

39 Hall & Cohn, *Eating without Fear*, pp. 23–6.

40 Sheppard, *Food Addiction*, p. 49, capitals in original.

41 Katherine, *Anatomy of a Food Addiction*, pp. 8–9.

42 Sheppard, *Food Addiction*, pp. 129–30.

43 Abraham & Llewellyn-Jones, *Eating Disorders*, p. 127.

44 Gronow, *The Sociology of Taste*.

45 Warde, *Consumption, Food and Taste*, p. 83.

46 National Food Authority, *Food for Health*, pp. 5, 6, 55.
47 Woteki & Thomas, *Eat for Life*, pp. 33, 6, 133.
48 Kenton & Kenton, *Endless Energy*, p. 60.
49 The Bottom Line, 'Grape Juice as Effective as Wine in Preventing Heart Disease'.
50 Steinman, *Diet for A Poisoned Planet*, p. 10.
51 Ibid, pp. 26–7; Fischler, 'Food Habits, Social Change and the Nature/Culture Dilemma', p. 946.
52 Schlundt & Johnson, *Eating Disorders*, pp. 322–3. See also Reichert, *Nutrition for Recovery*.
53 See: Schlundt & Johnson, *Eating Disorders*, p. 105; Abraham & Llewellyn-Jones, *Eating Disorders*, p. 86.
54 Crawford, 'A Cultural Account of "Health" '.
55 Steinman, *Diet for A Poisoned Planet*, p. 3.
56 Way, *Anorexia Nervosa and Recovery*, p. 17, emphasis in original.

6 Sex and Love Addiction: The Ethics and Erotics of Intimacy

1 Groult, *Salt on our Skin*, pp. 32–3.
2 Carnes, *Contrary to Love*, p. 5.
3 American Psychiatric Association, *Diagnostic and Statistical Manual of Mental Disorders*; Irons & Schneider, 'Differential Diagnosis of Addictive Sexual Disorders Using the DSM-IV'.
4 As illustrated in the chapter on gay and bisexual husbands in Schneider & Schneider's *Sex, Lies and Forgiveness*.
5 Carnes, *Contrary to Love*, p. 3.
6 Foucault, *The History of Sexuality, Volume One*; Irvine, 'Reinventing Perversion', pp. 444–6.
7 Foucault, *The History of Sexuality, Volume One*, p. 18, emphasis in original.
8 Earle & Earle, *Sex Addiction*, p. 44.
9 Griffin-Shelley, *Sex and Love*, pp. 21, 122–3.
10 Carnes, *Don't Call it Love*, pp. 42–4; *Contrary to Love*, pp. 80–1, 100–1, 'Sexual Addiction Screening Test'.
11 Carnes, *Contrary to Love*, p. 217; Schneider, 'How to Recognize the Signs of Sexual Addiction', p. 180.
12 Carnes, *Contrary to Love*, pp. 4, 45.
13 This figure of 3–6% is quoted from Carnes, *Don't Call it Love*. As Irvine notes in 'Reinventing Perversion' (p. 436.), sex addiction experts often cite figures without specific references or information about how they were arrived at.
14 Schneider, 'How to Recognize the Signs of Sexual Addiction', pp. 171, 180.
15 Irvine, 'Reinventing Perversion', p. 431.
16 Griffin-Shelley, *Sex and Love*, pp. 7–8, 79.
17 Ibid, pp. 11–22.
18 Ibid, p. 56.
19 Griffin-Shelley, *Sex and Love*, pp. 3.
20 Schneider & Schneider, *Sex, Lies and Forgiveness*, p. 48.
21 Kasl, *Women, Sex and Addiction*, p. 73.
22 Carnes, *Out of the Shadows*, p. 32; Griffin-Shelley, *Sex and Love*, p. 25. Also see: Schaef, *Escape From Intimacy*, pp. 102–6; Kasl, *Women, Sex and Addiction*, pp. 50–4; Arterburn, *Addicted to Love*, pp. 108–9; Carnes, *Don't Call it Love*, p. 67.

[23] Dworkin, *Pornography*; Griffin-Shelley, *Sex and Love*, p. 25.

[24] McClintock, *Imperial Leather*; Kasl, *Women, Sex and Addiction*, p. 147.

[25] Arterburn, *Addicted to Love*, pp. 115, 116.

[26] Schneider, 'How to Recognize the Signs of Sexual Addiction', p. 181; Sexaholics Anonymous, 'What is a Sexaholic and What is Sexual Sobriety?'.

[27] Diamond, *Looking for Love in All the Wrong Places*, p. 139.

[28] Sedgwick, 'Jane Austen and the Masturbating Girl', p. 106; Bennett & Rosario, 'Introduction', p. 2.

[29] Sedgwick, 'Jane Austen and the Masturbating Girl', p. 107.

[30] Schaef, *Escape From Intimacy*, p. 137; See also Coleman, 'Chemical Dependency and Intimacy Dysfunction' for a description of intimacy as communication.

[31] Griffin-Shelley, *Sex and Love*, p. 206.

[32] Solomon, *Love*, pp. xxxix–xxx.

[33] See: Grosz, *Sexual Subversions*; Derrida, 'Foreword' and 'Eating Well, or the Calculation of the Subject'.

[34] Schaef, *Escape From Intimacy*, pp. 13–18; Earle & Earle, *Sex Addiction*, pp. 47–8, 54–5.

[35] Schaef, *Escape From Intimacy*, pp. 140–1.

[36] Benhabib, *Situating the Self*, pp. 10, 159.

7 The Recovery Habit

[1] Rose, *Inventing Our Selves*, pp. 4, 17.

[2] Foucault, *The Use of Pleasure*, p. 11.

[3] Foucault, 'Technologies of the Self', p. 18.

[4] See Rapping, *The Culture of Recovery*, for an insightful account of the influence of feminism on the recovery movement. She argues that much of what is appealing in the recovery movement is borrowed from the women's movement, namely the recognition and articulation of women's pain and a focus on personal relationships and experiences. The catch is that instead of seeing the social order as the problem and offering a program of political action as the solution, recovery discourse tells women they are unhappy because they have a disease. Haaken, 'From Al-Anon to ACOA', also describes the appropriation of feminist ideas and ideals by codependency literature. Also see Rapping, *The Culture of Recovery*, pp. 69, 91–2, 95–102 and Valverde, *Diseases of the Will*, pp. 21, 29–32, for discussion of general differences between AA and the recovery movement.

[5] Leonard cited in Knaster, 'From Addiction to Creativity', p. 56.

[6] Cocores, *The 800-Cocaine Book of Drug and Alcohol Recovery*, p. 222; Carnes, *Contrary to Love*, p. 256; Moran, *Lost Years*, p. 196.

[7] Alcoholics Anonymous, *The Big Book*, pp. 83–4.

[8] Nowinski & Baker, *The Twelve-Step Facilitation Handbook*, pp. xvi.

[9] McDonald, 'Step Twelve'.

[10] Nowinksi & Baker, *The Twelve-Step Facilitation Handbook*, p. 72.

[11] See: Geller, *Restore Your Life*, pp. 364–7; Sheppard, *Food Addiction*; Griffin-Shelley, *Sex and Love*, p. 123; Killinger, *Workaholics*, pp. 133, 217–18.

[12] Mumey, *The New Joy of Being Sober*, pp. 149–50.

[13] Alexander, *Sick & Tired of being Fat*, pp. 94, 108, 127–8, 118; Griffin-Shelley, *Sex and Love*, p. 125.

[14] Cocores, *The 800-Cocaine Book of Drug and Alcohol Recovery*, p. 4; Seymour & Smith, *Drugfree*, p. 7.

[15] Cocores, *The 800-Cocaine Book of Drug and Alcohol Recovery*, p. 5.

[16] Geller, *Restore Your Life*, pp. 187, 191–2.

[17] Ibid, p. 283.

[18] Rose, *Inventing Our Selves*, p. 98.

[19] Mumey, *The New Joy of Being Sober*, p. 177.

[20] Ibid, p. 181; Rose, *Inventing Our Selves*, p. 154.

[21] Mumey, *The New Joy of Being Sober*, pp. 183–95.

[22] Ibid, p. 103.

[23] Valverde, 'Governing Out of Habit', p. 219.

[24] Wegscheider-Cruze, *Another Chance*, p. 33.

[25] Katherine, *Boundaries*, p. 3.

[26] See: Hoffman, *Recovery from Smoking*, p. 86; Smith, *Set Yourself Free*, pp. 204–6; Greenberg, *Self on the Shelf*, p. 154; Lloyd & Fossum, *True Selves*, p. 25; Beattie, *Codependent No More*, p. 56. The serenity prayer, attributed to theologian Reinhold Niebuhr, was adopted by AA in the early 1940s, and has become a integral feature of AA meetings and literature. The founder of AA, Bill W., said of the prayer, 'Never had we seen so much of AA in so few words'. Bill W., *Alcoholics Anonymous Comes of Age*, p. 196.

[27] Smith, *Set Yourself Free*, pp. 15–16.

[28] Greenberg, *Self on the Shelf*, pp. 119–20.

[29] Sweet, *Off the Hook*, pp. 226–7.

[30] Lloyd & Fossum, *True Selves*, pp. 7–8.

[31] Greenberg, *Self on the Shelf*, pp. 240, 242.

[32] Smith, *Set Yourself Free*, pp. 5–6.

[33] Hazelden Foundation, 'Step Four', pp. 30–57.

[34] Sweet, *Off the Hook*, pp. 134, 9.

[35] Smith, *Set Yourself Free*, p. 109; Sweet, *Off the Hook*, pp. 44–5, 141–3.

[36] Ibid, p. 150.

[37] Bradshaw, *Homecoming*, pp. 254–5; Ivy, 'Have You Seen Me?', p. 237.

[38] Smith, *Set Yourself Free*, pp. 116–21.

[39] Freud, 'The Unconscious'.

[40] Sweet, *Off the Hook*, pp. 152–63.

[41] Sweet, *Off the Hook*, pp. 35, 41; Hoffman, *Recovery from Smoking*, pp. 54–5.

[42] Bradshaw, *Homecoming*, p. 91; Hoffman, *Recovery from Smoking*, p. 49.

[43] Bradshaw, *Homecoming*, p. 117.

[44] Valverde, *Diseases of the Will*, p. 40.

[45] Kasl, *Women, Sex and Addiction*, pp. 25–7; Sedgwick, 'Epidemics of the Will', p. 591; Valverde, 'Governing Out of Habit', p. 225.

[46] Valverde, 'Governing Out of Habit', pp. 219–21.

8 Conclusion

[1] Sedgwick, 'Epidemics of the Will', p. 582.

[2] See: Stange, 'The Broken Self'; Keane, 'The Toxic Womb'.

[3] I borrow this phrase from Marguerite Waller's analysis of the rhetorics of cyberspace, 'If "Reality is the Best Metaphor," It Must Be Virtual', p. 91.

Bibliography

Abraham, S. & Llewellyn-Jones, D., *Eating Disorders: The Facts*, 3rd edn, Oxford University Press, Oxford, 1992.

Adam, B., 'Perceptions of Time' in T. Ingold (ed.), *Companion Encyclopedia of Anthropology*, Routledge, London, 1994.

Aggleton, P., *Health*, Routledge, London, 1990.

Alasuutari, P., *Desire and Craving: A Cultural Theory of Alcoholism*, State University of New York Press, Albany, 1992.

Albert, A., *Xenobiosis: Foods, Drugs and Poisons in the Human Body*, Chapman & Hall, London, 1987.

Alcoholics Anonymous, *The Big Book*, 3rd edn, Alcoholics Anonymous World Services, New York, 1976.

—— 'Is Alcoholism an Illness?' Literature obtained from AA National Service Center, Beaconsfield NSW (n.d.).

Alexander, E., *Sick & Tired of being Fat: A Man's Struggle to be OK*, Hazelden, Center City, 1991.

American Psychiatric Association, *Diagnostic and Statistical Manual of Mental Disorders*, 3rd edn, American Psychiatric Press, Washington DC, 1980.

—— *Diagnostic and Statistical Manual of Mental Disorders*, 4th edn, American Psychiatric Press, Washington DC, 1994.

Anti-Cancer Council of Victoria, 'Smoking: Your Questions Answered' in K. Healey (ed.), *Deadly Habits?*, Spinney, Wentworth, 1992.

Arterburn, S., *Addicted to Love: Recovering from Unhealthy Dependencies in Romance, Relationships and Sex*, Servant, Ann Arbor, 1991.

Australian Institute of Health and Welfare, *1998 National Drug Strategy Household Survey—First Results*, http://www.aihw.gov.au/publications/health/ndshs98/ndshs98-c01.pdf accessed 11 December 1999.

Barnao, T., 'I Woke Up . . . Cured of Heroin', *Australian Women's Weekly*, July 1997, pp. 30–4.

Barthes, R., 'Toward a Psychosociology of Contemporary Food Consumption' in E. Forster & R. Forster (eds), *European Diet from Pre-Industrial to Modern Times*, Harper & Row, New York, 1975.

—— *A Lover's Discourse: Fragments*, trans. R. Howard, Penguin, Harmondsworth, 1990.

Beattie, M., *Codependent No More*, Collins Dove, North Blackburn, 1989.

Benhabib, S., *Situating the Self: Gender, Community and Postmodernism in Contemporary Ethics*, Polity, Cambridge, 1992.

Bennett, P. & Rosario, V., 'Introduction: The Politics of Solitary Pleasures' in P. Bennett & V. Rosario (eds), *Solitary Pleasures: The Historical, Literary, and Artistic Discourses of Autoeroticism*, Routledge, New York, 1995.

Berridge, V. & Edwards, G., *Opium and the People: Opiate Use in Nineteenth Century England*, Allen Lane, London, 1981.

Bill W., *Alcoholics Anonymous Comes of Age*, Alcoholics Anonymous World Services, New York, 1957.

Bittoun, R., *Stop Smoking! Beating Nicotine Addiction*, Random House Australia, Milsons Point, 1993.

—— *You Can Quit*, Gore & Osment, Rushcutters Bay, 1995.

Blocker, J., *American Temperance Movements: Cycles of Reform*, Twayne Publishers, Boston, 1989.

Bordo, S., 'Anorexia Nervosa: Psychopathology as the Crystallization of Culture' in I. Diamond & L. Quimby (eds), *Feminism and Foucault: Reflections on Resistance*, Northeastern University Press, Boston, 1988.

—— 'Reading the Slender Body' in M. Jacobus, E. F. Keller, & S. Shuttleworth (eds), *Body/Politics: Women and the Discourses of Science*, Routledge, New York, 1990.

—— 'Whose Body is This?: Feminism, Medicine and the Conceptualization of Eating Disorders' in S. Bordo (ed.), *Unbearable Weight: Feminism, Western Culture and the Body*, University of California Press, Berkeley, 1993.

Bottom Line, The, 'Grape Juice as Effective as Wine in Preventing Heart Disease', *The Bottom Line*, vol. 16 (1), 1995, pp. 87–91.

Bradshaw, J., *Homecoming: Reclaiming and Championing Your Inner Child*, Bantam Books, New York, 1990.

Bridgwood, A. et al., *Living in Britain: Results from the 1998 General Household Survey*, The Stationery Office, London, 2000.

Brigham, J., *Dying to Quit: Why We Smoke and How We Stop*, Joseph Henry Press, Washington, 1998.

Brisman, J. & Siegel, M., 'Bulimia and Alcoholism: Two Sides of the Same Coin?', *Journal of Substance Abuse Treatment*, vol. 1, 1984, pp. 113–18.

Brown, S., 'What Adult Children of Alcoholics Need to Know' in V. Johnson, *Everything You Need to Know About Chemical Dependence*, Johnson Institute, Minneapolis, 1990.

Bruch, H., 'Four Decades of Eating Disorders' in D. Garner & P. Garfinkel (eds), *Handbook of Psychotherapy for Anorexia Nervosa and Bulimia*, Guilford Press, New York, 1985.

Brumberg, J. J., *Fasting Girls: The Emergence of Anorexia Nervosa as a Modern Disease*, Harvard University Press, Cambridge, 1988.

Butler, J., *Bodies That Matter: On the Discursive Limits of 'Sex'*, Routledge, New York, 1993.

Cahalan, D., 'Implications of the Disease Concept of Alcoholism', *Drugs
and Society*, vol. 2 (3/4), 1988, pp. 49–68.

Canguilhem, G., *The Normal and the Pathological*, trans. C. Fawcett,
Zone Books, New York, 1989.

Carnes, P., *Out of the Shadows: Understanding Sexual Addiction*, Comp-
Care, Minneapolis, 1983.

—— *Contrary to Love: Helping the Sexual Addict*, CompCare, Minneapolis, 1989.

—— *Don't Call it Love: Recovery from Sexual Addiction*, Bantam, New
York, 1991.

—— 'Sexual Addiction Screening Test', *SexHelp.Com: Dr Carnes' Online
Resources for Sex Addiction and Recovery*, http://www.sexhelp.com/
sast.cfm#sast accessed 25 October 1999.

Centers for Disease Control, 'Targeting Tobacco Use: The Nation's Leading
Cause of Death', http:/www.cdc.gov/tobacco/oshaag.htm accessed
11 December 1999.

Christen A. & McDonald J., 'Safety of Nicotine-Containing Gum' in
O. Pomerleau & C. Pomerleau (eds), *Nicotine Replacement: A Critical
Evaluation*, Pharmaceutical Products Press, New York, 1992.

Cocores, J., *The 800-Cocaine Book of Drug and Alcohol Recovery*,
Villard Books, New York, 1990.

Cohen, P. D. A., 'Desires for Cocaine' in D. Warburton (ed.), *Addiction
Controversies*, Harwood Academic Publishers, Chur, 1990.

Cohen, S., *The Chemical Brain*, Care Institute, Irvine, 1988.

Coleman, E., 'Chemical Dependency and Intimacy Dysfunction: Inextri-
cably Bound', *Journal of Chemical Dependency Treatment*, vol. 1,
1987, pp. 13–26.

Concar, D., 'Prisoners of Pleasure', *New Scientist*, vol. 1945 (1 Oct.),
1994, pp. 26–31.

Cooper, T., 'Anorexia and Bulimia: The Political and the Personal' in
M. Lawrence (ed.), *Fed Up and Hungry: Women, Oppression and
Food*, The Women's Press, London, 1987.

Covey, S., *The Seven Habits of Highly Effective People: Restoring the
Character Ethic*, Simon & Schuster, New York, 1989.

Crawford, R., 'A Cultural Account of "Health": Self-Control, Release and
the Social Body' in J. McKinlay (ed.), *Issues in the Political Economy
of Health Care*, Methuen, New York, 1985.

Dana, M. & Lawrence, M., *Women's Secret Disorder: A New Understanding of Bulimia*, Grafton Books, London, 1988.

Dance, P. & Mugford, S., 'The St Oswalds Day Celebrations: Organised
Ritual in an Australian "Drug Enthusiast" Group', *Journal of Drug
Issues*, vol. 22, 1992, pp. 591–606.

Davies, J. B., *The Myth of Addiction: An Application of the Psychological Theory of Attribution to Illicit Drug Use*, Harwood Academic Publishers, Chur, 1992.

Davis, C. & Claridge, G., 'The Eating Disorders as Addiction: A Psychobiological Perspective', *Addictive Behaviors*, vol. 23 (4), 1998, pp. 463–75.

DeGrandpre, R. & White, E., 'Drug Dialectics', *Arena*, vol. 7, 1996, pp. 41–63.

Deleuze, G., *Spinoza: Practical Philosophy*, trans. R. Hurley, City Lights Books, San Francisco, 1988.

—— 'Ethology: Spinoza and Us' in J. Crary & S. Kwinter (eds), *Incorporations*, Zone Books, New York, 1992.

Deleuze, G. & Guattari, F., *A Thousand Plateaus: Capitalism and Schizophrenia*, trans. B. Massumi, University of Minnesota Press, Minneapolis, 1987.

Dennison, S., *Diagnosing Chemical Dependency: A Practical Guide for the Health Care Professional*, Charles C. Thomas, Springfield, 1993.

Denzin, N., *The Alcoholic Society: Addiction & Recovery of the Self*, Transaction Publishers, New Brunswick, 1993.

Derrida, J., 'Plato's Pharmacy' in *Dissemination*, trans. B. Johnson, Athlone, London, 1981.

—— 'Foreword: Fors: The Anglish Words of Nicolas Abraham and Maria Torok', trans. B. Johnson, in N. Abraham & M. Torok (eds), *The Wolfman's Magic World*, University of Minnesota Press, Minneapolis, 1986.

—— 'Eating Well, or the Calculation of the Subject: An Interview with Jacques Derrida' in P. Cadava, P. Connor, & J. L. Nancy (eds), *Who Comes After the Subject*, Routledge, New York, 1991.

—— 'The Rhetoric of Drugs: An Interview with Autrement', trans. M. Israel, *Differences*, vol. 5 (1), 1993, pp. 1–25.

Diamond, J., *Looking for Love in All the Wrong Places: Romantic and Sexual Addictions*, G. P. Putnam & Sons, New York, 1988.

Douglas, M., *Purity and Danger: An Analysis of Concepts of Pollution and Taboo*, Routledge & Kegan Paul, London, 1978.

—— 'Risk as a Forensic Resource', *Daedalus*, vol. 119 (4), 1990, pp. 1–16.

Doweiko, H. F., *Concepts of Chemical Dependency*, 2nd edn, Brooks/Cole Publishing, Pacific Grove, 1993.

DuCharme, D., 'The Cigarette Papers' in L. Hall & L. Cohn (eds), *Recoveries: True Stories by People who Conquered Addictions and Compulsions*, Gurze Books, Carlsbad, 1987.

Duden, B., *Disembodying Women: Perspectives on Pregnancy and the Unborn*, trans. L. Hoinacki, Harvard University Press, Cambridge, 1993.

Duker, M. & Slade, R., *Anorexia and Bulimia: How to Help*, Open University Press, Milton Keynes, 1988.

Dworkin, A., *Pornography: Men Possessing Women*, Women's Press, London, 1981.

Earle, R. & Earle, M., *Sex Addiction: Case Studies and Management*, Brunner/Mazel, New York, 1995.

Edwards, G., 'Alcoholism Treatment: Between Guesswork and Certainty' in G. Edwards & M. Grant (eds), *Alcoholism Treatment in Transition*, Croom Helm, London, 1980.

—— 'Drinking in Longitudinal Perspective: Career and Natural History', *British Journal of Addiction*, vol. 79, 1984, pp. 175–83.

Edwards, G. & Gross, M. M., 'Alcohol Dependence: Provisional Description of a Clinical Syndrome', *British Medical Journal*, vol. 1, 1976, pp. 1058–61.

Edwards, G. et al., 'Nomenclature and Classification of Drug- and Alcohol-Related Problems: A Shortened Version of a WHO Memorandum', *Australian Alcohol/Drug Review*, vol. 3 (2), 1984, pp. 76–85.

Ettorre, E., *Women and Substance Use*, Macmillan, Basingstoke, 1992.

Farquhar, J. W. & Spiller, G. A., *The Last Puff: Ex-Smokers Share the Secrets of Their Success*, Norton, New York, 1990.

Farrar, S., 'Editors Foreword' to *Smoker: Self Portrait of a Nicotine Addict*, Harper & Row, San Francisco, 1990.

Fingarette, H., *Heavy Drinking: The Myth of Alcoholism as a Disease*, University of California Press, Berkeley, 1988.

Fischler, C., 'Food Habits, Social Change and the Nature/Culture Dilemma', *Social Science Information*, vol. 19, 1980, pp. 937–53.

Flegal, K. et al., 'The Influence of Smoking Cessation on the Prevalence of Overweight in the United States', *New England Journal of Medicine*, vol. 333 (18), 1995, pp. 1165–70.

Forbes, D., *False Fixes: The Cultural Politics of Drugs, Alcohol and Addictive Relations*, State University of New York Press, Albany, 1994.

Ford, B., *SmokeScreen: Guide to the Personal Risks and Global Effects of the Cigarette Habit*, Halcyon Press, Perth, 1994.

Ford, B., *Betty: A Glad Awakening*, Doubleday, Garden City, 1987.

Foucault, M., 'Orders of Discourse', *Social Science Information* vol. 10 (2), 1971, pp. 7–30.

—— *Discipline and Punish: The Birth of the Prison*, trans. A. Sheridan, Penguin, Harmondsworth, 1977.

—— *The History of Sexuality, Volume One: An Introduction*, trans. R. Hurley, Penguin, London, 1978.

—— 'Truth & Power' in P. Rabinow (ed.), *The Foucault Reader*, Penguin, Harmondsworth, 1986.

—— *The Use of Pleasure: The History of Sexuality Volume Two*, trans. R. Hurley, Penguin, London, 1987.

—— 'Technologies of the Self' in L. H. Martin, H. Gutman & P. H. Hutton (eds), *Technologies of the Self: A Seminar with Michel Foucault*, Tavistock, London, 1988.

—— 'The Ethic of Care for the Self as a Practice of Freedom', an interview with R. Fornet-Betancourt et al., trans. J. Gauthier, in J. Bernauer & D. Rasmussen (eds), *The Final Foucault*, MIT Press, Cambridge, 1988.

—— *The Birth of the Clinic*, trans. A. M. Sheridan, Routledge, London, 1989.

Fox, R. & Matthews, I., *Drugs Policy: Fact, Fiction and the Future*, Federation Press, Leichardt, 1992.

Freud, S., 'The Unconscious' (1915) in *The Standard Edition of the Complete Psychological Works of Sigmund Freud Volume XIV*, trans. J. Strachey, Hogarth Press, London, 1957.

Gamman, L. & Makinen, M., *Female Fetishism*, New York University Press, New York, 1995.

Geller, A., *Restore Your Life: A Living Plan for Sober People*, Thorsons, London, 1992.

Giddens, A., *Modernity and Self-Identity: Self and Society in the Late Modern Age*, Polity, Cambridge, 1991.

Gilbert, S. & Gubar, S., *The Madwoman in the Attic: The Woman Writer and the Nineteenth-Century Literary Imagination*, Yale University Press, New Haven, 1978.

Glassman et al., 'Cigarette Craving, Smoking Withdrawal and Clonidine', *Science*, vol. 226, 1984, pp. 864–66.

Gold, M. S. & Miller, N. S., 'How Effective is the Disease Model?', *US Journal of Drug and Alcohol Dependence*, vol. 11 (12), 1987, p. 7.

Goldberger, L., 'The Concept and Mechanisms of Denial: A Selective Overview' in S. Breznitz (ed.), *The Denial of Stress*, International Universities Press, New York, 1983.

Goodin, R. E., *No Smoking: The Ethical Issues*, University of Chicago Press, Chicago, 1989.

Goodman, A., 'Pragmatic Assessment and Multitheoretical Classification' in J. Sadler et al. (eds), *Philosophical Perspectives on Psychiatric Diagnostic Classification*, Johns Hopkins University Press, Baltimore, 1994.

Goodyear, B., 'Unresolved Questions About Alcoholism: The Debate (War?) Goes On—Is a Resolution Possible?', *Alcoholism Treatment Quarterly*, vol. 6 (2), 1989, pp. 1–27.

Gordis, E., *Alcohol Research: Promise for the Decade*, Rockville: US Department of Health & Human Services, 1991.

Gordon, R. A., *Anorexia and Bulimia: Anatomy of a Social Epidemic*, Basil Blackwell, Cambridge, 1990.

Gossop, M., 'Compulsion, Craving and Conflict' in D. Warburton (ed.), *Addiction Controversies*, Harwood Academic Publishers, Chur, 1990.

Graham, H., 'Surviving by Smoking' in S. Wilkinson & C. Kitzinger (eds), *Women and Health: Feminist Perspectives*, Taylor & Francis, London, 1994.

Grant, S. et al., 'Activation of Memory Circuits During Cue-Elicited Cocaine Craving', *Proceedings of the National Academy of Science*, vol. 93, 1996, pp. 12040–5.

Greaves, L. *Smoke Screen: Women's Smoking and Social Control*, Fernwood, Halifax, 1996.

Greenberg, G., *Self on the Shelf: Recovery Books and the Good Life*, State University of New York Press, Albany, 1994.

Griffin-Shelley, E., *Sex and Love: Addiction, Treatment, and Recovery*, Praeger, New York, 1991.

Gronow, J., *The Sociology of Taste*, Routledge, London, 1997.

Grosz, E. A., *Sexual Subversions: Three French Feminists*, Allen & Unwin, St Leonards, 1989.

—— *Volatile Bodies: Towards a Corporeal Feminism*, Allen & Unwin, St Leonards, 1994.

Groult, B., *Salt on our Skin*, trans. M. Teitelbaum, Hamish Hamilton, London, 1992.

Haaken, J., 'From Al-Anon to ACOA: Codependence and the Reconstruction of Caregiving', *Signs*, vol. 18 (3), 1993, pp. 321–45.

Hacking, I., 'Two Souls in One Body' in J. Chandler, A. I. Davidson & H. Harootunian (eds), *Questions of Evidence: Proof, Practice and Persuasion Across the Disciplines*, University of Chicago Press, Chicago, 1994.

Haddock, C. K. & Dill, M. S., 'The Effects of Food on Mood and Behavior: Implications for the Addictions Model of Obesity and Eating Disorders', *Drugs & Society*, vol. 15 (1/2), 2000, pp. 17–47.

Hafner, S., *Nice Girls Don't Drink: Stories of Recovery*, Bergin & Garvey, New York, 1992.

Hall, L. & Cohn, L., *Eating without Fear: A Guide to Understanding and Overcoming Bulimia*, Bantam, New York, 1990.

Hall, W. et al., 'Editorial: Rapid Opiate Detoxification Treatment', *Drug and Alcohol Review*, vol. 16, 1997, pp. 325–7.

Harris, J. E., *Deadly Choices: Coping with Health Risks in Everyday Life*, Basic Books, New York, 1993.

Hazelden Foundation, 'Step Four: Knowing Yourself' in *The Twelve Steps of Alcoholics Anonymous: Interpreted by the Hazelden Foundation*, Harper & Row, San Francisco, 1987.

Heller, R. & Heller, R., *The Carbohydrate Addict's Diet*, Dutton, New York, 1991.

Hillman, J. & Ventura, M., *We've had a Hundred Years of Psychotherapy and the World's Getting Worse*, Harper San Francisco, San Francisco, 1993.

Hoffman, E. H., *Recovery from Smoking: Quitting with the 12 Step Process*, Hazelden, Center City, 1991.

Huebner, H., *Endorphins, Eating Disorders and Other Addictive Behaviors*, W.W. Norton, New York, 1993.

Hughes, J., 'Craving as a Psychological Construct', *British Journal of Addiction*, vol. 82, 1987, pp. 38–9.

Husak, D., *Drugs and Rights*, Cambridge University Press, Cambridge, 1992.

Hyman, S. E., 'Drug Abuse & Addiction' in E. Rubenstein & D. D. Federman (eds), *Scientific American Medicine*, Scientific American Press, New York, 1996.

Irons, R. & Schneider, J., 'Differential Diagnosis of Addictive Sexual Disorders Using the DSM-IV', *Sexual Addiction and Compulsivity*, vol. 3, 1996, pp. 7–21, http://azstarnet.com/~jschndr/diagnos.html, accessed 24 October 1999.

Irvine, J. M., 'Reinventing Perversion: Sex Addiction and Cultural Anxieties', *Journal of the History of Sexuality*, vol. 5 (3), 1995, pp. 429–9.

Ivy, M., 'Have You Seen Me? Recovering the Inner Child in Late Twentieth Century America', *Social Text*, vol. 37, 1993, pp. 227–52.

Jacobson, B., *Beating the Ladykillers: Women & Smoking*, Pluto Press, London, 1986.

Jaffe, J., 'Current Concepts of Addiction' in C. O'Brien & J. Jaffe (eds), *Addictive States*, Raven Press, New York, 1992.

Jay, L., 'Nicotine Anonymous' in J. Cocores (ed.), *The Clinical Management of Nicotine Dependence*, Springer Verlag, New York, 1991.

Jellinek, E. M., 'Phases of Alcohol Addiction', *Quarterly Journal of Studies on Alcohol*, vol. 13, 1952, pp. 637–84.

—— *The Disease Concept of Alcoholism*, Hillhouse Press, New Jersey, 1960.

Johns, A., 'What is Dependence' in H. Ghodse & D. Maxwell (eds), *Substance Abuse and Dependence: An Introduction for the Caring Professions*, Macmillan Press, Hampshire, 1990.

Johnson, V. E., *Everything You Need to Know About Chemical Dependence*, Johnson Institute, Minneapolis, 1990.

Julien, R., *A Primer of Drug Action*, 8th edn, W. H. Freeman & Co, New York, 1998.

Jurd, S., 'Why Alcoholism is a Disease', *Medical Journal of Australia*, vol. 156, 1992, pp. 215–17.

—— 'Alcoholism as a Disease' in C. Wilkinson & W. Saunders (eds), *Perspectives on Addiction: Making Sense of the Issues*, William Montgomery, Perth, 1996.

Kasl, C. D., *Women, Sex and Addiction: A Search for Love and Power*, Ticknor & Fields, New York, 1989.

—— *Many Roads, One Journey: Moving Beyond the 12 Steps*, Harper Perennial, San Francisco, 1992.

Katherine, A., *Boundaries: Where You End and I Begin*, Parkside Publishing, New York, 1991.

—— *Anatomy of a Food Addiction: The Brain Chemistry of Overeating*, 3rd edn, Gurze, San Francisco, 1997.

Keane, H., 'The Toxic Womb: Fetal Alcohol Syndrome, Alcoholism and the Female Body', *Australian Feminist Studies*, vol. 11 (24), 1996, pp. 263–76.

Kenton, S. & Kenton, L., *Endless Energy: For Women on the Move*, Random House Australia, Milsons Point, 1993.

Killinger, B., *Workaholics: The Respectable Addicts*, Simon & Schuster, London, 1992.

Kinney, J., *Clinical Manual of Substance Abuse*, 2nd edn, Mosby, St Louis, 1996.

Kirk, S. & Kutchins, H., *The Selling of DSM: The Rhetoric of Science in Psychiatry*, Aldine de Gruyter, New York, 1992.

Kleiman, M. R., *Against Excess: Drug Policy for Results*, Basic Books, New York, 1992.

Klein, R., *Cigarettes are Sublime*, Picador, London, 1995.

Knaster, M., 'From Addiction to Creativity', *East West*, June 1990, pp. 54–1.

Kozlowski, L. & Wilkinson, D. A., 'Use and Misuse of the Concept of Craving by Alcohol, Tobacco and Drug Researchers', *British Journal of Addiction*, vol. 82, 1987, pp. 31–6.

Kramer, P., *Listening to Prozac*, Penguin, New York, 1993.

Kreeger, K. Y., 'Drug Institute Tackles Neurology of Addiction', *The Scientist*, vol. 9 (16), 1995, http://www.thescientist.library.upenn.edu/yr1995/august/drugs 950821, accessed 28 July 1998.

Krivanek, J., *Addictions*, Allen & Unwin, Sydney, 1988.

Krogh, D., *Smoking: The Artificial Passion*, W. H. Freeman, New York, 1992.

Landry, M., *Understanding Drugs of Abuse*, American Psychiatric Press, Washington DC, 1993.

Lawrence, M. & Dana, M., *Fighting Food: Coping with Eating Disorders*, Penguin, London, 1990.

Leccese, A., *Drugs and Society: Behavioral Medicines and Abusable Drugs*, Prentice Hall, Englewood Cliffs, 1991.

Leser, D., 'The Way Out?', *Good Weekend*, 31 January 1998, pp. 14–23.

Leshner, A., 'NIDA's Brain Imaging Studies Serve as Powerful Tools to Improve Drug Abuse Treatment', *NIDA Notes*, vol. 11 (5), 1996, http://www.nida.nih.gov/NIDA Notes/NNVol11N5/DirRep Vol11N5.html, accessed 17 July 1998.

—— 'Addiction Is a Brain Disease, and It Matters', *Science*, vol. 278 (5335), 1997, pp. 45–6.

Levine, H. G., 'The Discovery of Addiction: Changing Conceptions of Habitual Drunkenness in America', *Journal of Studies on Alcohol*, vol. 39 (1), 1978, pp. 143–74.

Lilienfeld, S., 'Reply to Maltzman's "Why Alcoholism is a Disease"', *Journal of Psychoactive Drugs*, vol. 27 (3), 1995, pp. 287–91.

Lloyd, R. & Fossum, M., *True Selves: Twelve-Step Recovery from Co-dependency*, Harper Collins, San Francisco, 1991.

MacAndrew, C. & Edgerton, R. B., *Drunken Comportment: A Social Explanation*, Aldine, Chicago, 1969.

McClintock, A., *Imperial Leather: Race, Gender, and Sexuality in the Colonial Conquest*, Routledge, New York, 1995.

McDonald, P. C., 'Step Twelve: Language of the Heart' in *The Twelve Steps of Alcoholics Anonymous: Interpreted by the Hazelden Foundation*, Harper & Row, San Francisco, 1987.

McManus, A., *They Said I Was Dead: The Complete Alternative Cure for Addiction*, Scarlet Press, London, 1993.

Madden, S., 'Effects of Drugs of Dependence' in H. Ghodse & D. Maxwell (eds), *Substance Abuse and Dependence: An Introduction for the Caring Professions*, Macmillan Press, Hampshire, 1990.

Maltzman, I., 'Is Alcoholism a Disease?: A Critical Review of a Controversy', *Integrative Physiology and Behavioral Science*, vol. 26, 1991, pp. 200–10.

—— 'Why Alcoholism is a Disease', *Journal of Psychoactive Drugs*, vol. 26 (1), 1994, pp. 13–31.

—— 'Reply to Lilienfeld: Why Alcoholism is a Disease', *Journal of Psychoactive Drugs*, vol. 30 (1), 1998, pp. 99–104.

Marlatt, G. & Rohsenow, D., 'Cognitive Processes in Alcohol Use: Expectancy and the Balanced Placebo Design' in N. Mello (ed.), *Advances in Substance Abuse Vol. 1*, JAI Press, Greenwich, 1980.

Matthews, R., 'Some are Born to be Smokers say Scientists', *Sunday Telegraph*, Source: Reuters Newsbriefs Health List, 11 June 1995.

Mattick, R. & Hall, W. (eds), *A Treatment Outline for Approaches to Opioid Dependence*, National Drug Strategy Monograph Series no. 21, Australian Government Publishing Service, Canberra, 1993.

Maxwell, D., 'Medical Complications of Substance Abuse' in H. Ghodse & D. Maxwell (eds), *Substance Abuse and Dependence: An Introduction for the Caring Professions*, Macmillan Press, Hampshire, 1990.

May, G. *Addiction and Grace*, Harper & Row, San Francisco, 1988.

Meyer, R., 'The Disease called Addiction: Emerging Evidence in a 200 year Debate', *Lancet*, vol. 347, 1996, pp. 162–6.

Milam, J. and Ketcham, K., *Under the Influence: A Guide to the Myths and Realities of Alcoholism*, Madrona Publishers, Seattle, 1981.

Milhorn, H. T., *Drug and Alcohol Abuse: The Authoritative Guide for Parents, Teachers and Counselors*, Plenum Press, New York, 1994.

Mill, J. S., *On Liberty*, ed. G. Himmelfarb, Penguin, Harmondsworth, 1974.

Miller, N. S., 'Drug and Alcohol Addiction as a Disease', *Alcoholism Treatment Quarterly*, vol. 8 (4), 1991, pp. 43–55.

—— *Addiction Psychiatry: Current Diagnosis and Treatment*, Wiley-Liss, New York, 1995.

Miller, W. R. & Kurtz, E., 'Models of Alcoholism Used in Treatment: Contrasting AA and Other Perspectives with Which it is Often Confused', *Journal of Studies on Alcohol*, vol. 55, 1994, pp. 159–66.

Mitchell, J., *Bulimia Nervosa*, University of Minnesota Press, Minneapolis, 1990.

Moore, D., 'Deconstructing "Dependence": An Ethnographic Critique of an Influential Concept', *Contemporary Drug Problems*, Fall 1992, pp. 459–91.

Moran, M., *Lost Years: Confessions of a Woman Alcoholic*, Doubleday, Garden City, 1985.

Morrison, J., *DSM-IV Made Easy: The Clinician's Guide to Diagnosis*, Guilford Press, New York, 1995.

Mugford, S., 'Controlled Drug Use Among Recreational Users: Sociological Perspectives' in N. Heather et al. (eds), *Self Control in the Addictive Behaviours*, Maxwell Macmillan, Sydney, 1991.

Mumey, J., *The New Joy of Being Sober*, Deaconess Press, Minneapolis, 1994.

Nakken, C., *The Addictive Personality: Roots, Rituals, and Recovery*, Hazelden Press, Center City, 1988.

National Food Authority, *Food for Health: A Guide to Good Nutrition with Nutrient Values for 650 Australian Foods*, by R. English & J. Lewis, Australian Government Publishing Service, Canberra, 1991.

National Institute on Drug Abuse, 'Moderate Drinking', *Alcohol Alert No. 16*, 1992, http://silk.nih.gov/silk/niaaa1/publication/aa16.htm, accessed 27 April 2000.

—— *Mind Over Matter: Teacher's Guide*, National Institutes of Health, Rockville, 1997.

Nelkin, D. & Lindee, M. S., *The DNA Mystique: The Gene as Cultural Icon*, W. H. Freeman, New York, 1995.

Nesse, R. & Berridge, K., 'Psychoactive Drug Use in Evolutionary Perspective', *Science*, vol. 278 (5335), 1997, pp. 63–6.

Nicotine Anonymous, 'How Nicotine Anonymous Works', *Nicotine Anonymous* (n.d.), http://www.slip.net/~billh/nicworks.html, accessed 15 January 1996.

Nowinski, J. & Baker, S., *The Twelve-Step Facilitation Handbook*, Lexington Books, New York, 1992.

Nowotny, H., *Time: The Modern and Postmodern Experience*, trans. N. Plaice, Polity Press, Cambridge, 1994.

Nutt, D., 'Addiction: Brain Mechanisms and their Treatment Implications', *Lancet*, vol. 347, 1996, pp. 31–6.

O'Connor, P., 'Routine Screening and Initial Assessment' in Kinney, J. (ed.), *Clinical Manual of Substance Abuse*, 2nd edn, Mosby, St Louis, 1996.

Orbach, S., *Fat is a Feminist Issue*, Hamlyn, London, 1979.

Orford, J., *Excessive Appetites: A Psychological View of Addictions*, John Wiley & Sons, Chichester, 1985.

Page, P. B., 'The Origins of Alcohol Studies: E. M. Jellinek and the Documentation of the Alcohol Research Literature', *British Journal of Addiction*, vol. 83, 1988, pp. 1095–103.

Patton, P., 'Metamorpho-Logic: Bodies and Powers in *A Thousand Plateaus*', *Journal of the British. Society of Phenomenology*, vol. 25, 1994, pp. 157–69.

Peele, S., 'A Moral Vision of Addiction: How People's Values Determine Whether They Become and Remain Addicts' in S. Peele (ed.), *Visions of Addiction: Major Contemporary Perspectives on Addiction and Alcoholism*, Lexington Books, Lexington, 1988.

—— *The Diseasing of America: Addiction Treatment Out of Control*, Lexington Books, Lexington, 1989.

—— *The Meaning of Addiction: Compulsive Experience and Its Interpretation* (1985), Lexington Books, Lexington, 1998.

Peele, S. & Brodsky, A., *The Truth About Addiction and Recovery: The Life Process Program for Outgrowing Destructive Habits*, Fireside, New York, 1992.

Peluso, E. & Peluso, L., *Women and Drugs: Getting Hooked, Getting Clean*, CompCare, Minneapolis, 1988.

Peterson, A. & Lupton, D., *The New Public Health: Health and Self in the Age of Risk*, Allen & Unwin, St Leonards, 1996.

Pope, H. & Hudson, J., *New Hope for Binge Eaters: Advances in the Understanding and Treatment of Bulimia*, Harper & Row, New York, 1984.

Pratt, C. T., 'Addiction Treatment for Health Care Professionals', *Addiction & Recovery*, Sept 1990, pp. 17–41.

Probyn, E., *Carnal Appetites*, Routledge, London, 2000.

QUIT Victoria, 'Introduction', *Tobacco in Australia: Facts and Issues* by M. Winstanley, S. Woodward & N. Walker, 1995, http: www.peg.apc.org/~vshp/intro.htm, accessed 20 June 1995.

Rajchman, J., *Truth and Eros: Foucault, Lacan, and the Question of Ethics*, Routledge, New York, 1991.

Rapping, E., *The Culture of Recovery: Making Sense of the Self-Help Movement in Women's Lives*, Beacon Press, Boston, 1996.

Redfield, M., 'Introduction', *Diacritics*, vol. 27 (3), 1997, pp. 3–7.

Reichert, K., *Nutrition for Recovery*, CRC Press, Boca Raton, 1993.

Reinarman, C. & Levine, H. G., *Crack in America: Demon Drugs and Social Justice*, California University Press, Berkeley, 1997.

Reinke, J., 'Counseling Techniques: Nutrition Intervention' in K. Clark, R. Parr & W. Castelli (eds), *Evaluation and Management of Eating*

Disorders: Anorexia, Bulimia, and Obesity, Life Enhancement, Champaign, 1988.

Robertson, N., *Getting Better: Inside Alcoholics Anonymous*, William Morrow, New York, 1988.

Ronell, A., *Crack Wars: Literature, Addiction, Mania*, University of Nebraska Press, Lincoln, 1992.

—— 'Our Narcotic Modernity' in V. A. Conley (ed.), *Rethinking Technologies*, University of Minnesota Press, Minneapolis, 1993, pp. 70–1.

Room, R., 'The Alcohologist's Addiction', *Quarterly Journal of Studies on Alcohol*, vol. 33 (4), 1972, pp. 1049–59.

—— 'Dependence and Society', *British Journal of Addiction*, vol. 80, 1985, pp. 133–9.

—— 'Alcohol and Drug Disorders in the International Classification of Diseases: A Shifting Kaleidoscope', *Drug and Alcohol Review*, vol. 17, 1998, pp. 305–17.

Rose, N., 'Governing the Enterprising Self' in P. Heelas and P. Morris (eds), *The Values of Enterprise Culture: The Moral Debate*, Routledge, London, 1992.

—— 'Medicine, History and the Present' in C. Jones & R. Porter (eds), *Reassessing Foucault: Power Medicine and the Body*, Routledge, London, 1994.

—— *Inventing Our Selves: Psychology, Power, and Personhood*, Cambridge University Press, Cambridge, 1996.

—— 'Authority and the Genealogy of Subjectivity' in P. Heelas, S. Lash and P. Morris (eds), *Detraditionalization: Critical Reflections on Authority and Identity*, Blackwell, Cambridge, 1996.

Rubin, G., 'Thinking Sex: Notes for a Radical Theory of the Politics of Sexuality' in C. Vance (ed.), *Pleasure and Danger: Exploring Female Sexuality*, Routledge & Kegan Paul, Boston, 1984.

Russell, M. A. H., 'Nicotine Intake and Its Regulation by Smokers' in W. R. Martin et al. (eds), *Tobacco Smoking and Nicotine: A Neurobiological Approach*, Plenum Press, New York, 1987.

Sansone, R. & Sansone, L., 'Bulimia Nervosa: Medical Complications' in L. Alexander-Mott & D. B. Lumsden (eds), *Understanding Eating Disorders: Anorexia Nervosa, Bulimia Nervosa, and Obesity*, Taylor & Francis, Washington, 1994.

Sartre, J. P., *Being and Nothingness* (1956), trans. H. E. Barnes, Washington Square Press, New York, 1992.

Schaef, A.W., *Co-dependence: Misunderstood, Mistreated*, Harper and Row, San Francisco, 1986.

—— *Escape From Intimacy: The Pseudo-Relationship Addictions*, Harper & Row, San Francisco, 1989.

—— *When Society Becomes an Addict*, Thorsons, London, 1992.

Schaef, A. W. & Fassel, D., *The Addictive Organization*, Harper, San Francisco, 1990.

Schlundt, D. & Johnson, W., *Eating Disorders: Assessment and Treatment*, Allyn & Bacon, Boston, 1990.

Schmidt, L., Room, R. & collaborators, 'Cross-Cultural Applicability in International Classifications and Research on Alcohol Dependence', *Journal of Studies of Alcohol*, vol. 60, 1999, pp. 448–62.

Schneider, J., 'How to Recognize the Signs of Sexual Addiction', *Postgraduate Medicine*, vol. 90 (6), 1991, pp. 171–82.

Schneider, J. & Schneider, B., *Sex, Lies and Forgiveness: Couples Speaking Out on Healing from Sex Addiction*, Hazelden, Center City, 1991.

Schuckit, M., *Drug and Alcohol Abuse: A Clinical Guide to Diagnosis and Treatment*, 4th edn, Plenum Publishing, New York, 1995.

Schultz, D. P., *Growth Psychology: Models of the Healthy Personality*, 4th edn, Van Nostrand Reinhold, New York, 1977.

Sedgwick, E. K., *Epistemology of the Closet*, University of California Press, Berkeley, 1990.

—— 'Epidemics of the Will' in J. Crary & S. Kwinter (eds), *Incorporations*, Zone Books, New York, 1992.

—— 'Jane Austen and the Masturbating Girl' in J. Chandler, A. I. Davidson & H. Harootunian (eds), *Questions of Evidence: Proof, Practice, and Persuasion across the Disciplines*, University of Chicago Press, Chicago & London, 1994.

Sexaholics Anonymous, 'What is a Sexaholic and What is Sexual Sobriety?', 1989, http://www.sa.org/b000english/b073sobriety.html, accessed 28 December 1998.

Seymour, R. B. & Smith, D. E., *Drugfree: A Unique, Positive Approach to Staying Off Alcohol and Other Drugs*, Sarah Lazin Books, New York, 1987.

Shaffer, H. J., 'The Disease Controversy: Of Metaphors, Maps and Menus', *Journal of Psychoactive Drugs*, vol. 17 (2), 1985, pp. 65–76.

—— 'The Epistemology of "Addictive Disease": The Lincoln-Douglas Debate', *Journal of Substance Abuse Treatment*, vol. 4, 1987, pp. 103–13.

—— 'The Most Important Unresolved Issue in the Addictions: Conceptual Chaos', *Substance Use and Misuse*, vol. 32 (1), 1997, pp. 1573–80.

Shaw, S., 'A Critique of the Concept of the Alcohol Dependence Syndrome', *British Journal of Addiction*, vol. 74, 1979, pp. 339–48.

Sheppard, K., *Food Addiction: The Body Knows*, Health Communications, Deerfield Beach, 1989.

Shiffman, S., 'Don't let us throw the baby out with the bathwater', *British Journal of Addiction*, vol. 82, 1987, pp. 37.

Showalter, E., *The Female Malady: Women, Madness and English Culture, 1830–1980*, Virago, London, 1987.

Siegel, R., *Intoxication: Life in Pursuit of Artificial Paradise*, Dutton, New York, 1989.

Singer, G., 'Introduction' in G. Singer and D. Graham (eds), *Decade of the Brain*, La Trobe University Press, Bundoora, 1995.

Smith, S., *Set Yourself Free*, Bantam, Sydney, 1990.

Solomon, R., *Love: Emotion, Myth, & Metaphor*, Prometheus Books, Buffalo, 1990.

Springborn, W., 'Step One: The Foundation of Recovery' in *The Twelve Steps of Alcoholics Anonymous: Interpreted by the Hazelden Foundation*, Harper & Row, San Francisco, 1987.

Stange, M., 'The Broken Self: Fetal Alcohol Syndrome and Native American Selfhood' in M. Ryan and A. Gordon (eds), *Body Politics: Disease, Desire, and the Family*, Westview Press, Boulder, 1994.

Stein, H. F., 'In What Systems do Alcohol/Chemical Addictions Make Sense? Clinical Ideologies and Practices as Cultural Metaphors', *Social Science Medicine*, vol. 30 (9), 1990, pp. 987–1000.

Steinman, D., *Diet for A Poisoned Planet: How to Choose Safe Foods for You and Your Family*, Harmony Books, New York, 1990.

Stockwell, T., 'Slaying the Disease Model Dragon—Again?', *Addiction*, vol. 90, 1995, pp. 1039–40.

Stockwell, T. & Saunders, B., 'Alcohol and Drug Dependence: Syndrome, Strong Attachment or Everyday Behaviour?', *Drug and Alcohol Review*, vol. 9, 1990, pp. 103–9.

Swan, N., 'NIDA Brain Imaging Research Links Cue-Induced Craving to Structures Involved in Memory', *NIDA Notes*, vol. 11 (5), 1996, http://www.nida.nih.gov/NIDA Notes/NNVol11N5/CueInd.html, accessed 17 July 1998.

Sweet, C., *Off the Hook: How to Break Free from Addiction and Enjoy a New Way of Life*, Piatkus, London, 1994.

Tai, B. & Blaine, J., 'Naltrexone: An Antagonist Therapy for Heroin Addiction', National Institute on Drug Abuse Meeting Summary, 12–13 November 1997, http://www.nida.nih.gov/meetsum/naltrexone.html accessed 25 October 1998.

Taylor, C., *The Ethics of Authenticity*, Harvard University Press, Cambridge, 1991.

Tournier, R. E., 'The Medicalization of Alcoholism: Discontinuities in Ideologies of Deviance', *Journal of Drug Issues*, Winter 1985, pp. 39–49.

United Nations International Drug Control Programme, *World Drug Report*, Oxford University Press, Oxford, 1997.

United States Department of Health and Human Services, 'Tobacco Use', *Preliminary Estimates from the 1993 National Household Survey on Drug Abuse: Advance Report No. 7*, 1994, http://www.health.org/pubs/93hhs/tobacco accessed 23 June 1997.

United States Public Health Service, *The Health Consequences of Smoking: Nicotine Addiction: A Report of the Surgeon General*, US Department of Health and Human Services, Rockville, 1988.

Unreich, R., 'Local Hero', *Mode*, February/March 1996, pp. 26–30.

Ussher, J., *Women's Madness: Misogyny or Mental Illness?*, Harvester Wheatsheaf, London, 1991.

Vaillant, G., 'Is There a Natural History of Addiction?' in C. O'Brien & J. Jaffe (eds), *Addictive States*, Raven Press, New York, 1992.

Valverde, M., 'Governing Out of Habit', *Studies in Law, Politics and Society*, vol. 18, 1998, pp. 217–42.

—— *Diseases of the Will: Alcohol and the Dilemmas of Freedom*, Cambridge University Press, Cambridge, 1998.

Van Dyke, C. & Byck, R., 'Cocaine', *Scientific American*, vol. 246 (3), March 1982, pp. 108–19.

Walker, E., *Smoker: Self Portrait of a Nicotine Addict*, Harper/Hazelden, San Francisco, 1990.

Waller, M., 'If "Reality is the Best Metaphor," It Must Be Virtual', *Diacritics*, vol. 27 (3), 1997, pp. 90–104.

Warburton, D., 'The Appetite for Nicotine' in C. Legg & D. Booth (eds), *Appetite; Neural and Behavioural Bases*, Oxford University Press, Oxford, 1994.

Ward, J. et al., *Key Issues in Methadone Maintenance Treatment*, University of New South Wales Press, Sydney, 1992.

Warde, A., *Consumption, Food and Taste: Culinary Antimonies and Commodity Culture*, Sage, London, 1997.

Warhol, R. & Michie, H., 'Twelve-Step Teleology: Narratives of Recovery/ Recovery of Narrative' in S. Smith & J. Watson (eds), *Getting a Life: Everyday Uses of Autobiography*, University of Minnesota Press, Minneapolis, 1996.

Way, K., *Anorexia Nervosa and Recovery: A Hunger for Meaning*, Haworth, New York, 1993.

Wegscheider-Cruze, S., *Another Chance: Hope and Health for the Alcoholic Family*, 2nd edn, Science & Behavior Books, Palo Alto, 1989.

Weiss, L., Katzman, M. & Wolchik, S., 'Bulimia Nervosa: Definition, Diagnostic Criteria and Associated Psychological Problems' in L. Alexander-Mott & D. B. Lumsden (eds), *Understanding Eating Disorders: Anorexia Nervosa, Bulimia Nervosa, and Obesity*, Taylor & Francis, Washington, 1994.

Wesnes, K., 'Nicotine Increases Mental Efficiency: But How?' in W. R. Martin et al. (eds), *Tobacco Smoking and Nicotine: A Neurobiological Approach*, Plenum Press, New York, 1987.

West, D. & Kinney, J., 'An Overview of Substance Use and Abuse' in Kinney, J. *Clinical Manual of Substance Abuse*, 2nd edn, Mosby, St Louis, 1996.

Westreich, L. M. & Rosenthal, R. N., 'Physical Examination of Substance Abusers: How to Gather Evidence of Concealed Problems', *Postgraduate Medicine*, vol. 97 (4), 1995, pp. 111–20.

Wilde, O., *The Picture of Dorian Gray*, Oxford University Press, Oxford, 1974.

Wilson, E., 'On the Nature of Neurology', *Hysteric*, vol. 2, 1996, pp. 49–63.

—— 'Introduction: Somatic Compliance—Feminism, Biology and Science', *Australian Feminist Studies*, vol. 14 (29), 1999, pp. 7–18.

Wise, R., 'The Role of Reward Pathways in the Development of Drug Dependence' in D. Balfour (ed.), *Psychotropic Drugs of Abuse*, Pergamon Press, New York, 1990.

Wodak, A. & Owens, R., *Drug Prohibition: A Call for Change*, University of New South Wales, Sydney, 1996.

Wooley, S. & Wooley, O., 'Overeating as Substance Abuse' in N. Mello (ed.), *Advances in Substance Abuse Behavioral and Biological Research Volume 2*, JAI Press, Greenwich, 1981.

World Health Organisation, *The ICD-10 Classification of Diseases and Related Health Problems*, World Health Organisation, Geneva, 1992.

—— *The ICD-10 Classification of Mental and Behavioural Disorders: Diagnostic Criteria for Research*, World Health Organisation, Geneva, 1993.

World Health Organization Expert Committee on Drug Dependence, *WHO Expert Committee on Drug Dependence: 28th Report*, WHO Technical Report Series 836, World Health Organization, Geneva, 1993.

World Health Organization Expert Committees on Mental Health and Alcohol, 'The "Craving" for Alcohol', *Quarterly Journal of Studies on Alcohol*, vol. 16, 1955, pp. 33–66.

Woteki, C. & Thomas, P. (eds), *Eat for Life: The Food and Nutrition Board's Guide to Reducing Your Risk of Chronic Disease*, National Academy Press, Washington, 1992.

Yates, A., *Compulsive Exercise and the Eating Disorders: Toward an Integrated Theory of Activity*, Brunner/Mazel, New York, 1991.

Yuker, H. & Allison, D., 'Obesity: Sociocultural Perspectives' in L. Alexander-Mott & D. B. Lumsden (eds), *Understanding Eating Disorders: Anorexia Nervosa, Bulimia Nervosa, and Obesity*, Taylor & Francis, Washington, 1994.

Zimberg, S., 'Principles of Alcoholism Psychotherapy' in S. Zimberg et al. (eds), *Practical Approaches to Alcoholism Psychotherapy*, Plenum Press, New York, 1978.

Zinberg, N., *Drug, Set and Setting: The Basis for Controlled Intoxicant Use*, Yale University Press, New Haven, 1984.

Zraly, K. & Swift, D., *Anorexia, Bulimia and Compulsive Overeating: A Practical Guide for Counselors and Families*, Continuum, New York, 1990.

Index

Compiled by Kerry Biram